The *Essence of Herbs*
An Environmental Guide to Herb Gardening

Globular flower heads of salad burnet, *Poterium sanguisorba*

THE ESSENCE OF HERBS
An Environmental Guide
to Herb Gardening

BY

Ruth D. Wrensch

🌿　　　🌿　　　🌿

Photographs by Bernard E. Wrensch

Drawings by Patricia Kozik

University Press of Mississippi
Jackson and London

The paper in this book meets the guidelines for permanence and durability of the Committee on Production Guidelines for Book Longevity of the Council on Library Resources.

95 94 93 92   4 3 2 1

Library of Congress Cataloging-in-Publication Data

Wrensch, Ruth D.
    The essence of herbs : an environmental guide to herb gardening / by Ruth D.
Wrensch ; photographs by Bernard E. Wrensch ; drawings by Patricia Kozik.
        p.   cm.
    Includes bibliographical references and indexes.
    ISBN 0-87805-604-1 (alk. paper) — ISBN 0-87805-605-X (pbk. : alk. paper)
    1. Herb gardening. 2. Herb gardening—Southern States. 3. Herbs.   4. Herbs—
Southern States. I. Title.
SB351.H5W74   1992
635'.7—dc20   92-18800
                                                                                    CIP

British Library Cataloging-in-Publication data available

But when from a long distant past nothing subsists,
after the people are dead . . . taste and smell alone . . .
remain poised a long time, like souls, remembering,
waiting, hoping, amid the ruins of all the rest; and
bear unflinchingly . . . the vast structure of recollection.

—Marcel Proust
Remembrance of Things Past

Contents

Preface

This book about herbs grew out of repeated recastings of a series of illustrated lectures, demonstrations, and field trips to herb gardens and natural landscapes. The subject matter has been presented in herb study programs sponsored by botanical gardens, colleges, and groups having herbal interests in the Midwest and the Southeast. For many years my overall title of the subject has been "The Essence of Herbs."

The writing, like the herb study programs, is addresed to those interested in exploring the captivating world of herbs at many levels. I have integrated personal observations with information from appropriate historical, herbal, botanical, and horticultural literature.

For wide usefulness the presentation aims to provide a sound foundation of environmental thinking. To this end, I have given special attention to native habitats of specific herbs. I believe this information will be appreciated by many herbists who want clues to the historical uses of herbs and optimum cultural requirements for success in the garden. One chapter offers garden designs that satisfy the needs of herbs from diverse environments. Although the functional design elements focus upon Southeastern environments, they can be used with equal success in other regions. Another chapter embraces ecologically valuable natural landscapes for spectacular gardens of native American herbs.

In this book some information appears more than once when it is relevant to several topics. Check in the general index and plant index to find what you need to know.

The standard reference for botanical and horticultural nomenclature in *The Essence of Herbs* is *Hortus Third* by the staff of the Liberty Hyde Bailey Hortorium, Macmillan Publishing Co. (1976). Other respected plant taxonomy publications are used when a herb is absent in *Hortus Third*.

The Descriptive Catalog is a straightforward guide to fill the needs of a beginner or an experienced herbist. It is arranged alphabetically by genera and usually alphabetically by species within each genus. Where there are considerable differences among the species within a genus, the species have been brought together in groups according to their described similarities. In each brief description I have attempted to give a picture of the herb in terms as simple and nontechnical as possible. Cultural directions are presented. Each entry identifies the part or parts of the plant utilized.

Any mention or notation of the medicinal use of a herb from folklore or otherwise, valid or invalid, does not imply that the University Press of Mississippi or the author of *The Essence of Herbs* suggest the use of the herb for medicine. Conscious of the many hazards involved in the indiscreet medicinal use of herbs, the author has purposefully withheld detailed reports from the many sources of medicinal usage. The herbist interested in herbal medicine is advised to pursue the subject with respect and to recognize and uphold the strict scientific disciplines involved with the subject.

It is inevitable that a descriptive catalog restricted in size cannot be all-inclusive. Limited space required deletions of some worthy herbs. Not all the herbs mentioned through the chapters have been allotted space in the Descriptive Catalog. To find their references, the reader is advised to use the plant index; for further references the bibliography is useful. However, a large number of native herbs are included to match the expanding interest in plants used by American Indian tribes.

Herbs are an inexhaustible subject. No book about them can ever be complete. Time and circumstances bring a writing to a close. The task into which I happened to be drawn is not finished, but the result will, I hope, prove useful to others.

One of the pleasures of authorship is to acknowledge one's gratitude to those who contributed directly or indirectly to the work. I am deeply aware

of my debt to former instructors. I cannot forget to thank the many participants in the herb study programs, especially those who over the years have
kept friendships alive and intact. The herbal connections they introduced
into the classes were appreciated, and I reveled in their enthusiasm. Their
contributions and questions influenced the development of the book. For
unfailing support and abiding interest in this project I gratefully name JoAnn
Crawford, Beverly Geist, Lillie Hilton, Patricia Johnson, Sue Dornfeld-Slater,
and the late Florence Woltman. Generous assistance and encouragement
were received from many wonderful people. Early on Margaret Lawler read
a number of chapters and made valuable suggestions and corrections. Members of The Herb Society of Hilton Head Island and Dorothy Spencer gave
me stimulating encouragement without which this book would not have
come into being. Ever since Catchy Tanner appeared in a North Carolina
community college herb study class, I have profited from her gardening heritage. Catchy's kind and unobtrusive manner of sharing her knowledge about
herbs and flora of Southeastern gardens informed me of facts and species
which have complemented my own Midwestern gardening experience. William J. Radler, director of the Boerner Botanical Gardens, has given me invaluable help whenever I sought his advice. Dorothy Bonitz supplied me
with a nursery list, a number of which have been included in the Useful
Addresses. Mark and Rima Dornfeld, archaeologists of the languages and
cultures of the ancient Near East and Middle East, read the ancient history
portion. Their comments on its treatment of herbs in antiquity were pertinent and welcome. And when I was searching for the source of an Egyptian
love poem, Mark provided it with remarkable speed. John Vining, able horticulturist in North Carolina, has been a valued consultant. His excellent
practice of collecting sound information from horticultural specialists gave
me an unfailing source of facts that have been placed in this book to benefit
herb gardeners. Amiable Patricia Kozik responsibly executed the pen & ink
drawings from photographs and written descriptions. To them all I give
heartfelt thanks.

Joan Janssen, Joy Johnson, James Mayberry, and Jane Warner gave singular
helpful attention to a detail in this book that has deeply touched me.

The author wishes to thank Houghton Mifflin Co./Ticknor Fields for permission to reprint lines from Cold Sassy Tree by Olive Burns.

I remember a father, Ernst Philipp Dornfeld, a bookish man who gardened for exercise and was adept at kindling my herbal curiosity by asking a question. I remember a brother, Ernst John, who suggested that I write a book of factual information.

Our son and daughter have been accommodating. Matthew has regularly mailed packages of typewriter ribbons and erasers to me. Elizabeth Jensen, after reading William Shakespeare in college, lightheartedly handed me a collection of quotes suited to my passion for herb gardening. A number have been put to good use.

To Bernard my spouse I owe a thousand thanks for assistance. He has patiently photographed herbs in gardens and in the wild—in the United States and abroad. The photographs of gardens and herbs in this book have been selected from our large collection. I have made practical use of his engineering knowledge which he shares with me when I plan herb gardens. To Bernard, for all he is to me, I dedicate this book.

🌿 The Essence of Herbs
An Environmental Guide to Herb Gardening

1 ✹ Introduction

In Touch with Herbs

Herbs possess a world of connections. The exchanges among herbists speak for themselves.

Perhaps you grow herbs; your friend uses them in cooking. The culinary expert states emphatically that there is an assurance of high quality and fine flavor when the seasoning herbs come directly from the garden to the kitchen.

Perhaps you lean to botany or horticulture and have become friendly with an artist who delights in sketching the fine lacy leaves of the *Artemisia* species (the wormwoods), or watercolors the blue-flowered hyssop, *Hyssopus officinalis*. The artist speaks of the intense blue color, the rakish arrangement of the flowers on one side of the spike, and the protruding stamens, long and curved, as worthy of the paintbrush. As a botanist you point out the defining characteristics of the hyssop plant, which place it in the mint family—to which many of the fragrant and culinary herbs belong. The artist's keen eye quickly notes that thymes, lavenders, and basils are members of the same family. A spirited conversation soon fills the fragrant garden.

Or, you are a gardener of patches of herbs and discover that gardening with them is therapeutic; your companion, who enjoys walking among the herbs, plucks the heavily scented leaves, and reminisces nostalgically about the thyme or mint that a favorite ancestor had tucked into a kitchen garden.

A historian eagerly tells how herbs have influenced the course of the world; the plant geographer expounds on plant environments; and the ethnobotanist discusses the association of herbs with culture patterns and ethnic ideals. Whatever the force drawing men or women, young or old, to herbs, one discovers, almost without exception, that the depth of one's friendship with the herbs must be communicated to some other person. This pleasure of herbs must be shared.

Herbs appeal to one's senses of color, taste, odor, and texture, as well as to thought and imagination. A great many herbists are drawn to the herbs for their aromatic or pungent odors—the rational and irrational perfume qualities. The lore of the plants used medicinally in the past leads to recent scientific research of plants by phytochemists bent on benefiting mankind. The dyer's-weeds are sought by followers of the ancient craft of vegetable dyeing. The numberless associations with natural history and civilization admit that herbs are not drab. Whatever the situation may be, many people think and talk about herbs.

Beauty exists in herb gardens as the poetry of all ages and languages reveals. Poets find pleasure and satisfaction in the less obvious and more subtle qualities of almost everything, including plants. Bards perceived beauty in the golden daffodil and other colorful blossoms, but also in patches of mint and wild thyme. Milton had known the "smell of sweetest fennel." Since the sixteenth century we have associated rosemary with remembrance because of the often quoted remark of Ophelia in Shakespeare's *Hamlet*: "There's rosemary, that's for remembrance." Throughout the history of English literature we find references to herbs. Herbs are in Chaucer and Spenser. Herbs abound in Shakespeare. Herbs can be followed right along with the history of the language. Tennyson referred to "purple spiked lavender." Dickens evidently was accustomed to eating caraway seed. In more recent times Walter de la Mare referred to parsley, sage, rosemary and thyme, a line he may have taken from a piece of medieval children's literature. The contemporary musicians Simon and Garfunkel, used the line in the lyrics for "Scarborough Fair." Ditties referring to herbs can be found in many languages—for example, this, from the German:

Petersilie, Suppenkraut, wächst in unserm Garten;
Unser Paulinchen ist die Braut, braucht nicht lang mehr warten.

Fig. 1. Dyeing skeins of wool. A woodcut from *Plictho de l'Arte Tentori* by Giaventura Rosetti, Venice, 1548.

Herbs for the most part possess no dazzling colors crying for attention but are plants in their simplest terms—leafy, sun-seeking, sweet-scented. In a herb garden the charm and endless delight of sense impressions are freely given to all passersby.

Few categories of plants have the universal appeal that herbs do. Who can deny the beauty and fragrance of the apothecary rose, the comeliness of sweet woodruff, or the joy of finding the first blooming bloodroot in the springtime? And yet the many settings of herbs and the uses that bond them to mankind are as important to a herbist as their appearances or fragrances.

What Is a Herb?

There is ever a war over precise definitions. Yet distinctions ought not to be neglected, even if they are, admittedly, not absolute. "Herb" may be and has been variously defined. Among botanists a herb is a nonwoody seed plant. A second principal definition is supported among herb gardeners, culinary experts, scent chemists, and researchers in pharmacy and medicine. It is also the definition to which this book conforms. In these domains herbs are distinguished from all other plants by the possession of certain properties which make them useful as a flavoring or garnish in cooking, for medicinal purpose, perfume, dyeing, insecticidal and industrial uses, and so on. A herb can be a nonseed producing plant as well as a seed producing plant, either nonwoody or woody. As nonwoody, the herb may be an annual, biennial, or a perennial; as woody, a tree or shrub. The certain property that makes a herb useful may be obtained from various plant parts that include the root, stem, leaf, flower, fruit, seed, bark, etc. A herb may be harvested in its natural environment or in a cultivated garden. Native habitats of herbs lie in temperate, subtropical and tropical zones in contrast to spices which are limited to the tropical zone; this distinguishing feature explains the contrasting economic and cultural roles herbs and spices have played through the history of mankind.

Just as herbs have been associated with man as long as he has been on earth, spices too have played a role. Spices have had a powerful influence on the course of history. Four thousand years ago, spices were transported along dangerous trade routes from the far Eastern tropics to the western markets. The gathering of the spices, the great distance to the markets by camel caravan and sea trade, plus the intrigue involved among those dealing in spices, always made them costly. By comparison, the aromatic herbs growing beside a humble dwelling or in a monastery garden, but in the temperate or subtropical zones, gave no cause to be so dear. Society at all economic levels could savor the aromatic plant that permitted itself to be domesticated.

The significance of distinguishing spices and herbs at the economic level broadens as one ponders the movements of Western man and his political orientations. The lure of spices after Marco Polo's reports inspired navigators like Columbus and Magellan to apply hypothesis concerning the shape of the earth and seek shorter routes to the East Indies, source of many spices. As a result Columbus came upon the Western Hemisphere, and by this twist it became the home of many European, African, and Asian peoples.

National powers rose and fell as nations engaged in rivalry for the spice trade, battling for control of the sea trade. The Portuguese lost out to the

Spanish and English. The Dutch entered the spice trade at the beginning of the seventeenth century and maintained a well-guarded monopoly until Yankee clippers entered the competition and the United States became involved. Man is all too well acquainted with the disquietude to which economic competition gives rise. It is recognized that spice trading provoked many evil days. Society has paid dearly for seeking spices instead of plebian herbs as seasonings.

Is the h in "herb" pronounced or not? In few words—it is a matter of choice. From a historical perspective the following can be added: The word "herb" is from the Latin *herba*, meaning a green plant, especially grass. Lack of an aspirator in the early Latin alphabet was apparently later supplied from the Greek, and when aspiration proceeded from fashionable to common, uneducated Romans frequently overdid it. Later the English borrowed the word from Old French which borrowed it from popular spoken Latin without the aspirator. Though not always, the letter h was retained in the spelling of "herb" by influence of ancient classic Latin. In the early nineteenth century fashionable English people began pronouncing "herb" with the h sound to avoid the Cockney dialect which dropped the h sound in all native English words. Towards the end of World War II a movement began in the United States that encouraged British English pronunciations; the h sound in "herb" became noticeable at herb meetings. Will you stay fashionable, or are those who say "erb" preserving tradition based on good evidence?

Herbs Then and Now

Herbs are a tradition, and like all traditions, have their origins in a particular kind of soil and climate. Plant geographers, who trace plants to the area where they originally grew, call this region the plant's native habitat. Information about a plant's native habitat provides clues for culturing it in a new environment; knowing the proper soil types, quality of light, rainfall, drainage patterns, and climatic conditions the herb is used to enables a gardener to reproduce a hospitable new home.

Plant geography and the movements of man have been intertwined since ancient times. Migratory movements of native races became the agencies for the dispersal of many herbal plants. Man's colonization of distant parts of

Fig. 2. The Mayan Rain God smoking a cloud-blowing tobacco pipe. From a carved tablet in limestone with hieroglyphics found in the ruins of Men-che in Southern Mexico.

the world brought the sowing of herbal seeds into regions far removed from their native habitats. Bound so closely to herbs for his well-being, man took them with him and cultivated them.

In the new environments many herbs became naturalized. "Naturalized," applied to a specific plant, signifies that the plant did not originate in the area where it is found growing today, but was introduced by purpose or accident and has successfully adapted itself to the new environment. The acclimation may be so successful that often the plant is termed a weed as it flourishes and spreads by natural means. Other transplants must be carefully nurtured.

Systematic botany has untangled the nomenclature of herbs from the multitudinous folk names and diverse plant classification systems of the ancients and the herbalists. It has given the world one correct name for each natural plant species in the form of the Latinized binomial; for example, *Salvia offici-*

nalis, common sage. This nomenclature is understandable and useful. Calling a herbal plant by its one and only correct name and avoiding the use of numerous and confusing common names in herbal writings satisfies the need of exactness. Moreover it enables gardeners to note similarities and (outward) differences among plants that are botanically related.

From ancient clues—from clay tablets, archaic manuscripts, herbal writings, and the cloister garths holding plants of the early apothecary—the botanists and pharmaceutical and medical workers of today seek clues to plants useful for human illnesses. In the New World, as well as the Old, ethnobotanists frequently search for green medicine used among primitive tribes without a written language.

Artifacts from many cultures substantiate not only the use of herbs in medicine, perfume, and flavoring but also their beauty as decorative motifs: in Egyptian tomb paintings, Sumerian cuneiform clay tablets, Chinese bronzes, Greek vases, frescoes of Pompeii, Persian paintings, stone stelae of the Mayas, woodcuts and botanical illustrations in herbals, and illuminated manuscripts from European monasteries. Egyptian temples are supported by pillars shaped like the lotus or the papyrus. Classical Greek artisans, skilled in working with metals and stone, were inspired by the fluid forms of acanthus leaves, and created the Corinthian capital.

Today the skillful blending of ancient plants with new herbal cultivars appear in herb garden designs. Tight English knots, parterres, and geometrical patterns echo fanciful patterns and embroidery shapes found in the decorative arts of the past. For favorable results herb gardeners in warm, humid climates avoid smothering herbs from arid climates with tight plantings and give preference to a loose form of planting in spaces of harmonious proportions. Most favor a naturalistic style of planting herbs that reproduces native environments. Keeping herbs in containers on a terrace is stylish and functional; it is easy to control soil and air circulation and thus combat problems associated with high humidity.

The general interest in herbs has expanded enormously in recent years, drawing on all its connections. It combines history and geography with the artistic uses of herbs in the garden and at the table. The essence of the culinary art is sought in traditional culinary herbs and the subtle flavors they impart to ethnic foods, as rich and diversified as the country of origin. The herbs in a country are the soul of its cuisine.

2 ❧ The Historical Account with Annotations

The practice of gathering, growing, and using herbs has existed among all cultures. Herbs and certain cereals have been collected and used longer than any other type of plants. For as long as man has been on this ecosphere, he has enjoyed herbs for flavoring his food, as medicine, and for the fragrances that bolstered his psyche.

Archaeology has discovered the remains of herb seeds in prehistoric sites, plus drawings of plants and the containers used for herbal products. Mustard seeds have been identified on refuse heaps of bones, because of which, it is believed that early man chewed mustard seeds with his meat to give it flavor. As the mustard seeds are joined with saliva, an enzyme in the seeds is released, a chemical change takes place, and a hot pungent flavor results; a similar reaction takes place when ground seeds are joined with water, vinegar, or the historic "must" (unfermented wine), which gives mustard its common name.

Most of the culinary herb seasonings, like the perfume herbs, make their contributions through the olfactory sense. Mustard's dominant hot flavor registers on the taste buds as well, just as we experience and enjoy the sour taste of acetous sorrel in tossed greens or in a well-prepared French sorrel sauce or soup.

Mustard has come down through the ages. We continue to savor it with a piece of meat or cheese, especially when the meat or cheese lacks flavor.

Elizabethan England was well acquainted with mustard. Note the following lines in *The Taming of the Shrew*:

> "What say you to a piece of beef and mustard?" asks the servant of Katherine, whereupon she replies: "A dish that I do love to feed upon."
> "Ay, but the mustard is too hot a little," remarks Grunio.
> "Why, then, the beef, and let the mustard rest."
> "Nay, then. I will not; you shall have the mustard, or else you get no beef of Grunio."
> "Then both, or one, or anything thou wilt," replies the exasperated Shrew, to which the witty servant counters, "Why, then the mustard without the beef."

Mustard plants are prolific, spread on all continents except Antarctica. No wonder every culture is familiar with mustard. When the purse is slim and you are reduced to eating a tasteless dish, prepare your own mustard. Gather seed from plants in the fields or waste places and follow a simple recipe:

> Grind or pound 3 tablespoons mustard seed or use purchased ground mustard. Blend the ground mustard with 3 tablespoons tarragon vinegar or dry white wine, 1 tablespoon flour, and 2 or 3 tablespoons honey. Permit the mixture to stand uncovered at least 1 hour. Cover and refrigerate.

The written acquaintanceship with herbs coming down from very remote times documented the plants or plant parts used as medicine, either in the cure of disease or in the treatment of wounds.

The Record from Sumer

Recorded history begins in Sumer. The Sumerians appeared in what is now Iraq 5,000 years ago. Ancient Sumerians were the world's first readers and writers. The world of Sumer gave us a literature in the form of small clay tablets on which their people, using thin cuneiform (wedge-shaped) reeds as markers, pressed their texts. Among the tablets left for us are prescriptions for medicine, delineating recognizable plants and giving instructions for their medicinal use. Sumerian clay tablets date from the late fourth millennium B.C. They are the earliest known written records about plants in Western civilization.

The Record from India

In the Sanskrit literature of India, names of herbal plants are used as a mode of symbolic expression.

Hymns from Vedic texts, early forms of the Indian Sanskrit literature, were composed in the latter half of the second millennium B.C. Soma, as a Bacchuslike god and at the same time a common name for a plant, *Sarcostemma brevistigma*, is lauded in 114 hymns called "purificational" because they were recited while the juice expressed from the soma plants was clarifying. Supposedly a celestial variety of soma, distinct from that of the earth, was drunk by the gods. It roused Indra, chief god of the early Hindu religion, to establish the universe. In later Vedic epics of India, soma, addressed as the moon plant, becomes the moon, waning when drunk by gods and replenished by the sun. The sap of soma, when fermented, is an intoxicant. It is native to India and Burma and was prized both in India and Iran as medicine conducive to longevity.

Like many herbal plants soma is entwined with an ancient literature of festive songs and tales, religion, gods, mystical powers, and medicine. The herb is strongly associated with ancient Indian culture.

The Record from Egypt

Art and symbolic hieroglyphs record herbs in ancient Egypt. A translated love poem from an original quotation in the recto of *Papyrus Harris 500* in the British Museum reads:

> I am thy beloved
> I am for thee like a garden
> Which I have planted with flowers
> And all sweet smelling herbs.

Deserving notice is an Egyptian manuscript from 1500 B.C. known as the *Ebers Papyrus*, a compilation of plants used medicinally at that time. Herbal writings throughout the centuries have referred to the *Ebers Papyrus*, and it continues to be studied. One ancient prescription uses squill, *Urginea maritima*, for heart disease and other illnesses. In our century the squill prescription in *Ebers Papyrus* has been compared to digitalis as a heart remedy, both made effective by the presence of glucosides. More familiar to the public is the utilization of red squill as a rat poison when given in large dosages. Squill is widely distributed in the sands and among rocks of the Mediterranean region. In a herb garden squill with its broad strap-shaped leaves growing out of an exposed, huge round bulb is complemented by a large semi-spherical clay container.

The Bible Period

Plants are frequently referred to in the Bible. Many plant names, used idiomatically or symbolically in the original Hebrew and Greek texts, are lost in translations. Although the Assyrian cuneiform clay tablets and the *Ebers Papyrus* confirm the use of medicinal herbs during the period covered by the Old and New Testaments, the Bible does not specify healing by plants. Instead, God is revealed as a source of faith and the divine healer exemplified by the lines: "The Lord sustains him on his sickbed: in his illness thou healest all his infirmities" (Psalm 41:3, Revised Standard Version).

In contrast, plants used for perfume and incense, in anointing oils and religious rites, are given detailed attention. The earliest known formula for incense includes spices, gums, and resins. Recorded in the Old Testament are the following materials to be assembled for the religious temple incense: "Take sweet spices, stacte [thought to be myrrh] and onycha, and galbanum, sweet spices with pure frankincense (of each there shall be an equal part), and make an incense blended as by the perfumer, seasoned with salt, pure and holy. . . ." (Exodus 30:34–36). References for the preparation of costly, perfumed, holy anointing, and embalming ointments are included in the Laws of Moses.

Aromatic plants were cultivated as early as the third millennium B.C. in Egypt, Assyria, and Sumer for sensuous pleasure, religious rites (holy ointments), embalming, and assumed magical qualities.

Ancient caravans traversing ancient ways created centers for international commerce and thus affected the distribution of herbs and spices. The Mediterranean littoral, Assyria, Mesopotamia, Sheba (modern Yemen and Hadhramaut), Ophir (possibly in East Africa), Egypt, and North Africa were linked by camel caravan as well as by sea lanes. Articles of commerce moved through the bustling international trade routes. Commodities like frankincense, balm, galbanum, myrrh, and drugs were readily traded.

A Milestone in Ancient Greece

Early studies of plants centered on the discovery and recording of their usefulness in medicine. In the fourth century B.C., Aristotle introduced the study of plants as a branch of natural philosophy and founded a botanical garden. His studies of plants included ecology, and plant classification systems were attempted. Theophrastus, his pupil, continued the work. Gradually attention was transferred from no more than recording medicinal uses of plants to the plants themselves. An important advance in plant study was made by the writing Enquiry into Plants—credited to Theophrastus, but acknowledged as writings of scholars who attended his lectures. The Enquiry attempted the first approach to a scientific study of plants for their own identity, instead of merely giving a plant's application in medicine. For this reason Theophrastus is acknowledged father of botany. The Enquiry investigated plant distribution and recorded native habitats, provided information on the cultivation of transplanted plants and the application of economic plant uses. Experimental knowledge began to free plant study from dogmatism.

Plants from countries outside Greece were made available to Theophrastus through Alexander the Great. Alexander, a student of Aristotle, was alive to the value of science. He advocated fraternization between conqueror and conquered, and these associations furthered an exchange of herbs and herb uses from the whole then known world. From the distant lands Alexander had conquered, bundles of plants were brought into Greece (300 B.C.) by his scientific personnel. Theophrastus and his students recorded descriptions of the introductions, taking into account their origins. The plants were propagated throughout the Mediterranean region and wherever Greek culture dominated.

The origin of basil, Ocimum basilicum, in India is supported in writings credited to Theophrastus. This large, shiny-leaved, sweet herb became known to Greeks as the royal plant, basilikon, from the word for "king," basileus. Basil was in such short supply at first that only royalty could afford to savor it. From Greece it was introduced to the Greek colonies of southern Italy, eventually to be permanently associated with Italian cuisine.

In Greek cuisine today bush basil, O. 'Minimum', is preferred, and small pots of it are commonly seen on windowsills. Members of the Greek Orthodox Church place containers of the herb on the church altars, and return home from services with sprigs of basil.

Despite widespread acceptance in the Mediterranean region after its introduction, basil is not recorded as naturalized in the Mediterranean environment. The rain-bearing southwest monsoon periods in India, basil's native habitat, supply a quantity of moisture to which basil is genetically adapted; the amount of moisture in the arid Mediterranean region is not sufficient.

The Roman Period

A landmark manuscript in book form (codex) among herbal writings is Dioscorides' De materia medica. Dioscorides, a Greek born in Asia Minor early in the Christian era, served in the Roman military as a physician. He compiled De materia medica as a pharmacological account of about 500 medicinal plants, identified by the names used at the time and their healing virtues. Descriptions of the plants themselves are slighted, which makes recognition with certainty difficult. In spite of this lack, the treatise was granted almost infallible authority up to the sixteenth and seventeenth centuries.

The manuscript has been many times copied and translated, elucidated, expounded upon by later herbalists, and transfused into herbals without question. The possibility of errors was manifold. Nevertheless, De materia medica remained a Bible of herbal medicine for 1,500 years.

Pliny the Elder (A.D. 24–79) of Roman antiquity wrote long treatises on plants in his Natural History. His essays on agriculture give information for a larger number of plants than writings limited to plants used in medicine. Pliny described the phenomenon of certain plants having a deleterious effect on plants growing nearby as a result of toxic substances given off through the root system, and suggested planting basil at a distance from rue, Ruta graveolens. This claim has never been proved, but the advice has been followed by some herbists to this day. In other instances, evidence of toxicity through the soil has been validated.

Pliny also suggested wool be washed before dyeing in water containing leaves of soapwort, Saponaria officinalis, to remove the grease. Saponin in the leaves and roots of soapwort produces a lather that dissolves grease, and because of its gentle action, soapwort continues to be used for cleaning and revitalizing fine historic fabrics, tapestries, etc.

Grain-paste, a discovery of prehistoric time, is a solid, nutritious food eaten unbaked. Essentially, it consists of roasted or dried sprouted grains pounded in a mortar and kneaded with a liquid into a paste. Palatable, more digestible than a baked product, and having excellent keeping qualities, grain-pastes continued into the Classical Greek and Roman periods. In the Mediterranean region unbaked pieces of grain-paste eaten with olives, a few figs, or some goat's milk cheese was the peasant's diet. A sophisticated Greek grain-paste recipe from Pliny the Elder reads:

> Soak barley in water for a few days; then leave it for a night to dry. Next day dry it by the fire and grind it in a mill. Mix with 3 pounds of flaxseed [which produces linseed oil when warm and pounded], half a pound of coriander seed and 1/8 pint of salt, previously roasting them all.

The recipe is sketchy as to the yield, but the amounts of coriander and flaxseed seem enormous.

Imperial Rome left us a work of gastronomy known as Apicius (after a first-century epicure). Cookery has long been acquainted with these recipes in various Latin renditions. The appeal of the book for cooks who grow and use herbs is immense. But many of its herbs and seasonings have fallen into disuse, or their identity forgotten. These we want to rediscover and perhaps adapt to our modern kitchens.

The Roman legions not only returned home with booty from campaigns, but like all military forces, left marks in the lands they conquered. Soldiers carried with them plants required for flavoring, medicine, and fragrance from regions around the Mediterranean Sea and introduced them to the conquered peoples: the Gauls in France, the Iberians in Spain, the Teutonic tribes of northern Europe, and the Celts in Britain.

The ancients of Egypt, Greece, and Rome knew the dye made from the indigo plant, Indigofera tinctoria, native to central Asia and northern Africa. From the ancient Picts in Britain (possibly a pre-Celtic people) Julius Caesar's men learned of the blue dye obtained from a plant called woad, Isatis tinctoria, native to their island and to the European continent.

Caesar's legions brought packets of sweet lavender to Britain from southern France, its native habitat. Soldiers' sweethearts liked to tuck lavender into their garments, where the warm bodies brought out its pleasing fragrance. The Romans also added lavender to wash water and gave us such words as lavender and lavatory, from the Latin lavare, "to wash." Today lavender grows and thrives in England's soil, and English grown lavender is recognized as the finest.

Aromatic plants from the Mediterranean regions able to withstand northern Europe's colder climate and heavier soils were accepted by its peoples and were cultivated; many became naturalized.

Not all the aromatic plants that have come down to us are natives of the Mediterranean region. Many herbs have moved into our herb gardens from their homes in central and northern Europe and Asia. Wild chive is native to central Europe and Siberia, the cultivated type to the Swiss Alps. Sweet angelica is a native of the cool, moist climates of northern Europe and Asia. French tarragon comes out of Siberia. Sweet woodruff and German chamomile are cherished fragrances of middle Europe.

Herbs in the Middle Ages

In the fifth century, the barbarians overran Roman Europe. Unlike the Romans, the Goths, Vandals, Franks, and Alemanns lived a simple life. Milk, cheese, meat, bread, porridge, and herbs gathered along the way completed their diet, and between the fifth and twelfth centuries there was a great return to the land. The Dark Ages closed in.

Organized trade began to disintegrate, affecting rural kitchens around the Mediterranean and all of Europe. Long-distance trade, by then centuries old, became almost nonexistent. Men began to cultivate herbs for flavoring along with the root vegetables, to take the place of the no-longer-available spices. Local areas had to be entirely self-supporting.

It became the responsibility of the monasteries and royal gardens to preserve medicinal and other such special plants. Thus, throughout the Middle Ages, the monasteries of Europe, such as the Abbey of St. Gall in Switzerland near Lake Constance (around A.D. 830), gave sanctuary to native and introduced herbs in orderly gardens. The medieval herb garden of the monastery was the forerunner of the botanical garden and the physic garden of a later era. It was an extension of the artistic and scholarly minds of the monks who laid out gardens in harmonious fashion. We owe them thanks for many functional design patterns. The monastery garden was a source of culinary delight, and it was a study garden, where medicinal plants were investigated. It served as a kind of early pharmacy shop.

In A.D. 800 Charlemagne was crowned emperor of the Holy Roman Empire. Achievements and attentiveness to the needs of his subjects made him a legendary figure. As a young man he is supposed to have given his tutor the frequently quoted definition of a herb: "Friend of the physician and the praise of cooks." Complete inventories survive of plants grown in the royal gardens and lists of plants (today classified as herbs) ordered to be grown on the imperial lands. All document the prominent status of herbs in the Middle Ages.

Like Roman soldiers' sweethearts, women of the medieval period placed packets of redolent herbs near their warm bodies, releasing the volatile oils to perfume the surroundings. To scent the air at public assemblages, herbs, mainly the mints, were strewn on the floor. Trampled underfoot, crushed herbs emitted pleasant aromas to combat the unsavory odors prevailing in communities lacking sanitation. Specific herbs were used to mask tainted meats. Thyme, *Thymus vulgaris*, was used as a meat preservative; its essential oil, thymol, is now acknowledged as an effective antibacterial agent. Herbs gave variety to an otherwise plain diet, which was all that most people could afford.

Today, we too use herbs to ease a monotonous diet, perking up the prosaic chicken, for example, with many flavors and combinations of herbs. The hen is a polygamist. She marries well to French tarragon, rosemary, parsley, sage, thyme, bay; with oregano she is presented at the barbecue altar. We prepare chicken in East Indian fashion (where the bird was first domesticated) with garlic, cardamom, coriander, turmeric, cumin, cinnamon, and cloves—spices and herbs all nicely blended.

Herbals and Botanic Gardens

From the fourth century B.C. onward, herbal documentations appear in the ancient texts of hieroglyphic, Greek, Latin, and Arabic papyruses and parchments, on sheets and in rolls. "Codex" (plural, "codices") is the name applied to the early manuscript of a classic text in book form—that is, a collections of written pages stitched together. By the fourth century A.D. the use of parchment and vellum in place of papyrus put an end to the scroll form. By A.D. 751 the Arabs had learned the art of making paper from the Chinese and become masters qualified to introduce the art into Spain and Italy, parts of which they occupied in the middle of the twelfth century. By the second half of the fourteenth century, the use of paper for writing purposes had become well established in all western Europe.

The development of botany and medicine can be traced in the manuscripts of classical antiquity and the Middle Ages. Speculations into natural

Fig. 3. A sheet of a ninth century manuscript copied from the fifth century work of Apuleius.

philosophy are foremost in the early texts and eclipse the writings of scientific investigations. By the fourth century B.C. a faint manifestation of botany had begun to appear in Greek manuscripts, and a branch of natural philosophy to take shape. In *Enquiry into Plants*, Theophrastus demonstrates the power of observation and deductive reasoning, based on a careful study of living plants, both native and foreign.

Far-reaching medicinal and botanical information probably developed and found its way into ancient manuscripts out of primitive man's speculations on life and its cessation, death. In his observations of nature, he gathered empirical folk knowledge, and this joined the mystical and magical practices of Babylon's magicians, sorcerers, and priests. The practice of medicine was born alongside utilitarian botany.

A number of ideas were acquired on physiology and pathology; pharmacognosy (study of drugs) and its unrefined experiments with plants proved some plants to be poisonous, others capable of effecting cures. To the herb gatherers, who combined the observation of plants with religious symbolism, myths, witchcraft, incantations, and superstition, was left the practical work of treating ills. It is in herbal manuscripts and early printed herbals based chiefly on practical knowledge, mythology, superstition, and magic, that the repression of botany as an independent discipline is discovered.

Many herbal manuscripts and early printed herbals are similar to the writings of Dioscorides and Pliny, recording plant uses, but limited in accurate plant descriptions. To this extent the writings were unsatisfactory and stifled advances in both medicine and botany. The scientific development of botany was further hindered during the thirteenth century when the natural philosophical interpretations of Aristotle's botany, presented by the Arabs, were introduced into Europe.

Before the invention of printing in the middle of the fifteenth century, herbal manuscripts in Latin, Greek, and Arabic were given close study in monasteries. These manuscripts included much pagan lore from the early Greek and Roman cultures and Islamic teachings from the Arab world, and thus many were declared heretical and burned. Fortunately, monks became the preservers of knowledge, diligently and secretly copying manuscripts. The Benedictine library at Monte Cassino in Italy was for centuries the depository for such valuable early manuscripts. Moved for safety to the Vatican, this precious collection escaped destruction in the Allied bombing of Monte Cassino in World War II.

In *Herbals, Their Origin and Evolution*, author Agnes Arber lists the principal herbals and related botanical works published between 1470 and 1670, totaling approximately 144. Arber admits that this list is probably incomplete.

Not surprisingly, the earliest printed herbals were either transcriptions of earlier manuscripts or contained information borrowed from them. Latin was the language of the first printings, and such Latin texts printed before 1501 were called incunabula (from the Latin for "swaddling clothes"). Later, because the first printing took place in Germany, German began to replace it. An early incunabulum is *Hortus* (*Ortus*) *Sanitatis* or *Gart der Gesundheit*, the Garden of Health. It was published by Peter Schoeffer in 1485 at Mainz where printing with movable type is believed to have originated between 1440 and 1450. Like other herbals of the Middle Ages it embraced medical and household uses for plants along with folklore and superstition, and included recipes for the preparation of foods, for preparing poisons for pests, for cleansing the scalp of lice, and suggestions for preserving sweet-smelling herbs to lay among clothes. One reads of herbs that should be used for "drunkenness," for "wicked unchaste dreams," for "wicked spirits," "to have grace," "to be fruitful."

Arber defines the herbal thus:

> A book containing the names and descriptions of herbs, or of plants in general, with their properties and virtues. The word is believed to have been derived from the medieval Latin adjective, herbalis, "the substantive "liber" (book) being understood. It thus simply means "herb book."

Accordingly, a herbalist is a writer or student of herbals, not necessarily a herb gardener.

Some herbists find a serene joy in the seclusion of a garden with herbs all about them, whereas others experience ecstasy in the seclusion of a library with herbals on every side. Still others enjoy both. They find that nurturing a herb, perhaps a rosemary, has more meaning to them when they are aware of the significance the herb has had in human affairs throughout the ages.

Among the outstanding German herbals of the sixteenth and seventeenth centuries are Otto Brunfels's *Herbarium vivae eiconis*, 1530, Hieronymus Bock's *Neu Kreuter Buch* (*Kräuterbuch*), 1539 (the first work to note the mode of occurrences and localities of plants), and Leonhard Fuchs's *De historia stirpium*, 1542. In the work of Fuchs, a German physician, plants are described scientifically with each individual character and habit, and the woodcuts are exact like-

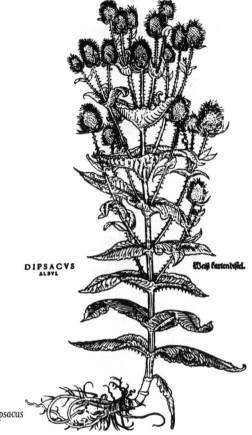

DIPSACVS
ALBVS

Fig. 4. A woodcut of fuller's teasel, *Dipsacus sativus*, from Fuch's *De historia stirpium*.

nesses of plants and splendid pieces of art. Many of its woodcuts were copied by later herbalists. Plants are arranged in alphabetical order, no attempt being made to form natural groupings or a system of plant classification, but in *De historia stirpium* Fuchs made a first attempt to establish a botanical terminology from which later scientific terminology and morphology were developed. The beautiful fuchsia was named for him.

An early Italian herbal is Mattioli's *Commentarii*, 1544, frequently translated into other languages. Reprints of the woodcuts are still popular decorative items.

Perhaps the best-known English herbal is John Gerard's *The Herbal*, pub-

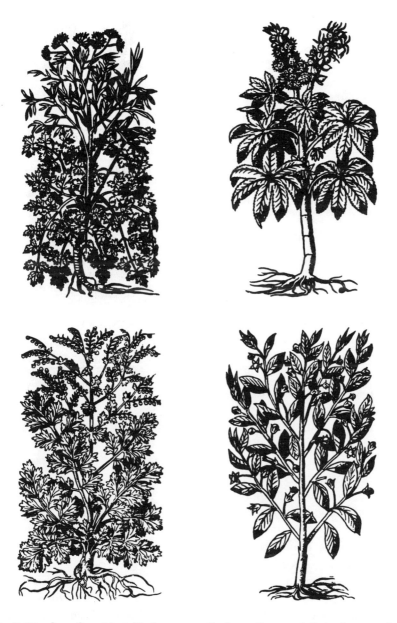

Fig. 5. Woodcuts from Mattioli's *Commentarii*. Clockwise from top left: Parsley, *Petroselinum crispum*; castor bean, *Ricinus communis*; belladonna, *Atropa belladonna*; bitter wormwood, *Artemisia absinthium*.

lished in London, 1597. Although Gerard is credited with the work, it is generally conceded that much of the work was done by the Belgian botanist Rembert Dodoens. One Dr. Priest in London was making a translation of the writing into English but died before it was finished. Gerard rearranged the work, brought it to completion, and put his name on the book (plagiarism was commonplace among herbalists). A revised and enlarged edition of The Herbal was published by Thomas Johnson in 1633 and is acknowledged today as an enduring and exemplary document of Renaissance botany in excellent Elizabethan prose. The 1633 edition is a gold mine of accumulated plant lore, including medicinal uses as known in the early seventeenth century. In 1975 Dover Publications republished the 1633 edition, so that it is still available outside libraries.

In discussing herbals, one must mention two pseudoscientific themes popular among the herbalists: the doctrine of signatures, and botanical astrology. According to the doctrine of signatures, a plant's color, form, or size gives a clear indication—a "signature"—of its medicinal use. For example, a yellow-flowered plant was to be used for jaundice; mottled leaves, as found in lungwort, Pulmonaria officinalis, resembled lung tissue, and therefore lungwort would be effective for respiratory diseases. The plant's habits also counted; sage, Salvia officinalis, a long-lived plant, was thought to lengthen the life span, whereas short-lived plants ought to be avoided. Some herb historians hold that the doctrine of signatures was introduced into Europe by the Arabs from China in the Middle Ages.

Astrological thinking has long held sway over human minds, so it is not surprising that men of medicine made a connection between the zodiac and the plants. Herbal writers advocated selecting specific healing plants according to the position of certain constellations in the sky. Astrological calendars gave information on the appropriate time for gathering other herbs. Perhaps the planting advice in modern farmers' almanacs descends from astrological botany.

Theophrastus Bombastus von Hohenheim, 1493–1541, of Switzerland, better known by his adopted name, Paracelsus ("Beyond Celsus," an early Roman encyclopedist), was an exponent of the erroneous doctrine of signatures as well as astrological botany. His writings influenced men well into the seventeenth century. Paracelsus studied alchemy and gained medical experience by caring for the poor, a nonconforming practice for a physician of the period. On the positive side, his speculations introduced the concept of chemical processes in the human body, unknown at his time and ignored by the schools of medicine. He comes down to us as the forerunner in the association of chemistry with medicine.

Among the seventeenth century English herbalists who extolled the doctrine of signatures and astrological botany were Nicholas Culpepper in *A Physical Directory*, 1649, William Cole in *Adam in Eden: or, Natures Paradise*, 1657, and Robert Turner in *The British Physician: or, The Nature and Vertues of English Plants*, 1664. Culpepper continues to retain an appreciative audience among those who choose to be either humbugged or amused.

The medieval herbals, as well as those of the Renaissance, were compiled almost wholly by and for physicians; medical knowledge was dominated by the properties of plants. Throughout the Middle Ages Dioscorides's *De materia medica*, botanically worthless, was preferred to the more scholarly works of Theophrastus.

The medieval herbalist's chief stumbling block was his ignorance of plant geography. He did not understand that medicinal plants described by the ancients, particularly Dioscorides, were indigenous to the Mediterranean area and simply not to be found in Germany or the rest of Europe. He failed to realize that flora differed from region to region, and since he had little interest in exact investigations of plant relationships, his erroneous assumptions eventually led to a confusion of plant nomenclature.

A great advance was made to right these misconceptions when early German herbalists began going straight to nature for their information, describing the plants growing around them, and had figures of them carefully drawn or executed in woodcuts. These first botanical works were published in Germany and the Netherlands between 1530 and 1623.

Plant nomenclature used in the medieval and Renaissance herbals is often erroneous by the taxonomic systems of classification employed today. Although Latinized names were used, they did not consistently match scientific binomials.

Taken as a whole, the illuminated manuscripts and herbals, with their skillfully executed woodcuts and illustrations, lie in the realm of art history. They are also invaluable as historical documents studied by medical researchers, pharmaceutical houses, botanists, and historians. To anyone interested in old horticultural practices, herb gardening, folklore, and symbolism associated with plants, these lovely old volumes are full of interest, too. But they are not scientific.

The science of botany did not come into its own until the Renaissance when botanic gardens were created at universities with medical schools and chairs for professors of botany established. The Universities of Pisa and Padua founded botanic gardens in 1543 and 1545 respectively to support their schools of medicine. Likewise, distinguished botanical gardens of the sixteenth and seventeenth century were laid out in Bologna, Leipzig, Leyden, Montpellier, Oxford, and Edinburgh. London had its Chelsea Physic garden, founded by the Society of Apothecaries in 1673. All were created for the study of plants for use in medicine.

As these collections grew and began to include plants arriving from different parts of the world, knowledge of plants expanded rapidly. Soon scholars had launched a movement to establish exact identification of specimens, nomenclature methods, and systems of classification, and the study of medicinal plants slowly evolved into the study of plants per se. Today botanic gardens, established throughout the world, may be dedicated to pure botanic research or attached to medical schools and pharmaceutical houses for scientific investigation. Or they may be there just to be enjoyed. The plant world has come a long way from mere "simples" used in the art of healing.

Herbs in America

From the sixteenth century onward, settlers arriving in America from the rest of the world brought with them packets of herbs and seeds for planting. Herbs served as medicinal comforters on the long sea journeys to the New World. In the chests of linens were tucked such miscellaneous seeds as tansy, santolina, and wormwoods, as insecticides and vermicides. Few, if any, of the European, Asian, and African herbs were indigenous to America, but as introduced species they flourished in the kitchen gardens or escaped into the fields and roadsides to become part of the American landscape. Today many are so common that we call them weeds.

The earliest herbal bearing upon medicinal plants native to the Western Hemisphere is the *Badianus* manuscript composed in 1552 by two Aztecs, Martin de la Cruz and Juannes Badianus, who translated it into Latin. After its discovery in the Vatican Library in the 1930s the manuscript was translated into English by Emily Emmart and published in a facsimile version in the United States.

American Indians employed all manner of native American plants as medicines, but since their languages were unwritten, they passed on herbal lore by word of mouth. Eventually settlers from the Eastern Hemisphere began to learn plant lore from skilled natives, and American Indian herbal medicine became a part of the early settlers' lives.

The Indians borrowed freely from the newcomers as well, utilizing plants from the Eastern Hemisphere. In time the foreign origins of such plants were forgotten, and the introduced species became jumbled together in more than one writing about Indian herbal plants. They were assigned Indian usages, despite being set apart according to ethnobotanical accounts of primitive American Indian tribes. For this reason collectors of native American herbs are advised to work with references placing emphasis on precise documentation of native habitats.

Rituals of the Indian medicine men in regard to plants were not far removed from superstition, the doctrine of signatures, and astrological botany associated with herbal cures among Europeans. But they knew genuine remedies as well. Indians treated rheumatic pain with wintergreen oil from the plant *Gaultheria procumbens*, which has as one of its constituents methyl salicylate. Laboratory investigation has determined that this substance is indeed medically effective.

Some indigenous plants listed as medicinal produce toxic components about which qualified pharmacognosists and pharmaceutical researchers warn us. While a fair amount of native herbal plants are confirmed and safe dosages are prescribed, a quantity are declared more toxic and magical than useful.

Many herb gardeners treasure and collect native American healing plants. Bee balm, *Monarda didyma*, is a familiar favorite in nearly every garden. During the famous pre-Revolutionary boycott of tea, American Indians suggested the rebellious Americans substitute bee balm for China tea. As a flower, the attractive bee balm made an impression on the French court in the seventeenth century, and rapidly all Europe became pleased with the large red floral heads. Recently pokeberry, or pokeweed, *Phytolacca americana*, has appeared in English herb gardens. Seeds of the mountain mints, *Pycnanthemum* spp., and anise hyssop, *Agastache foeniculum*, are becoming favored. Throughout the United States there is a strong trend toward placing American native herbs in the garden. Perhaps our enthusiasm for the indigenous plants is a reflection of current interest in ecology and preservation of our American natural heritage.

America has been described as a melting pot. Its people join hearts and minds once they arrive on its shores. But the cooking pot distinctly retains with pride the basic ingredients and herbal seasonings of a mother country. Herbs tied to cooking traditions of forebears continue to be grown near the kitchen door. Descendants from the British Isles allot space for clumps of sage; a German-American family keeps parsley, chive, summer savory (Bohnenkraut), thyme, and sweet marjoram; Italian-Americans culture garlic and sow basil when the weather warms; Greek-Americans cherish potted rosemary and, like Latins, seek out a specific oregano known to them from their homeland.

Americans in rural areas, through the nineteenth century, continued gathering native Indian medicinal plants and used them as their own in addition to remedies brought from the Old Country. When they could not find or afford Old World remedies, they substituted those of the new. Blossoms and bracts of American basswood replaced European linden blossoms and were blended with leaves of wintergreen to make an evening tea. Red bay and sweet bay of the southeastern coastal plain substituted for Mediterranean bay. Dried sassafras leaves became filé, used to thicken gumbo.

Organized collective farms, particularly the Shakers, grew and supplied medicinal and culinary plant materials. Shakers were advocates of functionalism and simplicity, so ornamental herb gardens had no place in their settlements, but they stocked druggists' shelves with Old World botanical remedies and native Indian plant medicines. Decline in the number of Shakers plus gradual changes in the direct application of plants to medicine reduced availability and demand.

During World War I, 1914–1918, embargoes kept necessary plant materials from entering our country, resulting in a dearth of medicinal herbs. The United States government hurriedly subsidized the growing of medicinal plants on a field scale. By the time the war was over, some participants in the government program had become herb devotees. In addition, many Americans had been captivated with English garden styles, and a great fervor for historic garden restorations came into vogue, especially for colonial houses of the seventeenth and eighteenth centuries with their lovely adjoining gardens enclosed with boxwood. New herbists absorbed the style for making gardens with herbs. Rekindling a herbal orientation not only brought into existence ornamental herb gardens, but a revival of many herbal connections.

During the 1930s and 1940s herb publications began to appear in book-shops, written in a popular style and soon became classics. Rosetta E. Clarkson, Helen M. Fox, Helen N. Webster, and Louise B. Wilder were among the writers who roused interest in herbs, all genuine herbists writing directly from their own gardening experiences. In 1933 the Herb Society of America was founded.

After World War II there was much new interest in ethnic cooking and exploring foreign cuisines. These were often dependent upon a herb season-ing. Enjoyment of these dishes was further stimulated by the return of American soldiers who often brought with them war brides from abroad. The period was marked by the crossing of ethnic lines in friendships and marriages. Through the war years American women entered the defense work force. Acquaintanceships formed in defense plants brought forward the heritage of American ethnic kitchens, many times with exchanges from a "brown bag lunch." Applause came to the ethnic cook who properly ap-plied herbs from his or her ethnic origin; it was not a pinch of this or that.

Relevancy of Herbs Today

Herbs have come down through the ages with little change in genetic con-tent—a contrast to the highly developed hybrids of the cultivated garden and tilled field which provide society with foods or handsome, large colorful blooms. Herbs of the garden, or in the wild, are essentially natural species. Seed harvested from such plants give assurance the progeny will be similar to the parent plant.

The only exception to this is where natural hybridization has occurred. An assortment of variations (not genetic) can be seen among herbs growing in an environment markedly different from their native habitats. The modifi-cations demonstrate a genetic ability to adapt and survive.

As natural species, herbs can be expected to have greater genetic resis-tance to diseases than artificially developed hybrids. If herbs are grown in an environment that mimics their natural habitat, they may produce inhibitors that repel specific insects. Sprigs of bee balm or pennyroyal in the gardener's hat make excellent mosquito repellents.

A garden of interplanted vegetables, flowers, and herbs—gardeners call it companion planting—not only give aesthetic satisfaction, but also provides food and flavors, and reduces plant disease by the efficacy of the herbs' inhibitors and the scattered arrangement, because pests and diseases do not spread as rapidly as they do in crops planted in neat orderly rows. The phenomenon was described by Pliny the Elder of the first century, and George Washington practiced it in the Mount Vernon kitchen garden. Even so, the variableness of climates, soils, and insect populations, influenced by weather conditions are factors for consideration before acknowledging all the reputed positive effects of companion planting.

Today, rational man's attitude toward herbs as medicine has changed from unquestioning acceptance, blended with superstition, to a scientific approach. Botany and medicine, so closely linked for the greater part of mankind's history, are now treated as separate scientific disciplines.

Organic chemists have unlocked the chemical structures of plant drugs. We call it phytochemistry and ally scientific investigation with ethnobotanical accounts and folklore, to find ways of treating physical ailments, of prolonging life, or of making it more endurable. The "active principles" of toxic substances are isolated by the phytochemist from sometimes poisonous plants. Thereby toxicity is controlled, and safe dosages are standardized. Using isolated essential principles of plant material in controlled dosage avoids the dangers of treatment with crude drugs, or imbibing parts of the plant that contain harmful chemicals.

Today, direct use of plant drugs has been replaced by their synthesized forms. Plant material is not sufficient to supply the world's population, nor is it affordable. Thus laboratories analyze plant parts to isolate the valuable molecules and then re-create the substance artificially. Moreover, the narrow margin between effective and toxic dosages is better discerned by laboratory testing than by orders of early herbalists or the Indian medicine man.

Nevertheless, we can learn a great deal from history to improve the quality of our lives. We embrace the great civilization of Greece, which left an indelible stamp on the art and thought of the Western World. Rome became victorious to be gently conquered by defeated Greece through its culture and the power of its ideas. Grecian thought moved west. As inheritors of the classic tradition we turn with some hesitancy, therefore, to Oriental culture now influencing Western thought and patterns of living. From the ancient history of herbs can we find answers by examining the trade routes of the ancients linking East and West and the cargo of herbs and spices? The 1977 publication of *A Barefoot Doctor's Manual* introduced the West to Chinese herbal remedies derived from its native flora. American pharmacognosists are finding some medical justification for the drugs of the Orient, and Asian herbs, arriving with people from all parts of the Far East, are adding an important dimension to our gardens and kitchens.

Food should not be merely nourishment. It should be one of the amenities that make life a joy. When we take delight in food, that contributes to its digestibility and healthfulness. Savory herbs contribute enormously to making nutritious but insipid foods palatable and pleasurable.

Until recently, land was thought too valuable and our production costs too high to consider herb growing profitable enterprise. That attitude has changed. Many people are now engaged in growing herbs and furnishing them fresh to the markets. By distillation or solvent extraction essential oils are separated from the vegetable base for culinary or perfume use. For culinary usage the process destroys a certain character of the herb, although economically it is worthy.

A herb garden accommodates our spatial and sensory needs. Space is not perceived with the sense of vision alone. All the senses are here involved and not the least is the sense of smell. Thermal effects also are created in a herb garden where the color tones of silver, blue, refreshing greens and gray provide an oasis of coolness, a relief from glare and tension. It is important to create environments that satisfy all the senses in the limited amount of territory available.

Life in a city bars man from nature. Urban ecologists emphatically state that the crowding of men into cities and the uniformity of their occupations produce a craving for an extraordinary incident. Might not a pot of herbs in the small space allotted an urban dweller produce a token of satisfaction? The green aromatic plant becomes an extraordinary incident—a decorative factor, a culinary delight, a healing balm, and a developer of a wholesome psyche.

3 ❧ Nomenclature for the Herbist

Beginning herb gardeners are usually interested in the basics of the learning process—seeing, touching, smelling, tasting, listening, doing—before they learn the vocabulary. Trying to learn botanical names of herbs first, in fact, is a fine way to kill the pleasure in herb gardening. As one's interest and knowledge increases, however, so does one's desire to call herbs by their correct names. As a Chinese proverb states, "The beginning of wisdom is to call things by their right names."

A recent meeting of herb gardeners became shockingly embarrassing when two members fell to quarreling over the name "rue." One spoke about the rue in her herb garden, and her counterpart "corrected" her, basing her statements on plants growing in her area commonly called meadow rue. The membership made an effort to explain the apparent contradiction by distinguishing the two by their botanical names. Because the meadow rue gardener was reluctant to accept the concept of botanical names, an impasse resulted.

The rue of the herb gardener is *Ruta graveolens*, of the rue family, to which the citrus fruits also belong. It is native to south Europe, has attractive blue-green, deeply segmented leaves, each segment spoon-shaped, and was used as a vermifuge. Oil in the leaves causes dermatitis in some people. Meadow rue is Thalictrum dioicum and belongs to the buttercup family, is native to North America, and was used medicinally by the Cherokee Indians.

At a public herb cooking session, a speaker included in her custard recipe yellow petals of pot-marigold to give the custard a deeper yellow color and a delicate flavor. A newspaper writer covering the meeting included the recipe in an article, but failed to specify pot-marigold, Calendula officinalis. Readers mistook "marigold" for ordinary garden marigolds, Tagetes spp., which have tightly packed petals, finely cut leaves, and an unpleasant odor. The resulting custards were understandably unsavory and brought many complaints to the local botanic garden. Use of the correct botanic name, Calendula officinalis, would have made all the difference.

Botanical names are important. They do not change from region to region or country to country. Botanical names enable a nursery to satisfy you properly, describe the herb for someone in a distant land who speaks a language you do not know, and open the doors of factual information in the literature.

Using a common name may cause difficulties for you. You may be looking for the plant that provides "bay leaf" for cooking. Perhaps your mother of European lineage referred to it as "laurel." Or, you know "sweet bay" and "red bay," both native to low areas and swamps in the warm southern climate. When scrutinizing plant catalogs you may find listed "bayberry" and "California bay." An order placed for "laurel" could be mistaken for the poisonous American mountain laurel, Kalmia latifolia; "bayberry," another American native and source of wax for bayberry candles, refers to Myrica spp. Neither belong in a stew. Classic "bay," native in the Mediterranean region and associated with the crown placed on a winning athlete or scholar, is Laurus nobilis and supplies the correct seasoning leaf. "Sweet bay," Magnolia virginiana, "red bay," Persea borbonia, and "California bay," Umbellularia californica, are native American plants that may be substituted for classic bay leaves when the latter are unavailable.

Among plants, herbs are notorious for having more common names than nonherbal species. These many names testify to their popularity through the centuries. Common names are an important part of our cultural heritage. Sometimes they are fanciful; at other times accurately descriptive. A single species may have two or more common names in a single location and many others in other areas, depending upon the geographical distribution of the herb and the languages spoken where it grows and/or is used. A friend asked me recently about names. She had read of "fennel-flower," "black cumin," and "Roman coriander" as being names of the plant, Nigella damascena. What really identified this herb if it had common names drawn from a number of different herbs?

I pointed out that N. damascena is the ornamental love-in-a-mist of the buttercup family, as is the herb correctly known as N. sativa, an annual historically used as a peppery seasoning and in ancient times grown in Mediterranean fields of wheat and barley for its insecticidal properties. It is also known as nutmeg flower "faux cumin, quatre épices, toute épice" in French, "Schwarzkümmel" in German, "kazha" in Arabic, "ketzah" in Hebrew; in the Bible it is erroneously translated as "dill" (RSV) and "fitches" (KJV) (Isaiah 28: 25 & 27). A gentleman and his wife who were members of my herb class, brought us sweet breads pleasantly seasoned with the aromatic black seeds of N. sativa, plus a supply of seeds to start plants in the garden. The ornamental love-in-a-mist, N. damascena, known not to have been cultivated in ancient time and having a very inferior flavor, is hardly a substitute.

Common names are confusing because they are so numerous, and in some herbal connections their use is hazardous. Without scientific basis and not governed by any code, common names are without authority and have no legal standing. They also fail to define relationships in an order of succession to other plants.

It was when men noted similarities and differences among plants and began to group them in families that shared common characteristics that scientific classification became possible. A plant's name is its pedigree.

Beginning with the ancients, classification and identification of plants followed many diverse courses. By the seventeenth century nomenclature and synonymy had reached a state of extreme confusion because different authors employed awkward, unstable, and inconsistent methods of identifying plants. The impact of movements through the world, including the New World, brought attention to the increased number of plants. There was a need for a simple and unified classification system. Today over 300,000 types of plants inhabit the earth. To be able to think, study, and talk about them requires a systematic approach.

Simplicity and consistency were brought into the naming process when

the work of the Swedish systematic botanist Carl Linnaeus (1707–1778) became known through his writings, *Genera Plantarum* (1737) and *Species Plantarum* (1753). He established a two-word name for individual plants and animals, *genus* and *species* (or specific epithet).

Before Linnaeus died, the binomial (two-name) system of nomenclature
had been accepted as the best means of identifying and classifying living
things. Linnaeus used Latin for his system and so made it available to the
learned world of his day. However, his Latin was not classical Latin, but a
technical form derived from renaissance and medieval Latin that included
borrowings from Greek and other languages. Thus the genus and specific
epithet in botanical nomenclature are Latinized words formed from many
languages and the system remains international in scope.

The process of identification and labeling rests on a plant's natural relationships to other plants. Often it is difficult to decide whether two or more
plants are the same or not. It is not a matter of the plants being identical,
merely similar enough to be grouped together. Are the two fundamentally
and uniformly alike, potentially capable of interbreeding and producing fertile offspring, reproductively isolated from other groups? Such a group of
closely similar individuals is called a species, the basic unit in the hierarchy
of plant classification.

A secondary unit of classification is the genus. A *genus* (plural, *genera*) consists of different species which, while differing from each other in some characters, are brought together by a certain common resemblance; for example,
most members of the genus *Allium* have flowers arranged in a round head
(umbel). Think of onions, *A. cepa*, leeks, *A. ampeloprasum*, Porrum group, and
chive, *A. schoenoprasum* in bloom.

The species name is an adjective—or a word used as one—and it may be
descriptive of a distinctive feature, (*odoratum*, "odorous"), or it may record
place of origin (*canadense*, Canada), commemorate a person (*requienii*, for Es-
prit Requien), or be a former genus name (*majoranum*).

In binomial nomenclature, common sage is *Salvia officinalis*, and this botanical name distinguishes it from all other species of the genus *Salvia*, of
which there are more than 700. Herb gardens may hold, in addition to
S. officinalis, *S. sclarea*, clary sage, *S. viridis*, red-topped sage, *S. pratensis*, meadow
sage, *S. dorisiana*, *S. elegans*, pineapple sage, and *S. lyrata*, cancerweed.

The binomial is italicized; the genus name is always capitalized, the species is in lower case. In this book the option to capitalize is not taken when a specific epithet commemorates a person or is a generic name used as a specific epithet. After the first use in a paragraph the genus name may be abbreviated to its initial as in the preceding paragraph.

Just as species are grouped into genera, so genera sharing basic similarities are distinguished as plant families; they are capitalized, but not italicized: Ranunculaceae, the buttercup family. In the naming of families, eight have been known for such a long time by names formed in another manner that either of the two names may be and are used in classification systems. Because four of these families hold a vast number of herbs the use of one or the other used in references can be confusing. To avoid a possible difficulty for herbists, common family names are used in this book. Families, in turn, are grouped to form successively orders, classes, and divisions.

The taxonomy (classification) of Linnaeus was based on a so-called sexual system. His exact observations and long study confirmed that reproductive parts remain fairly stable so that plants will reproduce successfully. The investigations led him to classify plants into major groups according to their reproductive parts, based on numbers of stamens and pistils. Flower parts, apart from size and color, remain constant in structure and in number and arrangement: petals, sepals, stamens, pistils. These unchanging characters are used to distinguish families. On the other hand the size and hairiness of leaves are not constant and hence are diagnostically unimportant. But the ways in which leaves are arranged—always opposite along a stem or always alternate or in whorls—are important vegetative characters in some families.

Linnaeus's system is called artificial because it was arrived at by descriptive science and Aristotelian logic. Today, with the tools of modern science— genetics, morphology, ecology, chemistry—and markedly different presuppositions as a result of experimental approaches, systems of classification are "natural." That is, they attempt to bring the lines of descent (phylogenetic relationship) into taxonomy. As plants' phylogenetic positions become clearer, some name changes are necessary. This is annoying to herbists and other gardeners, who have grown used to the old term, but there is also cause to be thankful when a herb's position has finally been determined and a degree of error eliminated.

The abbreviation L. for Linnaeus is appended to about 12,000 binomials, indicating the man who first described and classified the plant. When a second author has made an accepted change in a binomial, the abbreviated name of the original author is placed in parenthesis, followed by the abbreviated name of the author who made the change—for example, *Arisaema triphyllum* (L.) Torr., jack-in-the-pulpit. The abbreviated authors' names serve as bibliographic reference.

It is astounding to discover the large number of American native herbs named by Linnaeus. Specimens were sent to Uppsala for identification by his student in America, Peter Kalm, and by a host of English and American collectors. If the item had not been previously described, Linnaeus properly named and placed them in their families. Today's herbists are aided in tracing medicinal plants by Linnaeus's habit of designating medicinal plants used in his time as *officinalis*.

In addition to genus and species, plant identifications often indicate varieties and subspecies. These are subdivisions of species, sufficiently similar to the species standard to belong in that category yet having some minor distinguishing element, such as a slight difference in form or color. The distinguishing element is usually associated with a specific geographical area or exists as a result of environmental influences and is sporadic. Factors independent of genetical inheritance may affect it. Some herbal varieties: *Allium sativum* var. *ophioscorodon*, rocambole; *Origanum vulgare* var. *prismaticum*, oregano; *Lavandula dentata* var. *candicans*, larger and hairier-leaved toothed lavender.

To indicate hybrid origin within a genus, rules for naming require that a cross sign precede the specific epithet: *Mentha* x *piperita*, peppermint.

Rules of botanical nomenclature are formulated by an international botanical congress, the first in Paris in 1867. After international accord was reached to maintain an international system in 1935 a third edition of the *International Code of Botanical Nomenclature* was published. Revisions by action of a congress continue to be published. By international agreement, no two kinds of plants may have the same name at the same time, nor can one plant have more than one correct name. Every kind of plant has a different combination of generic name and specific epithet. When official changes are made in botanical names, the earlier name(s) become legally invalid.

Horticultural plant varieties are governed by the *International Code of Nomenclature of Cultivated Plants*, adopted in the United States in 1959. Rules and regulations are published in booklet form by the American Horticultural Society.

Emphasis is placed on the cultivar name, a word derived from "cultivated variety." Cultivars are distinguished from botanical varieties in that they are known only in cultivation. The cultivar, which may or may not be registered, is written with the initial letter capitalized. It is distinguished by the cv. abbreviation before it and/or by enclosing the name in single quotation marks. A cultivar name is assigned to a genus name or to a complete binomial to which it belongs. Because Latin is not used for the cultivar name, it is written in Roman type: *Pelargonium crispum* 'French Lace', a variegated lemon-scented geranium.

For a herbist a little knowledge of Latin is helpful, especially noun and adjective endings, and a Latin dictionary is often a help in deciphering esoteric names. But for the enthusiast, a guidebook to the botanical names is a must.

The attachment of virtues to herbs is often reflected in their generic names; *Alchemilla* is from the Arabic word *al-kimiya*, "alchemy," and refers to the use of dew gathered from this plant in alchemy; *Asclepias* (genus of milkweed) commemorates the Greek god of medicine and healing; *Pulmonaria* (genus of lungwort) from the Latin *pulmo*, lung, reflects its early application for respiratory disorders; *Salvia* from the Latin *salvére*, meaning "to be in good health."

Species, as adjectives (descriptive), agree in gender and number with the genus name they modify: *Cistus incanus* (grayish), *Lavandula angustifolia* (narrow-leaved), *Eupatorium purpureum* (purple). Some common specific epithets: *vulgaris* (common or usual), *americanus* (American), *albus* (white), *niger* (black), *pubescens* (clothed, which in plant terms means covered with soft, downy hair), *arborescens* (becoming treelike), *virens* (green), *sempervirens* (evergreen). A specific Greek ending, *-oides*, means "resembling" or "similar to": *ambrosioides* (resembling *Ambrosia*). Botanical names are much easier to keep in your memory when you are aware of what they mean.

If Latin pronunciation disturbs you, consider that it is more logical than English. It is phonetic, with no silent letters. Each consonant has only one sound. As a rule, if a word has two syllables accent is placed on the first syllable; if more than two syllables accent is placed next to the last syllable if that syllable is a long one either in spelling or pronunciation; otherwise the accent is on the third from the last syllable. While Latin academicians change pronunciation rules as they investigate pronunciation changes made by the Romans in their time, and audio communications make us aware of pronunciation changes in the language we speak, there are no hard-and-fast rules in pronunciation. Don't be afraid to use the Latin botanical names; let them roll off your tongue as you see them in print, and repeat the sounds in the herb's name as you place it in the ground. Correct spelling is essential in writing.

One may wish to, but one cannot always couch botanical names in English. In writing and speaking botanical terms are essential for providing accurate, precise information and to eliminate confusion. But when potatoes need a garnish, take a sprig of parsley from the garden. And may you catch a whiff of lemon verbena leaves on the way back to the kitchen.

4 ❧ Design and Environment

Designing and creating a herb garden is an art which gives form to space. The space is perceived as a composition for the accommodation of herbal plants in harmonious alliance with adjacent spaces. Styles of herb gardens work best when blended with the natural environment of the property and the architectural features of the surrounding buildings. The "spirit of the place" is regarded. It is pleasing when the garden follows the natural terrain, and the size of areas set apart for herbs and focal points are planned to relate to one another. In this wise the shapes and lines of a herb garden become echoes of the interior and exterior architectural features of the house. The garden is an extension of the house; house and garden are seen together. Climatic suitability and seasonal values are given attention.

A herb garden need not be very large or impressive, but, as conceived by the owner, it is very personal. Small postage-sized herb gardens are often hidden from public view; like a cloistered monastery garden, they are enjoyed as very private retreats, sheltering a keeper from social whirls and plants from unfettered winds.

By tradition and function herb gardens are located near a doorway to the house; snipping herbs for a dish in preparation demands few steps. A garden can be fully appreciated when the herbs can be viewed from windows through all seasons. Draw plans with winter, as well as summer, in mind. A lovely herb garden in winter can pleasantly stir our sensibilities when we look out on soft gray and green-foliaged evergreen plants. A herb garden close to daily outdoor activities or along pathways and terraces adjoining a house is beauty close-up, to see, touch, and smell.

There are guidelines that result in a garden whispering kindly. There is wisdom in taking plants' native habitats into consideration, in selecting herbs in accordance with the climate, light exposure, and soil type of the potential garden site. Garden designs developed as reflections of native habitats, however formalized, are sensible for successful herb cultivation. Attempts to create perfect environments for specific herbs is sound ecological practice. In a garden herbs grow better and look better if planted as nearly as possible within the range of environmental factors to which they have adapted in their native habitat.

Grouping herbs according to their native habitats and developing a concern for ecosystems makes good sense. Individual plant species and their environment are not linked by accident. Ecosystems are the archetypical gardens; they select plants for adaptive fit. The preservation of a herb species is difficult and at times impossible without preserving or re-creating its ecosystem. A species is what it is where it is; a papyrus without water is a compromised papyrus. Landscapes and gardens designed ecologically, with a particular region as the basic plan, draw attention to the aesthetic value of herbs, to analogies, cross-relationships, and to the historical and ethnic connections of herbs. A self-reproducing natural association inevitably produces spatial configurations different from a preconceived scheme; the collection of herbs unfolds naturally, developing into a pleasing scene, reminiscent of a region.

All too frequently we are tempted to heed contrived garden designs prepared for climates and soil types unlike the climates or soil types of the site chosen for our garden. In popular writings excessive emphasis is placed on stereotyped patterns, and little attention, unfortunately, is paid to designs that uphold the connections of herbs with their origins. Look for references that describe environmental factors as soil type, moisture, nutrients, temperature, wind, and light quality of specific herbs you want to grow. Helpful brief native habitat descriptions are given in the Descriptive Catalog of Herbs in this book. Such information is valuable in developing a successful herb garden. Observe herbs growing in your garden or in the wild to decide on sites, site preparation, and design to suit their needs. It is possible to create one or more environmental habitats varying enormously from yours. Successful cultivation of a visually agreeable garden lies in formulating designs from the herb's point-of-view or in reproducing a native habitat to as great a degree as possible.

A low dry-stone wall with a full sun exposure offers an excellent site for herbs from the sun-baked Mediterranean region; prepare an alkaline soil and place it between the stones. Rosemary, *Rosmarinus officinalis*, lavender, *Lavandula angustifolia*, sage, *Salvia officinalis*, winter savory, *Satureja montana*, or common thyme, *Thymus vulgaris*, inserted between the stones or rising on top of the wall, flourish and add grace to the structure. Gray, hairy borage, *Borago officinalis*, once planted, self-seeds on the ground below the wall. Perhaps a clump of horehound, *Marrubium vulgare*, is nearby. The stones, heated by the sun in the wintertime, keep the soil warm. Drainage is excellent. The colors, shapes, and scents identify the scene as a natural Mediterranean herbal association.

Herbs exist wherever plants grow and people find a use for them. A great number of plants designated herbs, however, have their origins in the Mediterranean region—that is, southern Europe, parts of southwest Asia, and northern Africa, the cradle of Western civilization. Herbs growing on the Mediterranean landscape are heavy with fragrant oils, chiefly by virtue of the Mediterranean climate and its soil. The climate is warm and sunny, heated by hot winds from the Sahara Desert. Cooler temperatures exist at higher altitudes. The air is dry; there is little rainfall in summer. The long summer drought is followed by a short, mild winter with rains. Because the summer is so dry, Mediterranean plants grow in late winter when water is available, and survive the dry, hot summer by the adaptive features of their leaves, which protect them from aridity and heat. The land is for the most part sloping. The soil is thin with rocky outcroppings, alkaline, calcareous. (See plate 1.)

In contrast, the American Southeast includes a variety of climates and soil types. At higher elevations of the Cumberland Plateau and the Blue Ridge, temperatures for all seasons are lower than on the piedmont and along the coastal plain. Temperate, subtropical, and tropical temperatures of the Southeast are influenced by a combination of latitudes and elevations, but four well-defined seasons occur in all of them except a very limited tropical region.

In the foothills, on the piedmont, and in the coastal plain the air in summer can become quite humid. High humidity and heavy rainfall during spring and summer create favorable conditions for fungus diseases among plants from arid climates. Such Mediterranean herbs as *Thymus* spp., lavenders, rosemarys, *Helichrysum* spp., and *Santolina* spp. are vulnerable. Gardens containing these plants should be designed to permit the best possible air circulation, in order to avoid blights and stem rots. Herbs from arid climates respond favorably when planted on hillocks and well apart from one another rather than juxtaposed.

In the Cumberland Plateau and westward, lime soils appear in conjunction with limestone, and farther south there are other spots of alkaline soil, which support a distinct native flora. But for the most part soils in the Southeast are acid. Heavy clay soils hold water from heavy rainfalls, and drain poorly. Native American herbal plants of the Southeast, as one might expect, consort happily in this acid soil with the native rhododendrons. A great number of herbs having dissimilar origins show no correlation with the alkalinity or acidity of the soil, but, a considerable number need alkaline or calcareous soil in order to grow more luxuriantly and resist fungus and insect infestations. But herbs originating in regions with alkaline soil require that acid soil be treated with sufficient lime to raise the pH level to about 7.5.

Good drainage is of great importance in growing herbs, unless they are aquatic in nature. Drainage is improved by incorporating sharp sand into a soil of clay. (Avoid beach sand, which is smooth, packs, and does not permit air and water to pass through.) In the coastal areas and sandy countries, the procedure is reversed; to hold water, humus and even clay are combined with the sand, in addition to heavy liming.

If it is impractical to correct surface level soil, the herb gardener may circumvent the problem by building up a suitable soil in raised beds, preparing mounds or berms; using containers as pots and troughs on a terrace; designing paved gardens; or building walls of calcareous stone, adding a proper soil to the crevices, and tucking in herbs. Introducing a "made to order" soil for growing herbs in raised beds is easier than coping with the unwieldy offerings of a plot. Costwise it may not be out of line. Moreover, herbs planted above ground level respond favorably to the improved air circulation.

Raised Beds

To bring into being a well-composed, architectural pattern, plant herbs in raised beds of pleasing proportions varying from a few inches to 2 or 3 feet in height, nicely balanced with empty spaces. The raised beds are complemented by herbs tumbling over walls, low growing herbs tucked about the base of the supporting walls, and upright growing herbs topping the beds. The feast for the eye is close-up; beguiling fragrances are not far from the nose.

Supporting materials for raised beds should be selected to blend with the site and nearby structures. In the fifteenth-century, as paintings and woodcuts show, raised beds were supported with wooden planks or bricks.

For a raised bed 8 to 12 inches above the ground lay 8 to 12 inch-wide planks of cedar or treated wood, nontoxic to plants, lengthwise and sawed to the bed's dimensions along the sides of the planned bed. Keep them in an upright position by attaching them on the inside to vertical stakes driven about a foot into the ground, one close to each end of the plank for an average sized bed.

For a higher raised bed many gardeners use 4 x 4 inch treated timbers sold at garden centers and lumber supply outlets. Saw the timbers into the lengths and widths that meet the dimensions of your planned bed. Stack one on another to the planned height, and secure them with vertical stakes on both the inside and outside for support. It is important that the stakes are treated and of a size and shape that not only support, but also enhance the outside appearance. Some gardeners use concrete reinforcement rods on the inside for support and longer life; others drill aligned holes through the timbers, insert measured and sawed concrete reinforcement rods, and pound them about a foot into the ground; stakes are thus eliminated, but appearance is dull.

For a good effect let the architectural features of nearby structures and the garden space influence your choice of place for raised beds, their sizes, shapes, and materials used to support them. If beds exceed 5 feet in width reaching and working among the herbs is difficult. Design for an agreeable balance of empty space with shapes and sizes of beds; keep maneuverability in mind. Raised beds of all brick or wood impose a regularity. Offset the strictness by combining materials, or plant with overhanging foliage along the inside edges.

Fig. 6. An engraving in wood makes known that raised beds supported with wooden planks and platforms for pots were in sixteenth century herb gardens when such woodcuts were used in *Kreuterbücher* (German herbals) published by Christian Egenolph of Frankfurt and later edited by his son-in-law, Adam Lonitzer.

By laying bricks, cut flagstone, or strips of rough concrete with or without small pebbles between timbers the regularity of all timber tiers is minimized. Mortar binds all the materials and outside supporting stakes are not necessary.

For a bed large in length and breadth and approximately 2 feet high, used railway ties are useful. On a brick terrace lay several courses of brick between two tiers of horizontally laid railway ties. A top layer of thin slate (used slate blackboards are an inexpensive source of slate), cut to fit looks good. Herbs like creeping thyme, *Thymus herba-barona*, cascading over the supporting wall, are protected from moisture absorbed by the wood. (See plate 2.) A supporting wall of stone is fitting when there is a stone counterpart on the site.

In a large raised bed with a supporting wall, drainage is improved by installing drainage pipes, laid in crushed stone, at the bottom of the bed. The pipes, below the surface-soil level, are directed to the outside at a lower level. In a garden of raised beds, the needs of herbs from different environments can be satisfied with comparative ease. Prepare a soil mixture to satisfy drainage requirements, maintain a proper pH value, and make available the nutrients necessary for the herbs you plan to plant.

Working with small plants, enjoying their pleasant fragrances, and taking a harvest from single plants in a herb garden, are invaluable for hortitherapy. Raised beds can be assets for the physically handicapped; 27 inches is a suitable height for wheelchair occupants, allowing them to tend the herbs without effort.

Raised beds are harmonious architectural components suggesting a sense of order and permanence. Although designed to be functional, a garden of raised beds can also soothe and delight the spirit with their unaffected and lovely scents and forms.

Fitting Herbs into the Environment

Like all plants, herbs have built into their genes requirements for different light intensity and temperature, to maximize growth and reproduction. The first consideration in selecting a garden site is whether it will have full sun, partial shade, or shade. A south, southeast, or southwest exposure naturally satisfies sun lovers. A bright sun warms the garden and dries the soil. If the house adjoins the garden on its north or northwest border, that will shield the herbs from harsh winter winds; a microclimate develops in the garden when southerly exposed walls absorb heat from the sun and reflect it into the area.

Tight hedges of evergreen herbal shrubs and trees have long served as windbreaks for herb gardens in cold climates, and they may also block an objectionable view. In the higher elevations of the Blue Ridge or Cumberland Plateau, wrap a herb garden in a waist high, unclipped or clipped hedge of yew, Taxus sp., for protection and an attractive winter effect.

Although a tight hedge of evergreens gives shelter from cold winds and contains subtle aromatic scents, it encourages stagnant air and little air circulation. In a muggy climate, a "dot and dash" hedge is preferable; air circulation is improved, and there is no feeling of being totally enclosed.

Narrow-leaved (needlelike) evergreens, planted singly, command attention in a herbal backdrop of mingled native deciduous and broad-leaved evergreen trees and shrubs. The evergreen red cedar, *Juniperus virginiana*, and white cedar (arborvitae), *Thuja occidentalis*, are good choices for obelisks to provide vertical accent among golden flowering witch hazels, *Hamamelis virginiana*, in November. Purple star-anise, *Illicium floridanum*, wax myrtle, *Myrica cerifera*, sweet bay, *Magnolia virginiana*, and red bay, *Persea borbonia* will sparkle in the winter sun. Some herbal trees and shrubs used for enclosures or backdrops are notorious feeders, depleting the soil of nutrients; to avoid competition keep small herbs away from the greedy trees and shrubs.

The bounteous multiformity of herbal trees and shrubs give Southeastern herb gardens interest, character, and function all through the year. Small trees, well-placed, provide cool temperatures for plants from cooler origins and relief from the strong glare of a hot sun. Shrubs and trees introduce height and mass into garden beds, as well as shade, and thus give depth to the garden. When they blossom and are stirred by a light breeze, their delicate scent pervades the grounds.

Plant chive and parsley under a standard cornelian cherry tree, *Cornus mas*, or a little-leaved linden, *Tilia cordata*, or a standard dwarf fruit tree. The cooler temperature under the canopy of summer leaves satisfies their genetic makeup. By the same token the absence of leaves in early spring, when herbs that need cool temperatures have their start, allows efficient photosynthesis and rapid growth, not unlike spring-blooming woodland plants. The increased moisture and cooler temperatures within a close periphery of partially shaded or fully shaded patches are favored by numerous mints, *Mentha* spp.: sweet woodruff, *Galium odoratum*, hyssop, *Hyssopus officinalis*, catmint, *Nepeta cataria*. Admittedly, herbs planted under trees will require extra doses of fertilizer to meet the competition of tree roots.

Finding or arranging a cool microclimate for such growing herbs as sweet angelica, lovage, French tarragon, and chervil in a warm climate is, to a degree, possible. Sweet angelica, *Angelica archangelica*, from cool northern Europe, grows best on or near a naturally shaded wet site similar to the environment of its American cousin, *A. atropurpurea*, found near swamps in eastern portions of zone 6 and northward. Prepare a bog or build a small pool in a shaded lower level of a planned site. (See plate 3.) Close to the pool plant lovage, *Levisticum officinale*, and French tarragon, *Artemisia dracunculus* var. *sativa*, hardy, fast-growing perennials in cold climates, and the annual chervil, *Anthriscus cerefolium*, close to the pool. If the soil holds too much moisture, utilize hillocks. In the very early, cool spring when growth is rapid, indulge these plants with doses of liquid fertilizer or composted manure; this will stimulate root development for sustenance during the hot summer. In late spring take a harvest of lovage and French tarragon by cutting back, repeat the doses of fertilizer, water well, and look for new growth through the summer. Establishing healthy root systems by fertilizing and cutting back in late spring induces continued growth of the perennials during hot periods. Sweet angelica, as a biennial, comes to maturity in the second or third year with a spectacular globular umbel. Chervil, an annual will not produce much during the hot summer.

At higher elevations in the Southeast, where temperatures are cooler, herbs from cooler regions of the world will grow larger than they do in the warmer regions of the piedmont and coastal plain. On the other hand, herbs from warmer habitats will grow large in the piedmont and the coastal plain. Beware of catalog descriptions suggesting a herb will grow in a different climate to the same height as in the region where it has its origin. In the Southeast, more often than not, the herb will set buds, bloom, and flower before the standard height is reached.

Borage, *Borago officinalis*, calendula, *C. officinalis*, coriander, *Coriandrum sativum*, chervil, *Anthruscus cerefolium*, dill, *Anethum graveolens*, sweet cicely, *Myrrhis odorata*, prefer cool temperatures for seed germination and growth to maturity. If you intend to grow these plants from seed, sow them in the autumn with the first of the season's rain; this permits the seeds to germinate according to their time schedule, to winter over, and produce full green patches of herbs in early spring. A substantial number of these herbs—those that require cool temperatures for seed germination—self-seed. For that matter, self-seeding is both a blessing and a curse. Promoting the blessings has its returns. Seedlings of perilla, *P. frutescens*, a Japanese culinary and medicinal herb of the mint family, once introduced into the garden, appear in great numbers. The unpretentious charm and the deep burgundy foliage of its cultivar, 'Atropurpurea', makes an excellent filler for the unintended empty pockets you find when all else is planted. But it's a good idea to move seedlings of self-seeding herbs to a storage area until you need them. See also Chapter 6 covering propagation methods.

If your herb garden does not provide a suitable cultural environment for certain herbs but your other garden categories can, do not hesitate to plant herbs wherever they will succeed. The association of herbs with plants of another garden class is often highly attractive. In our garden, sweet cicely shares a woodland floor beneath plumleaf azaleas with the native American herbs galax, G. urceolata, and Virginia bluebells, Mertensia virginica. The sweet angelica is vigorous in a shaded bog garden. In the foreground of a perennial border soft, silver-foliaged lamb's ears, Stachys byzantina, heightens contrast among vivid flower colors. An apothecary rose, Rosa gallica officinalis, gives a perennial border the look of a medieval tapestry as well as the gift of perfume. Various textured and fragrant leaves of scented geraniums, Pelargonium spp., offer welcome scents among the often odorless but large, colorful flowers of the perennial border.

In addition to taking environmental needs into consideration when developing a herb garden, gardeners can benefit by noting how some herbs are fitted to the demands and stresses of their native habitat by genetic adaptations. And then there are herbs that adapt to new environments. These are the many naturalized herbs in parts of the world to which they have been moved from their native habitat by natural means or by man's intervention; many we term "weeds."

Certain herbs native to the Mediterranean region reveal survival stratagems that enable them to survive in an arid climate. Under stress of a hot sun, they increase the production of hairs on their upper leaf surfaces, which trap moisture and reduce the leaf's temperature, and that in turn lowers the transpiration rate and reduces the plant's moisture requirements. The multiple hairs mask the chlorophyll in the leaf cells, and this gives the foliage a light gray color, which is capable of reflecting heat. The phenomenon is demonstrated when dittany of Crete, Origanum dictamnus, is planted in a strawberry jar (a jar-shaped container with numerous openings around the sides) and positioned so that half the pockets are exposed to full sun and the remaining half to shade; plants in pockets exposed to full sun take on a grayer appearance than plants in pockets exposed to shade. If you look closely with a magnifying glass, you will see a difference in the number of hairs. Gray- and silver-foliaged herbs, by the presence of hairs on their leaves, seldom show distress in dry weather. The long narrow leaves of rosemary, Rosmarinus spp., and lavender, Lavandula spp., roll inward longitudinally. The phenomenon protects the stomata (pores in the leaf epidermis for the interchange of gases and release of water by transpiration) and prevents water loss.

On the Mediterranean landscape glabrous (hairless) herbs, known to grow upright in a less arid climate, hug the ground to retain moisture. Not having protective hair to lock in moisture, salad burnet, *Poterium sanguisorba*, follows the pattern, keeps close to the ground, and retains a rich green color. As an evergreen in the Southeast, it offers a pleasing contrast to the visual effects of the gray and white felted xerophytes in a collection of Mediterranean herbs. In temperate regions with sufficient moisture, salad burnet forms loose rhythmical tussocks and makes an attractive yearlong edging along a pathway through a garden of Mediterranean herbs. The adaptable habit of salad burnet was made evident during a severe drought in the North Carolina foothills. A sun-soaked garden of Mediterranean herbs took on aspects of a true Mediterranean landscape, with hairy plants turning grayish and salad burnet hugging the ground in rosette fashion. I had observed the same phenomenon on hot June days along roadsides in Spain. The herb gardener need fear periods of drought far less than heavy summer rains, which support fungus spores on the felted stems and leaves of arid herbs.

Adaptations to prevent water loss are found not only among herbs from arid climates but among those from areas where wet and dry alternate seasonally. Many of the basils, *Ocimum* spp., have their origins in subtropical India. In their native habitat they thrive during the rain-bearing southwest monsoon periods, and when moisture is scarce during the dry northeast monsoon periods of India, or in the dry herb garden, the small leaves of bush basil, O. 'Minimum', and hybrid varieties conspicuously display folded leaves like hands in prayer. In this manner, the entrances of the stomata in the upper epidermis of the leaf, where the stomata are in greater numbers than in the lower epidermis, close and preserve moisture. Thriving during a rainy spell, no amount of moisture or humidity causes fungus diseases among the chiefly glabrous basils.

In a garden containing herbs transported from assorted climates and soil types, the herbist must consider the special needs of tender and exotic plants. When you have difficulty with one particular plant, which apparently will not adapt to your garden, plant it in a container instead and give it individual attention. Pots have design potential; in groups of three, five, or seven, they can add a tableau to an empty space. (See plate 4.) Strive for interesting compositions, well-shaped and balanced. Place the tallest or boldest plant in the center of the arrangement or in the back, with the low or more delicate species in smaller pots in the foreground or in irregular fashion around the larger pot. Improve the balance of the composition by placing one pot on a small podium for height; allow space for the cascade of a prostrate rosemary. Movable pots can be arranged and rearranged to please the herbs—catch the sun or, during a hot spell, rest in the shade. But take care. Rays of a hot summer sun striking directly on the sides of clay or plastic pots during the morning and late afternoon can cause critical damage to the roots. Give them space where there is shade in the late afternoon. On hot dry days, water your potted herbs in the morning to keep root temperatures below the thermal-injury threshold.

A magnificent rosemary in a handsome container set on a circle of stone is distinctive; it is perhaps a spare herb garden but, none the less, attractive.

The vagaries of winter weather in zones 6–8 require that certain herbs be moved indoors. Moving potted herbs is a simple task, but when plants must be dug up from the soil and potted, there is danger of damaging the plant. Nevertheless, moving herbs indoors repays a little care and effort. The piney resinous aroma of a potted rosemary, perhaps clipped to a pyramid or trained as a bonsai, is a fine addition to indoor Christmas decorations. A pot of thyme indoors—though evergreen outdoors throughout the winter—produces more fragrant oil under good light conditions and indoor warmth.

Containers for herbs may be selected from a multitude of sizes, shapes, and materials, varying in style from handcrafted containers of wood, clay, or porcelain sinks treated with a covering of mixed cement, sand, and peat, to simulated stone troughs. Garden shops offer unique containers, new and old, difficult for gardeners to resist. Functional containers that harmonize with a garden design or architectural style of the house are marks of devotion to a garden. When one catches sight of ordinary pots of the potting shed planted with herbs under intensive care, one recognizes a devoted herbist.

Italian clay pots are classic, functional, and ornamental, for such large herbal plants as the classic myrtle, *Myrtus communis*, often trimmed and trained into topiary shapes or standards. (See plate 5.) A collection of shaped myrtles, their dark green leaves twinkling in the sun or the rain, stand as guardians for a home and garden. Admittedly, Italian pots are costly; when they break a garden's keeper weeps. But latex cement makes an excellent

Fig. 7. A trio of simulated stone troughs are a handsome and functional feature in the author's herb garden.

material for patching cracks and mending broken clay pots, so that the calamity need not be irremediable.

Containers of wood have special merit in warm climates; they insulate from heat better than pottery or plastic.

Gardeners with an eye for pleasing compositions, symmetrical or otherwise, utilize clay chimney flues. These are available in a number of dimensions and are excellent material for designing artistic gardens with pleasing variations in height and spatial proportions. Small herbs tumbling and sprawling at their bases introduce informality.

Stone animal troughs, much appreciated in English gardens, are functional and stylish as containers for herbs. Because genuine old stone troughs are scarce, you may prefer to make do with simulated stone troughs. These are simply and inexpensively fashioned from a mixture of Portland cement, peat moss, perlite, and water. Molds for casting troughs are made of corrugated cardboard boxes, used parchment lamp shades, or wooden forms. Because troughs are widely used by rock gardeners, you can find explicit directions for making them in rock gardening publications. (See bibliography.)

Mediterranean herbs thrive in a trough provided with drainage openings and a proper alkaline soil mix; the added leaching of lime from the trough guarantees alkalinity. Sizes and shapes of troughs may vary. A large trough with a substantial number of herbs will require less frequent watering than a group of single pots. A shallow trough suits an assemblage of herbs with small root systems. The thickness of trough walls and often larger size than clay pots offer some protection to the soil from the summer sun. Troughs also absorb sufficient heat from a winter sun to keep the soil warm and so prevent root damage. Unlike clay pots, cement or stone troughs are not vulnerable to cracking as a result of winter freezing followed by spring thaw, which causes expansion and contraction of moisture in the soil. An assortment of troughs in various sizes and shapes on a brick or stone terrace can create a wonderfully distinct garden room for all seasons. For added height in the garden or on a paved area, raise troughs on a base of bricks or ties.

For a papyrus, *Cyperus papyrus*, allot space in the garden for a container under the soil or paved surface to hold water. Utilize small troughs with stopped drainage openings for small aquatic or bog-preferring herbal plants like scouring rushes, *Equisetum* spp. Acquire used porcelain sinks and etch them with muriatic acid (a commercial term for hydrochloric acid, a strong corrosive which must be used with extreme care; wear rubber gloves, goggles to protect your eyes, and be fully clothed). Then apply a two-part epoxy adhesive to the inside surface and rims, strew sharp sand over it, and follow with a rough coat of the Portland cement mixture. Prepare an opening to accommodate the sink below the ground so its upper rim is even with the surrounding soil surface; seal the drainage holes, and keep filled with water. This is a trick a gardener can use to gain a surrounding cool microclimate.

Drawings and woodcuts of early gardens frequently show a standard herb in a pot on a paved area or sunk into the ground surrounded by low growing herbs. Avenues in Mediterranean cities are frequently lined with large standard bays, *Laurus nobilis*. Simply defined, a standard is a plant trained or grafted to have a simple, erect treelike stem. Essential steps in developing a standard without grafting are as follows: (1) select a herb that can be trained to form a strong woody erect stem, and plant a cutting of it; (2) stake it for support; (3) remove all side branches and new shoots as they rise at the base to promote upward growth of a single, unbranched stem; (4) give it exposure to good light; (5) when a stem reaches a desired height, cut off the growing tip to encourage top branching; (6) prune and pinch the leafy top and continue tip-pruning repeatedly to develop a full crown; (7) turn the pot frequently as the herb grows, so light reaches all sides for even growth. It may be necessary to repot, restake, and check the ties to prevent their cutting into the stem as it grows.

Herbs commonly standardized are upright rosemarys (pink-flowering *Rosmarinus* x *majorica* is especially pleasing), rose-scented geraniums, *Pelargonium graveolens*, classic myrtles, Peruvian heliotropes, *Heliotropium arborescens*, lemon verbenas, or tiny-leaved bush basils, *Ocimum basilicum* 'Minimum'.

For the Love of the Herb Garden

It is good sense to design a herb garden on a human scale. Permit it to be a place conducive to contemplation. Do not let it become a physical burden. Match enthusiasm with common sense. When the innately prolific herbs take over, share them.

Accept your herb garden as a constantly evolving arena. Adapt the design as the herbs grow and your herb collection increases. Admit your garden is an unfinished work, and pleasure lies in changing and improving it, experimenting with new plants and new arrangements of old ones.

An agreeable herb garden reflects the person who keeps it. Naturally, then, it allows for imperfection. Perfection is not an essential factor for the enjoyment of a garden. The distinguished American philosopher, George Santayana (1863–1952), said, "There is tragedy in perfection because the universe in which perfection arises is itself imperfect." And Santayana was a profound lover of nature and the garden. Tolerance for anything that upsets a garden—within acceptable bounds—is valuable. If a plant behaves impudently, like the "weed" or the creeping thyme, observe it carefully before concluding that it is an unworthy intruder. Volunteers that grow and bloom in chance places become graceful surprises, and we should learn to cherish them. A thoughtful gardener does not impose his or her implacable will upon nature's ways because, noteworthy observations may be overlooked. In a garden where there is harmony with nature and an indulgent gardener, things happen on their own—if you let them.

Working in a garden with tolerance is akin to love and can be the pathway to discovery. Many horticultural practices and horticultural varieties gained entrance into our gardens by means of natural selection, observed by curious gardeners. Gregor Mendel (1822–1884), an Augustinian monk in a Moravian monastery, after observing offspring of red-flowered and white-flowered varieties of the garden pea, *Lathyrus* sp., applied experimental methods in plant hybridization. The work laid the foundation for modern investigations on inheritance and established genetics as a science.

Historical Development of the Herb Garden

The designing of gardens follows the history of people. When man ceased to be a nomad, gardens began. According to archaeological evidence, early man observed the germination of seeds in his refuse heaps. The epoch-making discovery was applied by sowing seeds of plants selected for their healing properties in the refuse heaps (compost piles). Having herbs close at hand instead of out in the wild was an advance in primitive man's life-style.

To protect the plants from wild and domesticated animals, man began to enclose the plots with windbreaks of scrub and thorn or mud walls. As more plants from the wild were added to the plot, he developed practical garden plans and developed primitive hand tools. Soon the pattern was set for square beds within the garden. Square beds, often raised and accessible from all sides, so that plants were not trampled, became standard—form followed function.

The recorded history of Western gardens continued along a well-worn path. Elaborations and refinements of Assyrian, Babylonian, Egyptian, Persian, Roman, and Greek gardens of antiquity are well-documented by paintings, writings, and archaeological evidence.

Ornamental and fruitful plantings generally indicated periods of security from invasion or enclosed areas given to meditation, as in monasteries and temple or university enclosures. By the twelfth century the cloister garths of monasteries were filled with herbal plants in square or rectangular beds, sometimes raised, sometimes flat. Paths of handsome stonework adorned the gardens. As gardens supplying whole communities with food and medicine, they were functional. Even so, these lovely garths were and are acknowledged as decoratively effective.

By the sixteenth century, squares and rectangles gave way to all manner of geometric and fancifully shaped beds in European gardens. In southern Europe geometric designs were used extravagantly in complicated patterns, emphasized by edging plants and marked by contrasting leaf colors. The Elizabethan knot garden, fashioned with herbal plants, may well have had its impetus in the sweeping movement of pattern—preferred by the rich and fashionable to the square beds of common people or the physic garden of the apothecary. The fashion had its apotheosis in the complex French parterre of the seventeenth and early eighteenth centuries. Herb gardens shared in this design fashion. Herbs were planted in geometric beds outlined in box, santolina, germander, hyssop, or thyme—all formally clipped to traditional patterns.

When the site, architectural features of the house, and environmental qualities are appropriate for growing herbs in geometric beds, a spacious and decorative herb garden unfolds. An assemblage of rectangles, triangles, circles, arcs, and trapezoids of pleasing proportions become beds of herbs set apart by walks, allees, or alcoves. One needs some skill at balancing curved and straight lines if the garden is to leave a flowing and well-composed look. A variety of detail will prevent monotony.

Adaptations to Traditional Design Patterns

Such environmental factors as high humidity or an uncompromising soil must be taken into consideration when selecting a potential site for your herb garden, but if necessary, they can be mitigated by employing modifications. Raise the geometric-shaped beds to a uniform height and introduce the proper soil type. Or arrange beds to different heights, adding dimension to the design and concurrently increasing air circulation.

Loose, uncomplicated plantings of herbs from arid climates are preferred to close plantings. For mass plantings or for formal patterns with herbs laid out in neat lines, select herbs not vulnerable to stem rot and blights. Breaks in lines of gray santolina, lavender, or upright thymes are bound to occur during periods of muggy weather and are more conspicuous than a loss in a free-form planting pattern.

Almost all herb gardeners, at one time or another, believe they can plan and execute an Elizabethan knot garden. But creating a first-rate knot garden is fraught with difficulties unknown to the embroiderers whose intricate patterns inspired the "knot" (English for *parterre de broderies*) garden. A herb gardener may aspire to imitate the historical needleworker, have equal taste, sense of proportion and of color, but unless he or she knows the herbal plants and can predict how each herb will behave and what it will require in the way of soil, exposure, and, above all, the effects of unanticipated climatic factors, the herbist cannot be certain of producing a satisfactory knot garden.

Unless a knot garden is flawless, it is an offense to the herb garden and to its historical origins. By definition a knot garden requires tightly planted "intertwined" lines. During the humid summer herbs from arid habitats planted close together are vulnerable to diseases. As a result the eye focuses on sick plants instead of ribbons and knots. Keeping a storage bed for replacements is a possibility, but causes an unconscionable amount of work. Thus the utmost care and foresight must go into planning the design, for a beautiful result without excessive labor and frustration. In some areas of the Southeast an authentic Elizabethan knot garden can be cumbersome.

More feasible than a conventional knot garden with the traditional santolinas, lavenders, thymes, germanders, and marjorams from arid climates planted in tight ribbons is the conversion of the knot pattern to brickwork. Many garden-design books illustrate how to lay bricks, pavers, or cut stone in triangles, squares, or circles to form interlocking patterns on a small or large scale, similar to ribbons of clipped plants. (The concept is closely allied with the pathways of mazes, labyrinths, and parterres.)

An example is a 5 circular, interlocking brick bed, called a quincunx, illustrated in figure 8. To construct a quincunx, draw the design to scale based on the following dimensions and instructions: To balance planting beds with ribbons, circles of 7 or 8 feet in diameter are good. This is based on the dimensions of available and suitable brick pavers that you will want to use. These pavers are 7 1/2 inches long, 3 1/2 inches wide, and 1 5/8 inches deep. The pavers, when cut lengthwise in half and laid "on edge" can be satisfactorily used with a full-sized paver laid flat. Use a power driven masonry saw for cutting. When a site requires a narrower ribbon, cut pavers laid flat to suit the selected dimensions. In determining the width of the ribbon do not neglect to include the space required for the mortar. Prior to laying the pavers, pour a concrete base, level with the soil surface, in accordance with your scaled drawing. For effective "knots" have a skilled mason lay a single row of the pavers cut lengthwise "on edge," between 2 rows of the full-sized pavers laid flat. The skilled mason in binding the pavers with mortar and to

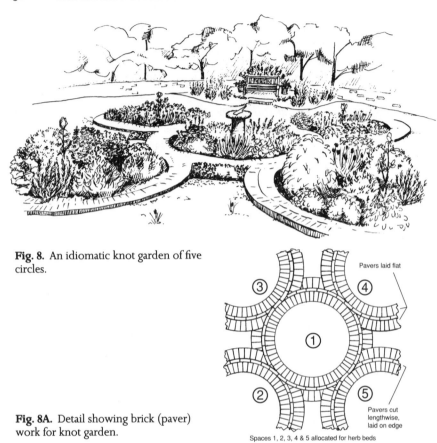

Fig. 8. An idiomatic knot garden of five circles.

Fig. 8A. Detail showing brick (paver) work for knot garden.

Pavers laid flat

Pavers cut lengthwise, laid on edge

Spaces 1, 2, 3, 4 & 5 allocated for herb beds

the concrete base, will use mortar and bind to guarantee a permanent and flat surface. Binding the bricks to a concrete base, level with the soil surface, raises the ribbon to the width of one brick above the soil surface.

Plant conventional knot garden herbs of contrasting leaf colors and textures well-spaced in the open areas. The soil should be slightly mounded and the herbs kept neatly clipped as mounds. Set off the focal point of the brickwork pattern and herb forms with sufficient unplanted space, so that the charm and loveliness of healthy herbs is set forth undisguised. The knot garden of brickwork injects an idiom of the true Elizabethan knot garden.

Broad, irregular unplanted spaces are more desirable than narrow passages between beds. Aside from creating necessary arenas for air movement, space is provided for a garden bench, large pots holding small herbal trees, potted herbs, and garden ornaments. The gardener can move his tools and carts freely while tending the herbs. Moisture-retaining materials, such as grass or wood chips, should be shunned in the unplanted areas. Better ground covers are stone, slate, brick, or gravel, matched or contrasting in texture and color, and blended with the architectural style of a nearby building.

In another garden a slightly raised circular structure planted around the base with lady's mantle, *Alchemilla vulgaris*, becomes a dais for potted scented geraniums, *Pelargonium* spp. Sniffing the floral, spicy, citric, resinous, and fruity scents is sheer contentment. The varied leaf forms and textures catch the eye as well as the nose. In the wintertime, brought indoors, their scent pervades the house, or harvested leaves are dried for potpourri.

After planning a design, it is essential to follow it through from preliminary drawings to final plantings by viewing it from all approaches, windows, porches, and angles in open spaces. Look for good composition from all viewpoints.

Squares and Rectangles

Fewer constraints are placed on the gardener when pattern shapes are limited to squares and rectangles than when the design is one of multiple geometric shapes. The regularity of the beds, raised or otherwise, with broad paths between them, tolerates treating each square or rectangle as a unique plot for a specific herb or for a collection of herbs. (See plate 6.) A pattern of squares and rectangles, planted with a single herb in each space, can present as formal an aspect of contemporary design as a Mondrian painting. Mixed herbal plantings in squares give a tone to an informal style of gardening fitted to a contemporary life-style.

In large squares or rectangles herbal shrubs or a tree offer sculptural effects and space for underplantings of herbs requiring part-sun, part-shade conditions. Large squares and rectangles convey a naturalistic, loose style of planting better than small squares.

The Checkerboard

A checkerboard pattern of alternating planted squares and surfaced squares is a welcome plan for improving air circulation among herbs, whether the

Fig. 9. A checkerboard design.

garden is small or large. Situated against a wall or an adjoining building, or a pergola for old roses, and with full sun exposure, a checkerboard pattern is planned for herbs requiring full sun. The alternating planted squares and surfaced squares allow air to circulate, a blessing for sun-loving herbs from arid climates. A microclimate is formed in the wintertime when unplanted spaces and a wall trap the sun's heat and give the garden environment a warmer temperature. Whether the checkerboard is large or small, the allotment of space unites the herbs without diminishing their individual forms. To assure that water runs off immediately and to avoid excess moisture, the garden requires a slight slope away from the a wall, adjoining building, or pergola. The soil of the squares, constituting contained areas, can be controlled to match the needs of specific herbs. The display of such marvelously aromatic, very gray and very green subshrubs as rosemary, lavender, santolinas, and rock roses, *Cistus* spp., is visually harmonious, especially when plants are all well-formed, in good health, and with blooms in pink to lavender to blue. A checkerboard plan also reduces competitive local plant species—weeds.

The straightforward framework of the checkerboard also makes a charming appearance when herbs spill over the plain squares. Mounded squares, 20 inches to a side, become patches of creeping thymes—species, varieties, and cultivars—in various shades of gray and green, variegated, glossy, and hairy leaved, for a handsome and almost evergreen collection. For a vivid carpet of rose crimson flowers, plant *Thymus praecox* 'Coccineus' on a low mound. Its brilliance is enhanced by keeping white flowered 'Albus' on a mound close by, with woolly thyme, T. *pseudolanuginosus*, interspersed and mounded for quiet contrast. At the Missouri Botanical Garden's herb garden, a mounded square of ample size is planted in quarter segments of creeping, golden-variegated lemon thyme, T. 'Aureus', and woolly thyme, a most effective focal point. (See plate 7)

Note the stress on "mound." Mounds and banks shed water, preventing thymes (of Mediterranean origin) from suffering during wet spells. "I know a bank where the wild thyme blows. . . ." says Shakespeare's Oberon, indicating that the poet was familiar with creeping thymes and their tendency to cascade over the dry hillsides and calcareous rocks. (See plate 8.)

Another attractive accent plant to use in zones 8–11, is the bold vertical grass vetiver, *Vetiveria zizanioides*, from subtropical India. It is most dramatic planted among squares of low and medium-sized herbs. (See plate 9.) Do not cut back the tall grass in the fall, but leave it standing for an almond-colored winter display. After several years of good growth, you may decide to dig it up, divide the clump, and replant. Save a handful of the aromatic roots, wash and dry them, and press them among linens for their exotic perfume.

An unplanted square of the checkerboard is a fit place to introduce height during the growing season with a potted, standard bay, *Laurus nobilis*, or lemon verbena, *Aloysia triphylla*.

The Paved Garden

Historical antecedents of the paved garden can be traced to Persia, Spain, Greece, and Rome. In the fiercely hot, dry climate of ancient Persia the garden was, more often than not, a partially or completely paved area, a patio, or a courtyard; size varied. It was designed with irrigation channels to cool the surrounding air and supply water for plants. The layout of these narrow channels, running between flat stone paving, resulted in geometric shapes. Channels varied from about 4 inches wide in small gardens to 4 feet for principal channels in very elaborate gardens. In low beds of the paved areas trees were planted for shade. Pots set on the stone paving held aromatic plants to scent the air, and low, moist beds held masses of herbaceous plants. During Alexander's conquest of Persia in the third century B.C., the Macedonian soldiers absorbed the spirit of the Persian garden and on their return to Greece introduced the stone courtyard.

Eight hundred years later Islam began to extend itself beyond Arabia to form the Muslim world of North Africa, southern Spain, Sicily, and Italy, and introduced the basically Persian paved garden (called moorish style) into Europe. Designed originally for outdoor living, Arab gardens were reflected in the patios of Spain, the atriums or central courtyards in Rome, and within castle walls of France and England; a paved herb garden was made in 1247 at Clarendon Palace in Wiltshire.

Like its predecessors, a paved garden for herbs is part of a living unit. Herbs make it seem the best and most preferable of outdoor living areas. Viewed from windows the paved herb garden is lovely, but, better yet is the pleasure of walking safely on firm surfaces among myriad scents.

An existing terrace can be turned into a paved garden by removing portions of stone or bricks and planting herbs in the openings. Removing stones in a regular pattern creates a formal garden; removing one here and one there in an irregular design develops into a pleasingly informal herb garden. For good drainage, remove material and subsoil in the opened portions to a depth of 18–24 inches, and fill the empty space with a soil suitable for the herbs selected. Choose herbs that tumble and sprawl and plant them on low mounds sloping to the level of the paved surface. Prepare slightly higher mounds for upright herbs adapted to arid climates; this improves air circulation at their base and helps them survive damp summers.

Top-dress with chopped oyster shells. White shells, reflecting light into the lower branches of a plant, impede fungus growth and hinder spores from reaching the plant. They also keep the soil alkaline.

Spacing herbs in small irregular beds between stones or flags, especially when they are planted with a consciousness of their mature heights in mind, lays the foundation for an attractive composition, not unlike a small Mediterranean landscape with stone outcroppings. A brick terrace converted into a paved garden is transformed into an entrancingly informal adjunct to a house. The design is not that of an English cottage affair with crowded plant-

Fig. 10. A paved garden for herbs.

ings, but equally pleasing to herbs, noses, and eyes. A paved garden fulfills the needs of many herbs, because the paving drys out quickly after rain and the distances of herbs between paved spaces promotes effective air movement. Around an entrance, door or gate, a paved garden extends a warm invitation to the garden and to the home.

When no previous pavement of stone or brick exists, the gardener has a choice of paving materials and can define a style. Reasonably smooth and level slabs of calcareous stone or flags look right in an informal setting. Brick is the most versatile paving material—alone, or in conjunction with stone (slate for effective color tones) or concrete slabs. It is also useful to incorporate areas of gravel with other paving material; it can be used as a planting medium for clumps of prickly pear cactus, a handsome agave or yucca.

It is essential to prepare the site in advance by careful grading, sloping the ground gently away from the house for water runoff, and compacting the bases on which the paving will be placed. Next comes consultation with a skilled mason. Techniques for laying paving materials vary, and unless you are personally skilled in masonry, the job is best left for a professional. To lay in sand, with or without mortar, to lay in concrete, and necessary edgings or framework are all best decided on by the mason. But you should do the planning and designing yourself for a unified visual concept, and this includes the choice of the surface paving material. Personal taste is important for a successful garden.

A collection of herbs in containers suits a paved garden very well. Genuine or simulated stone troughs with herbs tumbling from the rims or rising high introduce sculptural interest, and fit the scene exactly as one would wish. Moreover, the garden is extremely functional for herbs. Paved gardens offer many charms and surprises for both herbist and visitor.

A Rock Garden for Herbs

In Mediterranean countries, patterned herb gardens as accompaniments to private homes are uncommon. Instead, a common sight from the village street is the pot of bush basil on an outdoor windowsill. In a private garden, near the kitchen door, you may catch sight of a large flat clay pot planted with spearmint, *Mentha spicata*. The spearmint sits so near to the door, your host will explain, because of its common use in cooking. At the far end of the garden, growing in the wild, is a favorite mint used for a medicinal tea. He explains, quite correctly, that keeping the mints at a distance from one another prevents hybridization, which would result in progeny of undesirable poor quality. A bay tree and rosemarys grow in the garden as ornamentals and culinaries. Lavender, thymes, oreganos, savories, fennel, dill are gathered for use from the wild, where it is not unusual to stumble over them by accident.

How to re-create such an environment for herbs in regions where soils and climates are alien to them? A rock garden may be the answer. Rock gardeners, in laying out such a project, tend to follow nature. Rocks are selected and arranged to appear as a natural deposit. The choice is important: calcareous rocks of stratified limestone contribute alkalinity to the soil; granite rocks give an acid reaction to the soil. Then the variety of soil types is chosen and supplied, and stone troughs, genuine or simulated, are put to use as raised beds within the rock garden. A mulch of gravel or chipped oyster shells is appropriate, since it does not hold moisture.

A rock garden provides a home for herbs in which similarities, differences,

Fig. 11. Herbs in a rock garden.

cultural habits, and growth forms can be studied and enjoyed. Study rock gardening publications to develop techniques before you place the first stone; knowledge of the subject helps you avoid unnecessary physical effort.

A low wall of flat stones (preferably calcareous), constructed according to directions for rock garden walls (without mortar) near a house or adjoining it, is a potential herb garden. It may be free-standing or a supporting wall of an adjoining terrace. Good drainage is important for good plant development, so the wall should be sited for runoff. The herbs should be planted in open spaces as the stones are laid up. Inserting roots and soil into crevices after the stones are laid is difficult; the soil often drops away, and the roots dry out rapidly. The difficulty can be minimized by inserting into the crevice a wet package of soil and roots wrapped well in spagnum moss, but if possible planting should accompany the wall building.

A gentle slope at some distance from a house or along steps at an entrance can make a naturalistic rock garden site. A rock garden need not be large, but it should be balanced in relation to the home environment and placed so that it can be enjoyed from a porch, terrace, or window. The gentle slope allows for water runoff. Scale should determine the sizes of the rocks chosen in the construction; large boulders vanquish small herbs. Rocks placed strategically stabilize the soil on a slope. Moreover, rocks gather warmth from the winter sun and insulate nestled plants against strong winds. An existing rocky soil tends to drain rapidly, a prerequisite for most herb growing. Herbs inserted between crevices of a set of steps add to the informality of a naturalistic rock garden; trodden upon, they give off pleasant aromas. Select from flat growing, creeping herbs: in partial shade, English pennyroyal, *Mentha pulegium:* in sun, creeping thymes, *Thymus praecox,* or caraway thyme, *T. herba-barona,* golden oregano, *Origanum vulgare* 'Aureum'; or English chamomile, *Chamaemelum nobile* 'Treneague' of "chamomile bench" fame. Many more *Thymus* and *Origanum* spp. succeed in spilling over the dry, warm, calcareous rocks.

In the low sand country or coastal plain it is possible to contrive a rock garden for growing a variety of nonnative herbs. Alter a flat site into a berm (a landscaper's term for an artificial mound of a proper soil type that may be rounded, elliptical, or ridge shaped—straight or curved). More pleasing than one berm is a group of dissimilarly shaped berms for the undulating effect they present. For a pleasing composition balance the sizes and shapes of berms with the size of the site. On the mounds of alkaline soil with good drainage lay well-chosen calcareous rocks of varying sizes which you have collected. Lay them partially beneath the soil surface, the remainder just emerging from the soil as almost flat outcroppings. A rise of 2 to 3 feet, sloping gently, provides air circulation and a depth for good root development. A difficult task lies in successfully arranging chosen rocks of varying sizes for a berm's incline, prone to erosion. This requires skillful setting of rocks with well-rooted plantings to prevent washouts during heavy rains.

Steps of flat stones (outcroppings) provide easy movement through the garden. Create naturalistic interspaces between rocks, from gaps of various widths to small interstices. Plant large herbs like rosemary and lavender in pockets between stepping stones and outcroppings and diminutive herbs like thymes and *Calamintha cretica* in crevices on the rise. From a distance, their forms convey an image of a native habitat. A herbal shrub or tree close by is valuable for herbs that prefer partial shade or need a cooler temperature than the others. An illusion of undulating topography is created by planting the slopes with a combination of herbs of differing heights and shapes. Herbists can learn a great deal by visiting gardens and conservatories in botanic gardens set aside for plants from arid climates (xerophytes) and growing under the direction of qualified curators. (See plate 10.)

In the background, at a distance from the herbal rock garden but in full view, plant herbal shrubs and trees regularly cultivated in the coastal plain for their singular fragrance and beauty. Choices come from a large selection of native and introduced species. Notable among the evergreens are the camphor tree, *Cinnamomum camphora*, the loquat or Japanese medlar, *Eriobotrya japonica*, the native cherry laurel, *Prunus caroliniana*, sweet viburnum, *V. odoratissimum*, the devilwood of the Southern states, *Osmanthus americana*, the southern magnolia, *M. Grandiflora*, native purple anise, *Illicium floridanum*, and the gardenia, *G. jasminoides*. The deciduous China tree (Chinaberry), *Melia azedarach*, is naturalized in the warm South; the trifoliate orange, *Poncirus trifoliata*, is reputed to be a strong deciduous hedge. The above are only a small number of the many herbal shrubs and trees included in the Southern flora. They suggest an undeniable pride of place.

The concept of employing naturalistic landscapes in herb gardening bodes well for the herb gardener with a divided soul—half in love with order and pattern, half in love with undisciplined nature. Designing a herb garden according to naturalistic concepts follows from observing herbs growing in their natural environments and attempting to re-create those qualities in a cultivated garden. When a garden is planned for native American herbal plants an undisturbed natural environment or restoration of an environment becomes the garden, a preserve for native herbs and a healer for the gardener's divided soul. (See plate 11.)

Naturalistic styles of gardens and the preservation of native American species occupy center stage in America today. In deference to this interest in our native flora, Chapter 5 concentrates on them.

Of Old Roses

Old roses deserve tenure in the herb garden for their historic medicinal uses, culinary flavorings, and as suppliers of attar of roses for perfume. Their delicate primitive charm is reflected in the literature of all periods of history—from classical antiquity to modern time.

In moderate or cool climates, a sun-drenched spot is best for old roses. Where summers are hot, shade is needed in the afternoon. But if shade trees grow nearby, their roots may invade the rose beds, competing for water and nutrients. A pergola (arbor or trellis), constructed along a western exposure of a rose bed, matching or complementing the style of the garden and architectural features of the house, provides afternoon shade and, in season, a spot for the gardener to pause and imbibe the heady aromas. In sand country or the coastal plain, build berms for old roses and plant them in a soil that provides moisture retention and a pH of about 6.5.

Ancient writings may be the inspiration for your choice of old roses for your garden. William Shakespeare wrote much exquisite poetry about the unsurpassed beauty and incomparable fragrances of the old roses he knew. As did many other poets. Brilliant color and sophisticated multidoubling developed in modern roses by artificial hybridization are contrary to the expectations of old rose collectors. The unaltered true colors of natural species and natural hybrids of European ancestry are white, pale pink, rose-pink, and red. Flowers are single, semidouble, and double. In the most ancient roses, flowering is not recurrent. They bloom once, in their season, and then do not blossom again until the next year. Recurrent flowering and greater color range were introduced among European roses, when in the nineteenth century, the China rose, *Rosa chinensis* (introduced into Europe in 1768), and the recurrent tea rose, *R. gigantea*, hybridized, which was followed by their progeny crossing with the roses of Europe. Rising from these crosses and included among old roses are the Bourbons carrying the pink coloring of the European roses and the recurrent flowering of the China rose, the pale yellow to coppery Tea Noisette climbing roses, and the Hybrid Perpetuals displaying the dark crimson of the Chinese hybrids.

In the Southeast the time-honored, nonrecurrent, natural rose species and their hybrids with well-scented flowers are on display from early May through June. Masses of delicate color rise upward amid green foliage, ascend in arches, arbors, and obelisks, or follow, horizontally entwining, a post and rail fence. The air is so heavily scented that there is no need to get up close and sniff. In late summer the red and orange fruits (hips) appear to brighten the garden through the winter. The foliage offers varieties of textures from smooth and shiny to corrugated, as well as foliage colors from soft light-green through blue-green to dark-green. The natural species and their hybrids are hardier than modern hybrid roses and less susceptible to insect and fungus diseases.

As a group, herb gardeners are undimmed by the array of modern hybrids. Old roses—comely, exquisitely scented, replete with a long history of virtues—are their preference. Found among the descendants of ancient natural species are natural hybrids, mutations, sports (bud mutants), varieties, and cultivars (variants of horticultural origin) that came into existence before

1867. On this account, the Classification Committee of the Old Garden Rose Society in 1966 put it thus: "A rose is an 'old rose' if it belongs to a group which existed before 1867." The date is well before the advent of the artificial hybridization of the modern roses.

Acknowledged "starters" for a garden are the ancient roses of European descent. The acquisition of an apothecary rose, *Rosa gallica officinalis*, which puts forth 2 1/2-inch-wide semidouble deep pink to red flowers, and a delicious scent from both flowers and leaves initiates enthusiasm for old roses. (See plate 12.) The apothecary rose is believed to be a variant of the single-flowered R. *gallica*, native to southern Europe and western Asia, grown before rose history began and treasured because the petals retained their fragrance after drying. R. *gallica officinalis* was coveted because its semidoubled flowers supplied more petals with equally rich fragrance for the potpourri. Because petals and leaves were used in medicine and for conserves, it became known as the apothecary rose or the rose of Provins, because the industry supplying the dried material was at Provins in France. The shrub suckers heavily and reaches a height of 4 feet; hips are conspicuous, rounded, and red.

A sport of R. *gallica officinalis*, and similar to it in all respects except flower color, is 'Rosa Mundi'. The petals, striped red and white, are striking. Throughout the years 'Rosa Mundi' has been confused with the 'York and Lancaster', which has the pale pink and partly colored white petals, not striped; the 'York and Lancaster' is a variety of the damask rose, R. *damascena versicolor*, and differs distinctly from 'Rosa Mundi'. Both the apothecary rose and 'Rosa Mundi' are inclined to develop a harmless mildew on their leaves in late summer.

The damask roses, R. *damascena*, are of ancient lineage, thought to have descended from R. *gallica* and other species—natural hybrids whose foreparents are difficult to assign with certainty. (Roses, even from widely separated regions, hybridize readily, giving rise to types that overlap the parental forms and thus make it difficult to determine basic species.) From Pliny's writings, it is evident the damasks were known to the Romans. A cultivar of R. *damascena*, 'Trigintipetala', is the major source of attar of roses. The extraction from the flowers by distillation is principally carried on in Bulgaria, where the soil and climate are favorable for the production of a high quality oil. In the garden it and the recurrent 'Bifera' grow to 8 feet; support is required for the large lithe branches. An image of a sultan's garden and its seraglio is conjured up when the intensely fragrant perfume of the pink, semidouble flowers scents the air.

As ancient and favored as the damasks is the cabbage rose, R. *centifolia*; rich scent and warm pink flowers, very double and nodding. Two attractive derivatives of R. *centifolia* are the moss rose, 'Muscosa', in which the calyx and pedicels are covered with sticky glandular growths, "moss," intensely aromatic; the other, originating as a sport, is the crested moss, 'Cristata', with sepal edges mossy and aromatic. The lax open growth of cabbage roses suggests that it would be better to grow them along a wall for support. Without a wall support, provide a framework around the shrub of 3 or 4 sturdy stakes driven into the ground and connected horizontally by 3 or 4 sturdy stakes 3 feet above the ground. This permits branches to rise up through the framework and gracefully arch over the horizontal stakes, keeping nodding flowers well above the ground. R. *centifolia* is grown by the important perfume industry in France for the attar of roses distilled from the heavily scented fresh flowers.

The sweetbrier or eglantine rose, R. *eglanteria*, native of Europe and North Africa, is the most giving of roses. The loveliest of single warm pink roses, borne in clusters, it covers great arches over a pathway or an arbor. The delicious fragrance of the flowers, with undertones of apple scent, has an equal counterpart in the aromatic foliage. The scent is emitted of its own accord and will often drift in through a nearby open window. During a soft summer rain the fragrance pervades the garden. Linens hung out to dry near the eglantine absorb the released oils and give off the scent during ironing—a dull task made pleasant. In our garden even the bare branches give off the aroma on mild, moist winter days. Masses of orange to red prickled hips shine bright through autumn and winter. Because of its habit of dense growth, the sweetbrier adapts well as a hedge.

The dog rose, R. *canina*, is included in a garden of species roses. It is the dog brier of the English hedgerows and is naturalized in North America. Single flowers are a delicate blush pink about 2 inches across and grow on a large prickly arching bush that looks best in a naturalistic planting. From late summer through the winter, the eye is caught by the display of red ovoid hips, which can be used medicinally when fresh. According to some authorities, the original white rose, R. alba, sprang from a natural cross between R. damascena and R. canina, and its descendent is the favorite, vigorous stout shrub, R. alba semi-plena, whose large prickles and hard gray leaves it owes to R. canina.

The musk rose of the ancients, R. moschata, is famous for its unforgettable scent, reminiscent of costly perfume. Its origin, which predates 1600, is obscure but for the present R. moschata autumnalis is held to be the true musk rose. It is rare but on occasion available from Pickering Nurseries in Pickering, Ontario. R. moschata autumnalis begins to bloom in midsummer and continues till October with semidouble white flowers of strong fragrance. Since it can grow to 10 feet, you can treat it as a climber.

The word "musk" is often used misleadingly and thus causes some misunderstandings among collectors of old roses. The musk rose of Shakespeare is believed to be R. arvensis, the English musk rose. The Himalayan musk is R. brunonii. The so-called group of hybrid musks developed in England in the early 1900s are identified by such names as 'Buff Beauty', 'Moonlight', 'Penelope', 'Pax', and 'Felicia', but these hardly come under our pre-1867 definition of old roses.

The large choice of documented old roses is limited solely by the garden space the herbist has available. Because the dimensions of mature shrubs vary from small, low-growing plants to tall broad shrubs to climbers, it is well to anticipate how much space you will need to allot to them in your planning. When horizontal space is limited, use supports for vertical growth. Roses on French tuteurs (A tapering support made of 4 strips of metal, standing about 8 feet tall, and held together with spaced metal rings) become architectural features to an otherwise flat garden, adding height and sculptural effects from the base of the rose to the top. Rustic tripods of tree limbs or vinyl-covered metal stakes, 8 feet high, function equally well.

Beds of roses are enhanced with underplantings of gray-foliaged pinks, Dianthus spp., blue-flowering ornamental catnip, Nepeta mussinii, or variegated scented geraniums. Include clumps of Iris x germanica var. florentina and I. pallida 'Dalmatica' for the handsome contrast contributed by the glaucous, sword-shaped leaves and large flowers. Beneath a large rose that provides shade, plant sweet violets, Viola odorata. Around and about roses growing on tripods plant shrubby, evergreen Jerusalem sage, Phlomis fruticosa, with whitish pubescent leaves and yellow flowers, or shrubby, evergreen, and gray-green-leaved rock roses, Cistis incanus, with rose-pink flowers; the beauty of the tall, vertical roses will be enhanced.

Old roses have lived and produced beautiful flowers without attention for hundreds of years. However, simple pruning, begun two or three years after planting, is recommended to keep the shrubs strong and to shape them. In early spring before buds leaf out, all dead or injured wood should be cut out. Likewise weak, twiggy, and inward-growing branches or branches that cross or interfere with other branches. Keep the vigorous canes, cutting back to a height sufficient to retain the normal habit of the particular shrub. Cutting back canes by one third will force laterals to break and produce a heavy bloom. Make the cut at a 45 degree angle above a strong outward bud, and direct the cut upward from the center of the bush, to encourage outward growth of the bud. Climbers that bloom only once during the season are best pruned immediately after flowering. Ever-blooming (recurrent) climbers should be pruned at the end of the season, before cold weather arrives, or early in spring before new growth starts. Cut back side shoots 3 to 6 inches; keep five to eight main canes and tie them to the fence, trellis, or other support. Pruning is an art that can be learned from experience.

Old shrub roses, if their branches are to maintain the graceful arching form given them by nature, must be less frequently clipped and cut than are the rigid and graceless modern roses grown as bushes. Good pruning encourages new growth from the base, making a shrub healthier, more attractive in shape, and ensures flowering.

Although old roses are usually disease resistant, black spot, a fungus disease, may occur on specific old roses in regions where summers are warm and humid. Control of black spot begins when the gardener identifies the specific roses susceptible to infection by their black or brown spotted leaves. Then a regular spraying treatment with a fungicide is required throughout the growing season. In following years the susceptible roses are sprayed early—before the leaves have become spotted—and continued throughout the growing season. To minimize fungus infections, roses should be kept well-spaced and pruned, thus allowing good air circulation.

Insect infestations among old roses are not fatal. Fertilizers combined with insecticides usually give adequate control. For the most part, weather conditions, over which there is little control, influence insect invasions.

Color in the Herb Garden

Ever since hybridists have been seized by the mania to create plants with large flowers and in a riot of colors (but frequently devoid of fragrance), gardeners have become acutely sensitive to the use of harmonious colors or dramatic color contrasts in their gardens. They give attention to "proper" decorative colors and avoid clashing color contrasts. Their gardens proceed from a carefully planned flower color scheme. Without a detailed color scheme they fear subtleties of shadings and hues may be lost. By giving forethought to flower color combinations they achieve lovely flower color effects in dramatic contrast or close harmonies.

Herbists, on the other hand, unequivocally grow herbs because they appreciate and are committed to the simple, uncompounded beauty of natural species, in contrast to the artificial colorations of hybrids. For the most part, the ability of herbs to persevere, their remarkable influences on the senses and the mind, give the herb gardener more pleasure than do large flowers calling for attention by their exotic colors. Visitors to a herb garden, who might be missing vivid colors or enormous stiff blooms, often change their minds when a succession of small sample leaves or blossoms are passed into their warm hands and the volatile perfumes are released. Nothing beguiles the spirit so completely as scent; the nose knows. Small flowers with gentle colors and enticing fragrances are suddenly better.

The designing of a herb garden does not usually place emphasis on flower colors; instead, the diverse forms of herbs plus the colors and textures of their foliage are dominant in design. Compositions incorporate contours of the land to intensify natural height, depth, and distance.

In the garden where herbs are grouped for color, the proper layout is based on the natural associations of herbs in their native habitats. Their natural landscapes offer excellent models for well-conceived, low-key color combinations. Herbs are not dull. Threaded through a herb garden in an impressionistic fashion are herbs with foliage of silvery white to gray or monochromatic shadings of gray-green, blue-green, and yellow-green; gold, bronze, burgundy, and dark green are contrasting accents. Leaf textures—smooth, glossy, hairy, feltish, pebbly—and a variety of leaf shapes catch light to increase color shadings. The colors of herb foliage furnish an oasis of calm; they do not disturb.

Among herbal plants sought for varying leaf texture and foliage color in gray-green to silver and used to intensify the vividness of dark green, bronze, and burgundy leaf colors are the following: gray-green southernwood, *Artemisia abrotanum*, and the silvery wormwoods with divided leaf patterns, *A. absinthium*, *A.* 'Lambrook Silver', and *A. arborescens*; grayish lavender's narrow leaf blades; feathery-leaved, gray santolina, *S. chamaecyparissus*; silver and gray-leaved thyme, *Thymus x citriodorus* 'Argenteus'; gray, round-leaved horehound, *Marrubium vulgare*, or *M. incanum*; woolly, silvery-white lamb's ears, *Stachys byzantina*; mullein, *Verbascum thapsus*; and pebbly gray-leaved sage, *Salvia officinalis*. All are of dissimilar heights, and their leaf shapes and textures enhance the colors of other herbs. It is difficult to omit mentioning how pleased a small child becomes when a velvety leaf of lamb's ears is drawn gently across his check. The child's pleasure often doubles that of a visiting mother.

The well-known white garden created by Vita Sackville-West at Sissing-hurst in Kent, England, tempts many herbists to plan a herb bed solely in silver, gray, and light green-leaved plants flowering white. Such a garden is stunning in the moonlight when the night-blooming flowers of the South American jasmine tobacco, *Nicotiana alata*, perfume the air. The ghastly white flowers of an angel's-trumpet, *Brugmansia x candida*, from Ecuador, 12 inches long, are haunting seen from a window with a bright moon in the sky. The spectacle, coupled with the plant's well-documented reputation as a hallucinogenic agent, creates a haunting memory.

When laying out a winter garden, the herbist has to be particularly attentive to foliage. The dark-green, lustrous leaves of billowing box, *Buxus sempervirens*; the sparkling, classic myrtle, *Myrtus communis*, the proud bay, *Laurus nobilis*; the creeping caraway thyme, *Thymus herba-barona*; the glossy-toothed germander, *Teucrium chamaedrys*—all convey an image of stability among the lighter shades of gray and green. Where winter hardy and evergreen, they present an appreciated, distinct display in the winter garden design and a gainful contrast with gray-leaved evergreens as lavender, *Lavandula spp.* and santolina, *S. chamaecyparissus*. When choosing needle, scalelike, linear, or broad-leaved evergreen shrubs and subshrubs, give attention to winter hardiness especially in the climatic zones 6–7 and the higher elevations. In climatic zones 8–11 discrimination in choosing some of the listed evergreens is required because of high humidity with high temperatures. Match herbs to the climates and soils of their native habitats as much as possible.

Once introduced into the garden, self-seeding orache, *Atriplex hortensis* var. *atrosanguinea*, will freely present red strokes of color from zone 7 northward. A purple-bronze foliage is supplied by the self-seeding annual perilla, P. *frutescens* 'Atropurpurea', attached to the Japanese cuisine. In mid-summer I move self-sown perillas to fill voids of color created by the early, no-longer blooming flowers: blue meadow clary, *Salvia pratensis*; red Maltese cross, *Lychnis chalcedonica*; yellow dyer's Marguerite, *Anthemis tinctoria*; and white feverfew, *Chrysanthemum parthenium*. In this manner, colors are calendered around the time of year, and a garden is enhanced. As keeper, you enjoy the acclaim.

A herb garden, dependent upon foliage for color and the way in which nature lights it, can be lovely through all seasons; yet exquisite seasonal blooms catch the eye and nose in a legato style. Fragrant old roses form buds and come into full bloom. Spikes of pink, blue, and purple lavender flowers do not go unseen. We are cheered by flowers of the yellow pot-marigold, *Calendula officinalis*, and dyer's marguerite, *Anthemis tinctoria*. Wallflowers, *Cheiranthus cheiri*, Madagascar periwinkle, *Catharanthus roseus*, red valerian, *Centranthus ruber*, and many more charm herbists with bright colors. Gardeners in search of blue blossoms discover an abundance in the herb garden: The bright blue flowers of borage, *Borago officinalis*, alkanet (bugloss), *Anchusa officinalis*, hyssop, or rosemary cultivars dot the garden as stars stipple the sky. In early spring clustered pink buds of lungwort, *Pulmonaria officinalis*, open into handsome blue flowers. The great blue lobelia, L. *syphilitica*, offers its tall blue-flowered spikes after midsummer.

Add color harmonies to those of fragrance, and the herb garden becomes a citadel of pleasing sense impressions.

Garden Accessories

Many times the adornment of herb gardens with objects other than plants bear the stamp of a gardener's cultural taste, skill, or whim, and, oddly enough, these endow the garden with a character of its own.

A bench is the most traditional of garden accessories. There is no herb garden, small or large, that does not need a comfortable bench. A bench invites a gardener to pause amid pleasing scents and linger to survey the garden scene in comfort. A bench is equally valuable for enjoying the companionship of a friend. Benches are constructed of stone, metal, wood, or a combination of materials. Early man sat on a large stone or fallen tree trunk to rest, or he rested on the earth itself, preferably on a bed of low plants, which reduced the earth's hardness.

It is said chamomile benches had their origin in England where stone was plentiful and wood not. For a more comfortable seat, soil was placed in a shallow container and upholstered with a soft padding of dwarf chamomile; raised up on stone to the required height, it provided a comfortable bench and a fragrance fit for relaxation. Apocryphal or not, the chamomile bench was evident in Tudor England. The chamomile used for the living cushion is *Chamaemelum nobile* 'Treneague', nonflowering and known since Elizabethan times. A chamomile bench made of cedar or treated wood today may not be authentically Tudor, but can give equal pleasure. In a sunny corner of the garden or tucked into an alcove, the chamomile bench claims attention and is an aromatic treasure and a herbal earmark.

For use through all seasons, handsome English teakwood benches are difficult to match, and simple laundry or meetinghouse benches have Shaker charm.

Wattle fences enclosing a herb garden or portions within the garden are of European origin, historically employed by common men and women who kept the gardens in the Middle Ages. Perhaps the human touch gives them their appeal, for they are appropriate in very nearly all styles of herb gardens. In European tradition branches of the European osier are used in the weaving of wattle fences. The osier is not common in the American Southeast, but an available substitute is the commonly used landscape shrub, thorny elaeagnus, *E. pungens* 'Fruitlandii'. From midsummer onward it sends out rusty-brown branches, often 8 feet long. The supple branches, with thorns removed, if present, form an attractive wattle fence woven around and between upright stakes. Admittedly, the elaeagnus branches do not last as long as osier.

As historical and compatible as wattle fences are bee skeps. "Skep" is a word from Old Norse, *skeppa*, meaning "bushel." It is a domed basket of straw used formerly as a beehive. Because straw beehives present problems in the control of bee diseases, they are prohibited for use in the United States except as ornaments. Agrarian writings of antiquity tell us of the flavorful honey supplied from sweet herbs by bees. A bee skep is a nonfunctional focal point of historical interest in a herb garden. Protect it from moisture with a platform of wood or stone and a roof. (See plate 13.)

Sundials have served garden occupants through the centuries. Visit the herb garden at Callaway Gardens in Pine Mountain, Georgia, and you can become a living gnomon, with your shadow pointing out the time of day. For smaller herb gardens a variety of sundial styles are available to mount on a column, place close to the ground, or hang on a wall. Placement of a sundial is determined by where, in your garden, it will be exposed to the sun for a maximum number of hours. After setting it up, a sundial requires proper adjustment and orientation in accordance to the manufacturer's instructions.

Ornaments from which water trickles or splashes feed the eye as fine creative works of art. Historically they served to supply water to plants. But best of all are their therapeutic sounds. Nothing soothes like the tinkle, splash, or gush of moving water.

A gate gives a sense of cloistered ingress. A simple Gothic arch without pretensious decoration, marks an otherwise undistinguished entrance and hints at a *giardino segreto*; it may be a collector's treasure.

Handsome hand-thrown terra-cotta pots, new or old, make attractive accents. Plant them with well-formed herbs, perhaps standardized or made into a topiary. Or employ a shallow container for a mass planting of favorite herbal species. The bright earth shade of the terra-cotta sets off garden greens with great style.

An assortment of purely decorative garden ornaments may introduce an improper focus. Antique urns and garden statues—carved, cast, or of a composition stone—may reveal more of the gardener's idiosyncrasies than you would prefer. Nevertheless a bit of whimsy is sometimes welcome, and the garden's keeper may have an appreciation of garden adornments that surpasses the run-of-the-mill.

Intentionally naturalized concepts in herb garden designs, to be consistent, should omit objects that detract from nature or might complicate the beauty of simplicity. Accessories in a natural landscape may include a simple footbridge to span water, a natural stone of lovely proportion to mark a focal point or to serve birds with water in its concave cavity, and a bench of stone or one hewn from a log for rest and contemplation.

5 ❦ Natural Landscapes for Native American Herbs in Southeastern United States

Americana has arrived in the herb garden. Increasing numbers of genuine herb gardeners, like poets, are sensitized and rapturous over the beauty of a pastoral meadow, shaded woodland, bog, or sandhill studded with native American herbal species. A sensitivity to an environment leads to a respect for the way simple, unimproved natural species grow and are naturally fitted to a habitat (See plate 14.)

Natural landscaping with native herbs is an innovative approach for herb gardeners, which brings into view naturally splendid scenes. Herb gardeners are learning that gardens designed for native herbs with an environmental approach, in partnership with nature, require less maintenance and support than traditional designs planned for nonnative herbs. American native herbs, together with oral and written accounts of how American Indian tribes used plants for food, medicine, crafts, etc., are equal in historic background and virtues to the Asian, European, and African species commonly focused upon by herbists.

The unmatched diversity of naturally landscaped spaces increase interest and create an untroubled sense of calm. Think of the satisfying color and scent of the red-flowered bee balm, *Monarda didyma*, distributed south to Georgia and Tennessee. The sculptured contours of the woodland jack-in-the-pulpit, *Arisaema triphyllum*, with its handsome striped green and brown canopied pulpit, consorts with the dainty foliage of the North American and

East Asian maidenhair fern, *Adiantum pedatum*, and its counterpart, the Southern maidenhair, *A. capillus-veneris*, distributed worldwide in temperate and tropical regions; they are not limited in herbal use to American Indian tribes.

The profusion of native American herbs vividly colors a meadow in the summertime. To achieve an effect, sow seeds of purple coneflower, *Echinacea purpurea*, around a fence post and have the added joy of seeing the tiger and giant swallowtail butterflies the flowers attract. Sweet goldenrod, *Solidago odora*, planted nearby in acid soil, contributes both a contrasting golden color and the sweet fragrance of anise. A cheering yellow to crimson-brown annual, self-seeding, is the Plains coreopsis, *Coreopsis tinctoria*, used by the North American Indians as a dye plant and a medicinal. From mid-to late summer, the sourwood tree, *Oxydendrum arboreum*, offers sweet-scented flowers borne in spreading racemes, which lure the bees to create sourwood honey for good eating and sweet perfume. Our associations with our native herbs add a rich heritage to a lifetime.

In a search for native American herbal plants a study of the relationships of an American Indian tribe (as an ethnic group) to its environment is necessary. Information comes down through oral and written historical accounts. In the documentation of narrations passed on by the Indian hunter and gatherer of plants, the medicine man, the tiller of the soil, the craftsman, etc., the uses of plants for food, medicine, etc. are found. As the search for accurate documents about the native flora and its associations with the culture of an indigenous race is pursued herbal plants are brought into view. The study in its entirety is called ethnobotany.

Keepers of native American herbal plants are intrigued with plants close to the various American Indian tribes. They proclaim devotion for what is botanically American and are intrinsically conservationists. Their gardens are often a sanctuary for threatened indigenous species, but they are cautious in what and how they transplant from the wild.

Do not collect from the wild unless you do so wisely—take some seed, not all; take a cutting, not a root. Question whether or not the herbal species you are coveting is on an endangered species list or in a designated protected area. Ask permission before removing plants from a site about to be bulldozed; arrangements may have been made before you arrive for the rescue of plants by those in charge. If you are not skilled at propagating herbal plants, or are searching for native herbs difficult to propagate, buy only nursery-propagated material—and choose nurseries willing to make visible their propagation methods.

Consider the broad ecological role and economic benefits that plants in the wild provide. Plants work together in nature through complicated inter-relationships, and the removal or disruption of any one component of the ecosystem may have an adverse chain reaction that will effect countless or-ganisms throughout the ecosystem and may cause the loss of an economi-cally significant genetic resource by the extinction of one or more natural species. Many native plants are becoming extremely rare as undisturbed habitats continue to be lost to development.

Using Native Habitats for Native Herbs

A preserve limited to native American herbal plants, set apart and planned, is the start of a secure sanctuary for the indigenous plant inhabitants and their keeper. Such a garden is limited to natural species; invasive naturalized species are unwelcome.

By virtue of its diverse habitats, the Southeast supports a rich and diverse flora of herbal plants, most of them known and employed by the North American Indian and the early pioneers. The region is composed of temper-ate, subtropical, tropical (along the southern coastal areas of Florida), and subalpine flora. Woodland, prairie (meadow), sandhills, and wetlands (wa-terways, marshes, swamps, bogs, and tidal pools) occur in each climatic zone of the Southeast and support a distinct flora. Many native plant species of the southern Appalachian region are common to the central and northern Ap-palachian regions as well, or closely related species occur.

The southern region of the Appalachian Mountains extends from the in-terior low plateau eastward, through the Cumberland Plateau, the ridge and valley, and the Blue Ridge. The Blue Ridge Mountains have steep slopes where woodland shelters a large assortment of herbaceous plants under its canopy, and above that treeless balds (grassy summits) with subalpine flora; microclimates contain unique flora. The rising elevations of the Appalachi-ans and abundant rainfall produce a cool, moist climate.

In the foothills of the Blue Ridge thermal belts accommodate a flora from

Southern climatic zones, in spite of their northerly latitude. A herb garden in a foothill's thermal belt allows gardeners to assemble both temperate and subtropical native herbal species. Fifteen miles away at a higher elevation, there may be cold temperatures and heavy snow, while the thermal belt gardener tends his plants.

In contrast to the Appalachian regions, the coastal plain boasts arid sand-hills bordering rivers. Sand dunes, if they have no mat of vegetation to hold them in place, are vulnerable to winds. They blow about, constantly shift their pattern; and hold little water; moreover, their relative sterility further reduces the possibility of any vegetation or formation of a plant habitat. By contrast, sandhills, stabilized by vegetation, have less rainfall and higher temperatures than the mountain region, but are sufficiently stable to support a flora adapted to the environment.

Between the mountains and the coastal plain lies the piedmont, distinguished by its granite outcroppings and soil derived from metamorphosed rock.

Streams and rivers flowing from the mountains through the piedmont, form aquatic habitats of bogs, swamps, and tidal pools. Distinctive native plant communities mark these areas.

Along the Mississippi River and in valleys of rivers draining into the Gulf and Atlantic shelf, alluvial soils provide rich productive habitats. The lime soils and outcroppings of limestone of the Cumberland Plateau and westward support a distinct lime-requiring flora. The black belts in Alabama and Mississippi associated with lime soils are reflected in their flora; sinks of lime occur in areas of South Carolina, Georgia, and Florida. Elsewhere the soil is generally acidic and associated with granite rock.

Because of varied topographical features, amounts of rainfall, temperatures, and soil types, the Southeast embraces diverse native habitats with an accompanying multiformity of endemic plant species. Native plants are well adapted to their environment, an advantage over introduced or exotic species. Some species occur only in specific habitats and, because they demand special conditions, are usually difficult to cultivate elsewhere. On the other side, they are tolerant of their own region's climatic irregularities and require less maintenance in the way of fertilizing and watering. Once established, a region's native plants replenish themselves by self-sowing or asexual methods of propagation. By preventing the introduction of cultivars or aggressive species from other habitats, the herbist preserves the integrity of an ecological community and the singular beauty of a natural landscape.

The environment of a site for a potential ecological garden is basic to any plan. The natural association of distinct plants that have mutual relationships among themselves and to their environment (a plant community), whether it be woodland or meadow or wetland, present an inherent unlabored and unfettered character. These natural landscapes as gardens holding native herbs are sensuous escapes for civilized man; they are without architectural composition imposing formal order. Acknowledging the validity of an existing woodland, meadow, sandhill, bog, marsh, bald, or slope with granite or calcareous outcroppings as a natural garden site for native herbs suited to it is sensible. On each of these sites, optimal conditions of climate and soil prevail for the herbs adapted to these distinct environments. Herbs endemic to an arid climate bear the stress of drought; herbs endemic to a moist climate bear heavy amounts of rain. By growing the kinds of herbs that would naturally occur on the site you happen to have, you will create a garden that is in partnership with nature, thrives, and more or less cares for itself. You thus preserve the integrity, stability, and beauty of the plant community. Viewing this garden brings to mind the American Indians' attitude toward plants.

Once you have accepted a natural habitat as a garden site, the next step is to conceptualize its design. Permit nature to do the planning by making careful observations of the climate—minimum and maximum temperatures. Know the soil structure—the arrangement, amounts, and sizes of particles of sand, loam, or clay that give a soil its texture. Soil structure effects moisture holding capacity, aeration, and fertility. A porous soil of principally sand through which water drains rapidly will dry out more quickly than one of loam, and a non-porous clay soil will hold water and remain wet. The amount of organic matter increases water-holding capacity and supplies nutrients. (Think of a bog whose soils of organic matter have accumulated under the influence of excessive moistening and deficient aeration.) Know the acidity or alkalinity of the soil because it exerts a strong influence on the availability and transfer of nutrients to plants. Know the soil's fertility. A soil test gives all of this information. With the results of a test in hand you can select and plant native herbs whose native habitats match the environmental qualities of your site. Note whether or not the average rainfall for required moisture matches your site. Study the topography of the site to take advantage of slopes as microclimates. (South- and west-facing slopes are hotter and drier than the usually cooler north slopes. East-facing slopes are intermediate.) Remember that sloping sites require precautions to prevent erosion. By planting small herbal shrubs among partially imbeded rocks, soil can be held in place. Consider the tolerance of specific herbal plants to sunlight and shade conditions. Respect natural plant associations in the landscape by introducing only native herbal species naturally fitted to the habitat. Refer to the Descriptive Catalog of Herbs and the Bibliography in the back of this book for information pertaining to regions of herb origins and their native habitats.

Plan and garden with environmental sensitivity. If you intend to make alterations to the site, some destruction of the established ecosystem will occur. Minimize this disruption. Preserve all the parts, and allow these parts to maintain their interrelationships as naturally as possible; for example, common lousewort, *Pedicularis canadensis*, used by the American Indians medicinally and to delouse pups and sheep, is distributed from Quebec to Florida and occurs in rich woods, well-drained, and in the open. Lousewort is semiparasitic on roots of suitable host plants, usually grasses. Depriving it of its host by haphazardly changing its ecosystem or placing the plant under cultivation where it may not find the proper host may cause its extinction. In this way countless plant species are lost. Avoid clearing a plot. Instead, catalog and mark the existing plants; herbal plants may be among them, and at a later date you may realize that they are strategically placed, or their form is in counterpoint to another plant form. Moreover, eradicating plants may result in permanent losses of necessary organisms supporting the ecosystem.

It is a natural instinct to tame plants to please oneself. Restrain this instinct. Keeping a natural habitat for native herbal plants is in direct contrast to gardening centered on domesticating plants from the wild to please a human being. The tidy gardener may have difficulty in keeping a naturalistic garden, because nature is not neat. A certain disorder is almost unavoidable.

A garden of native plants should, however, be visually interesting. Study the existing relationship of natural focal points in the landscape—a small stream through shaded woodland, a mound of sand catching full sun, a bog in a sunny meadow, granite outcroppings or other rock formations. For these attractions, choose eye-catching mass plantings of herbal species naturally expected to be found in the site's environment. In so doing the dramatic rhythms of nature itself, so infinitely varied, provide sensory expectations. Settle on a boundary of the space allocated for your garden by correlating it with topographical features and nearby buildings.

Features like walks, steps, bridges, and enclosures should be planned and executed in context of the distinctive aspects of the site. There should be a minimum of manipulation. A walk or path should connect points of interest, reach a view, bring you to a bench for a pause—conduct a visitor through nature's display. Let paths follow the natural contours and avoid sharp, unnatural turns. Also make them safe, reasonably level and a comfortable width of at least 3 feet for yourself and your visitors. Delineate pathways with plants or other indigenous natural materials. Embellished neatness detracts from the beauty of a natural habitat, so avoid tight edgings or using single species as an edging. Nature is irregular. For the construction of a pathway, use indigenous materials that blend into the habitat—stepping stones, gravel, sand, pine needles, bark. Through shaded woodland, a path of moss conveys a mood difficult to match. Through a meadow, a winding path simply formed by a mower is fitting.

Consider making your garden of native herbs a private space and screen it from public view with native herbal shrubs and trees. Arrange for a view from the approach or from a window of the house. Providing an *Ausblick* (outlook or view) from the garden is equally appropriate; nature provides many grand overlooks of water or mountain ranges, or vistas through long passages of tall grasses, trees, or shrubs. At the end of a straight moss pathway, bordered irregularly with herbal ferns, plant a principal shrub like the flame azalea, *Rhododendron calendulaceum*, appreciated for its yellow to orange flowers, or strawberry bush, *Euonymus americanus*, with its vivid orange and red fruits. Seen from a distance, the view is a harmonious focal point blending with the woodland.

For crossing a dry or wet stream, set stepping stones—alternately rather than at right angles to the stream. Use large flat stones for steps leading down to the stream, and plant unrestrained vegetation around and about, to unify path and water. The following herbal species are suggested: yellow-eyed grass, *Xyris caroliniana*; blue iris, *Iris virginica* or *I. prismatica*; arrowhead, *Sagittaria latifolia*; common cattail, *Typha latifolia*; cardinal flower, *Lobelia cardinalis*; turtlehead, *Chelone glabra*; swamp milkweed, *Asclepias incarnata*; aquatic milkweed,

Fig. 12. Pen and ink drawing from *Sing Mit!* by Fritz Reuter (Zwickau: Saxony, 1914).

A. perennis, crested fern, *Dryopteris cristata*, and Virginia chain fern, *Woodwardia virginica*. A rustic pier reaching out over a bog or marsh garden is an essential appointment for herbists who enjoy watching and reflecting on the ecological processes taking place in bog or marsh. When bridges are necessary, let them be simple; use a plan of staggered or simple planks laid horizontally across supports.

Recall the joys of discovery you experienced as a child when you roamed the wild and renew that pleasure with endearing herbal species in a manner that surprises: a clump of dwarf iris, *Iris verna* or *I. cristata*; bloodroot, *Sanguinaria canadensis*, perhaps the double-flowered mutant that rises spontaneously; blue to white blooming phacelia, *Phacelia dubia*, on and around granite outcroppings; or, beside a natural spring, a patch of blue flag, Iris virginica. Tuck herbal plants between fallen timbers and rocks. Use one or two rocks carefully, instead of scattering many rocks.

Observe variations in heights, textures, and colors of native herbs and follow nature's examples. Plantings, particularly trees and shrubs, seem more natural if different sizes of the same species are grouped together. To achieve an effect, stagger sowing and planting time, or acquire plants in several stages of growth and plant them together. The beauty of native herbal plants is achieved by their association with one another in groups and colonies among trees and shrubs, rocks, and in other natural formations. Follow nature; do not cross her.

Contrived Natural Habitats

Although native herbs of meadow, wood, sandhill, marsh, or bog look best in their native habitat or resist ordinary attempts to domesticate them in the garden, habitats can be contrived. Moreover, with adaptations a design with overlapping habitats within a climatic range can be achieved. A feasible plan centers on an elliptical mound or berm of suitable soil, proportionate in size for the site. Rim this berm irregularly with rugged boulders, as elements of garden design derived from nature, to serve as structural supportive elements. (See plate 15.)

In a humus-rich soil on one side of the mound, preferably the cooler north or west slope, plant native herbal trees and shrubs to give shade for an array of herbaceous woodland native herbs. Since trees and shrubs rarely grow as single specimens in nature, plant as many of these natives as space permits. Your choices may give you the same delightful surprises: yellow flowers blooming in November on a witch hazel, Hamamelis virginiana; early spring flowers on the spicebush, Lindera benzoin, before the leaves appear; white clusters of flowers in April on black haw, Viburnum prunifolium; an evergreen holly, Ilex opaca; or an ample sweet gum, Liquidambar styraciflua.

In the shade underneath the lush woodland foliage of herbaceous herbs is protected and thrives: mayapple, Podophyllum peltatum; large Solomon's seal, Polygonatum biflorum or shrub yellowroot, Xanthorhiza simplicissima. The scene is enhanced when Virginia bluebells, Mertensia virginica and false Solomon's seal, Smilacina racemosa, are placed together in the same patch as they often occur in nature. Virginia bluebells blossom in early springtime, and after they have gone out of sight, false Solomon's seal appears in great masses with clusters of starry flowers and red fruits well into summer.

Plants should be positioned with care, out of consideration for their particular needs. Plants needing shade or cool temperatures should be shielded by shrubs or trees, and placed on the cooler side of the mound. Those requiring warmth and sun should be exposed to the south and east. Follow the same concept when tucking in small herbs among rocks at the base of the mound. Arrange for granite outcroppings among the natives at intervals, which will keep roots warm in winter and be stepping stones.

The sunny area on top of the mound welcomes drifts of tall meadow plants. Meadow plants will enjoy the sun and endure a cruel drought. Prepare a sandhill on the mound for plants from dry areas by spreading sharp sand over the existing soil. Include evergreen *Conradina canescens* with other species native to the sandhills of the coastal plain.

For bog plants whose roots need access to water at all times, fashion a portion of the mound as a bog. Remove a pie-shaped section of soil to a depth of 12–15 inches starting at the base and tapering upward on the slope to a point midway between the base and the top. Line the cavity with heavy-duty polyethylene sheeting—or, for longer life, butyl rubber. Lightly perforate the sheet and wet it, then fill the hole with a soil mixture of 2 parts soil to 1 part peat for water retention. Wet thoroughly before planting. The bog, situated on a slight slope, will accumulate more water at the base, useful for herbs having greater need of it. In it plant blue flag, *Iris virginica*, scouring rush, *Equisetum hyemale*, turtlehead *Chelone glabra*; and many more native herbs of wetlands not genetically adapted to survive in dry soil. Dot-and-dash the bog area on its shady side with indigenous herbal ferns.

Surround a mound with a broad path or driveway. Along the outer periphery of the broad path, if the environment and space permit, prepare an open or thinly wooded xeric habitat for an assemblage of Southeastern herbs from xeric habitats. Bear grass, *Yucca filamentosa*, with its dramatic sword-shaped leaves and tall white luminous flowers makes a fine sentinel at the entrance. In a region of coastal sands edged with brackish marshes, use Spanish bayonet instead, *Y. aloifolia* or *Y. gloriosa*.

The whole, enclosed with a split-rail fence, is an informal garden tending to obscure boundaries. It wraps nature around the house; and it presents a lovely view from a window all through the year.

The shapes and forms of berms or mounds are limited only by the topography of the site, its surroundings, and its size. Planted berms can effectively screen an undesirable view or separate one garden area from another. A mound plan, divided into portions treated as separate ecological systems, promotes success for growing native herbs from different environments. The slope permits excess water to run off. The choice of limestone or granite rocks helps to contribute alkalinity or acidity respectively to the surrounding soil; moreover, rocks keep the soil and plant roots warm through the winter.

A piece of land in the piedmont holding outcroppings of granitic rock is attractive when it accommodates waves of medium to tall native herbal grasses. America's grass roots movement toward fundamental concepts includes the grass roots themselves. Across America there is an increasing trend to plant native grasses, which once blanketed the land of temperate America and were found useful by the American Indian tribes. Broom sedge, *Andropogon virginicus*, is also adapted to sandy pine and oak woods.

Miniature areas can be transformed into microclimates. Areas where shade usually presides—nooks and crannies around and about a home or corridors between houses—can become intimate, captivating gardens for indigenous herbs of the woodlands. Sunny corners or recesses can be styled as sloping rockeries. A miniature sandhill can become an arid environment holding a few herbal species; form sandhills from a child's sandbox by redressing its composition to suit the plants. A raised planter can serve as an upland meadow, a lath shelter replaces a woodland; and a leaky wooden cask substitutes as a swamp. Developing miniature contrived habitats is an undertaking for children, enriching those of urban areas in particular. They grow to become citizens who understand, cherish, and respect the natural environments of our ecosphere.

A garden of native American herbs allies itself with the specific geographical and ecological distribution of native herbs; such a garden is valuable to any conservation plan. The American Indian gathered plants from the wild for use and is known to have propagated a number of them; today we are obliged to propagate plants and maintain ecosystems for their preservation.

Natural landscapes of native American herbal species are links to the lives and plant discoveries of botanists and plant collectors. The Spanish physician, Nicholas Monardes, recorded his discoveries of New World plants in three books published from 1569 to 1574. An English translation, titled *Joyful*

Fig. 13. Drawing of a sassafras tree in the English translation of Monardes' *Joyful News*.

News out of the New Found World, came in 1577. Monardes noted the existence of differences between plants of different regions; he expressed appreciation of new medicines and remedies found among the plants of the Americas. He described the sunflower and furnished a drawing of tobacco. Monardes wrote of the tea he prepared from the wood and root of the sassafras tree, *Sassafras albidum*, used by the Indians of Florida; it is now on the lists of herbs dangerous to our health. The genus name *Monarda*, assigned by Linnaeus, honors the Spanish botanist and physician. During the later part of the eighteenth century, a father and son, John and William Bartram of Philadelphia, and André and Francois Michaux from France, also father and son, spent many years in botanical explorations to leave for posterity vivid accounts of a bountiful flora in Southeastern habitats. In 1788 Thomas Walter of South Carolina published *Flora Caroliniana*, the first descriptive flora of the Carolinas.

During colonial days, the British were eager for plants and seeds from the Southern colonies, as is revealed in letters between British plant devotees and governors of the colonies, government botanists, and colonists like John Bartram. For example, upon request, the seeds of the aromatic Florida Illicium, star aniseed, and swamp magnolia were received by the Princess of Wales at Kew from John Blommart of Florida. A letter from John Foster of Dublin in 1768 thanks his correspondent for the account and drawings of *Dionaea muscipula*, Venus's-flytrap, and asks for seeds from America. The interest in native Southeastern herbal species continued from across the waters without abatement, while we in America often overlooked our native flora. Only recently have we learned to cherish "American natives."

Native plants used as substitutes in the cooking pots of colonists are referred to in Chapter 2 and listed in the Descriptive Catalog of Herbs.

There is a place for gardens with captivating herbal plants introduced into the United States from dissimilar regions of the world. But an existing habitat planted with native American herbs matched to it is an exciting garden. The plant species enhance the beauty and ecological integrity of the particular plant community, plants found useful to American Indian tribes of southeastern United States are conserved as part of our national heritage, and potential sources of genetic traits are in no danger of extinction.

6 ❧ A Time to Plant and Tend Herbs

The skills required for growing herbs are close to the heart and soul of human existence. From childhood to old age, the human race has been cheered by successes in the garden. In propagating and growing a difficult herb, there is adventure as both tradition and innovation are examined and tried. Preparing a herb garden, supplying herbs with their needs, and coddling seedlings to maturity are pleasant human endeavors—not completely selfless, but close to it.

Having imposed upon yourself a garden design in keeping with the maxim "Site dictates the design scheme," composition and planting follow. And the first chore is preparing the soil, for thorough soil preparation is fundamental, its major function to carry the garden into maturity with a minimum of setbacks.

Preparing the Soil

Soil preparation begins well before planting time and needs forethought. Physical and chemical changes occur in the soil after you have tilled, and, added organic and inorganic fertilizers, and materials to control the pH. Because the beneficial effects are not immediately effective, you must allow time for the soil to stabilize and settle. The familiar Biblical quote of Ecclesiastes, "To every thing there is a season, and a time to every purpose under

the heaven" speaks to the herb gardener, whose soil is prepared for "a time
to plant."

> Now 'tis the spring, and weeds are
> shallow rooted;
> Suffer them now, and they'll o'ergrow
> the garden,
> And choke the herbs for want of husbandry.
> —Shakespeare, Henry VI, Part II

Weeds must be controlled. If they are not thoroughly destroyed before
you dig, they will return and become so invasive as to make removal almost
impossible. Today many gardeners use herbicides developed for specific
weeds, before they do any digging.

Working with the soil can begin in late summer, fall, or early spring, providing the weather is dry and the soil is friable (sufficiently dry to crumble
rather than held by water in a mass). This is probably the most strenuous
part of gardening. Rototilling, double-digging, spading, or turning soil over
with a fork is the hardest kind of physical exercise, and laboring over uncompromising imbedded rocks, tight roots, or impenetrable clay can be exhaust-
ing. But the soil must be prepared.

The digging depth should be sufficient for the development of tap roots
present in the many herbs of the parsley family (root parsley, lovage, fennel,
caraway, etc). The greater the depth tilled, the better roots can reach deep
into the soil for moisture and good anchorage against heavy winds and rains.
Eighteen to 24 inches is a good depth when you are preparing ground-level
beds for the first time. Besides loosening the soil, digging will reveal the
porosity of the exposed soil type at the bottom, so that, if necessary, corrections can be made.

A nonporous soil will not permit water to drain through it. The water
collects, forces out necessary air between soil particles, and drowns plant
roots that reach into it. A serious drainage problem can be corrected by
removing a poorly draining soil to a depth of 18 or more inches, filling the
lower strata with a layer of cracked stones and sharp sand, topped by garden
soil mixed with sharp sand and humus. For a truly serious problem, lay
perforated drainage pipes in a bed of small stones at a depth of 24 inches,
tilting them gradually toward a lower level that leads away from the garden,
to expel excess water. We used this technique successfully in a bed to be

planted with old roses, which had a clay soil with a subsoil of nonporous red clay.

If you are in doubt about the classification of your soil type and its fertility, have a soil test made by your state agricultural agency and request suggestions for improving the quality of your garden soil. A soil test will include the soil type, amount of humic matter, soil pH value (reading of hydrogen-ion concentration expressed by an established scale and used to indicate acidity and alkalinity; the scale of pH values from 0 to 7 indicate acidity, from 7 to 14 indicates alkalinity, 7 being neutral), and amounts of nutrients in the soil. With suggested soil treatment in hand and information on special soil requirements for growing herbs, you can proceed to prepare your surface soils with assurance, not inclined to over- or underamend.

A soil compacted and made heavy by sticky clay is loosened by adding sharp sand. The irregularity of sharp sand particles provides air spaces and prevents the soil mixture from packing; drainage is improved. For further benefits, humus is added in the form of organic compost, leaf mold, or well-rotted stable manure. Humus is valuable for its water-holding capacity, as a fertilizer, and when joined with sharp sand, enlarges the air spaces, making the soil lighter and more porous. Incorporate the humus material thoroughly into the soil where it supplies foods for beneficial organisms that release chemicals not otherwise available to the plants. Because of its high acidity, avoid using sphagnum moss as humus.

In the coastal plain, or wherever the soil is sandy, heavy clay soil and humus are combined with the sand to increase the soil's water and nutrient-holding properties and give substance so roots can become firmly anchored.

Because a county agricultural extension agent is familiar with the local county soil types, drainage patterns, etc., he or she can offer helpful information and solutions for unique drainage problems, measurements of amending ingredients, and amounts of lime or powdered sulfur to change a pH value for specific plant categories.

Large trees like pines and oaks, majestic and lovely as they are, are not suitable for a conventional herb garden. Roots of trees alter the drainage pattern and deplete the soil of nutrients. Pine needles and oak leaves increase the soil's acidity and decrease fertility. Plan to lay out your garden well away from tall trees—or plan a garden of woodland plants, adapted for this environment.

Powdered lime from limestone is commonly added to acid soils to improve soil productivity. It helps the soil release such essential nutrients as calcium, phosphorus, magnesium, and other micronutrients. If a herb is genetically adapted to a calcareous soil, there are great advantages to growing it in a soil made neutral or slightly alkaline. Adjusting the pH value of a soil with lime, which aids in the normal decay of humus, increases the population of soil organisms, and it improves the structure of the soil so that water seeps through it more rapidly, thus helping control certain disease organisms.

Benefits of accessible calcium are considerable: (1) Longer and stronger root systems develop, and root hairs reach out to become more effective absorbing organs. (2) The formation of necessary insoluble calcium pectate in the middle lamella (a cementing layer of a wall between two adjacent plant cells) is not impeded; its presence prevents changes in the permeability of adjoining membranes and strengthens tissues, resulting in sturdy plants, less vulnerable to fungus and insect diseases. (3) An increase in hair production keeps leaf tissues cooler than air temperatures, which reduces water loss; hairs act as obstacles to insect attack.

Lime, to be most effective, should be applied at a proper rate, according to the soil-test suggestions. The reaction time of lime is slow, so time should be allowed between its distribution and the adding of fertilizers—both well before planting. The application of lime may not be necessary each season; a yearly soil test, however, is insurance for maintaining the correct pH.

Wood ashes from a stove or fireplace sprinkled on the soil when the garden is dormant, in addition to being a good source of potash, help keep the soil alkaline. Just as some herbs are genetically adapted to an alkaline soil, there are many herbs genetically indifferent to the pH of a soil. Their ability to flourish in a range of soil pH values makes them desirable in an assortment of garden categories.

Prepare the soil by double-digging if possible. Spade out the top 8–12 inches of soil in a few feet of bed and set it aside; then turn over the lower 8–12 inches. This enables you to add suggested amounts of organic matter and sharp sand to the lower part. Lime (amount dictated by the results of the soil test), and superphosphate or other fertilizer, whatever has been suggested, are added, and all ingredients are thoroughly mixed and forked over. The process is repeated by spading out the next few feet of bed 8–12 inches deep and turning that over onto the lower prepared layer; mix the additions into the second lower layer, then proceed to a third section of bed, and so on. At the end of the bed, the soil set aside from the first top layer is used to fill the final top layer. The softened, well-textured soil bed is graded with a rake, mounded into the center, and given time to settle.

After the prepared soil settles, your garden beds will be in good condition for planting. The soil can be easily worked and dug into without forming large clods of impervious clay; water will not remain on the surface or produce sodden black gumbo after a rain or after watering; nor, if it began with light, poor sand, will it dry out so quickly that young herbs suffer from an early spring drought.

Successfully changing the physical structure and the chemical content of a soil for herb growing is both science and art. Not to mention extremely hard work. When the transformation is made from heavy, impervious red clay, light, poor sand, or soil choked with silt, there is cause for both celebration and liniment.

Ah, my back, my back,
—Shakespeare, Romeo and Juliet

In regions where the indigenous soil greatly hampers drainage and corrections are physically unfeasible, it is a good idea to resort to containers of various sorts or raised beds, filled with a prepared soil. (See Chapter 4.) Building up free-form berms with a garden soil mixed with sharp sand is another approach. (See plate 16.) Large stone boulders can be attractive supports for large berms. The selection is influenced by the garden's style and surrounding architectural materials.

Fertilizers

In formulating a fertilizer program, a herb gardener must decide on either organic or inorganic fertilizers, or both, plus how much fertilizer to apply. Because soils differ in fertility and retention of nutrients, and herbs differ in nutrient requirements, no widely applicable guidelines can be offered. But it is helpful to be aware of the roles played by organic and inorganic fertilizers.

Both supply nutrients to the herbs, but there's a marked difference in concentration. Compared to soluble inorganic fertilizers, most organic fertilizers are in low concentration and in insoluble form. The macro- and micronutrients are taken up by plants at a slow rate. For this reason some gardeners choose to give young herbs a quick boost in spring with a soluble "complete" (nitrogen, phosphorus, and potassium) inorganic fertilizer. But this should be applied with care so as not to overfertilize. Organic fertilizers are steady in supplying both macro- and micronutrients essential for a balance in foliage and essential oils, and they present little danger of overfertilization. If you are uncertain about amounts, ask advice from fellow herb gardeners nearby. In time experience will teach you how to modify amounts and types on the basis of how well your herbs are growing, their condition, and aromas.

Drawings and woodcuts in medieval herbals show identifiable bleached white thigh bones of animals, partially imbedded in garden beds, apparently used as a source of fertilizer. Steamed bonemeal contains only 1 percent nitrogen and 20 percent to 30 percent phosphoric acid. It also supplies calcium. Bonemeal's low nitrogen content, in proportion to its phosphorus content, prevents interference with oil production in a ratio proper to the growth and volume of green leaf. One teaspoon to 1 tablespoon of bonemeal spread around an established herb in the spring or 1 teaspoon mixed into each pocket where a young herb will be planted is sufficient for the development of a strong root system and a healthy plant.

Compost is both fertilizer and soil conditioner, and is the least expensive and most convenient form of humus. Most herb gardeners today, like generations before them, allow space, (usually screened from view), where the vegetative refuse from their gardens and kitchens is left to decompose into a fertile humus. In addition to macronutrients, certain micronutrients and trace elements, difficult to obtain in a commercial fertilizer, are reintroduced into the soil through the decomposed plant material.

An essential feature in making good compost is keeping the material moist and aerated. Leave the top of the pile flat or depressed, rather than in a cone shape, to catch water. Regularly turn the piled material.

Plant and kitchen materials designated for use in a herb garden should be composted separately from other garden categories. Herb garden compost consists only of vegetative material from the herb gardens and the kitchen. To prevent weed seeds from getting into the garden inadvertently, no weed material should be placed in the compost or diseased herbs. Since composting results from the activity of countless millions of soil organisms in the soil and decaying humus, add layers of garden soil and doses of complete commercial fertilizers to support the life activities of these organisms. To maintain alkalinity in the compost, add agricultural lime. Compost material with adequate nutrients, aeration, and moisture is usually ready for shoveling out in six months.

Calcium-demanding herbs like lavender, thyme, and rosemary are well served with spoons of ground, dried egg shells scratched into the soil surface at their base. It satisfies their need and sweetens the soil. Like my grandmother, I save eggshells; unlike my grandmother I process them in a food processor before strewing the finely chopped shells around the calcium lovers. Chopped oyster shells serves in a similar capacity.

Herbs in containers have limited space for roots to branch out and absorb fertilizers in soluble form. In midsummer, container soils dry out rapidly and require frequent waterings, which leaches out the nutrients. They need to be replaced by watering at intervals with a liquid (20-20-20) fertilizer. The length of the intervals and the strength of the solution are determined by the size of the herb and the size of the container, plus the amounts of rainfall falling on pots outdoors; the herbist has to develop experienced judgment of the potted herbs' condition. Small herbs in small containers benefit from less frequent (bimonthly) applications and weaker doses of fertilizer than herbs in large containers. Just as contained herbs respond quickly to a rainfall or watering can when leaves droop and soil is parched, so they regain good color and vigor after a fertilizer watering. Eventually you should replant a contained herb in fresh potting soil, after trimming the roots; this will supply a fresh complement of nutrients and remove the herb from toxic salts that build up in a small, confined space.

Herb Propagation

Propagating herbs is the backbone of herb cultivation—fundamental, fascinating, and enormously stimulating. There is a bit of exciting midwifery in keeping alive an only seedling to have germinated from a quantity sown, or a single cutting, from a herb species long sought, showing a root.

Propagating herbs, whether by recommended methods or experimentation, makes a fledgling horticulturist of the herbist. A variety of herb species not available at nurseries can be added to your collection. Quantities of herbs can be produced with a small expenditure. You gain an acquaintanceship with herbs through all their growth stages and increase your ability to note details in form and structure, useful for identification and helpful in positioning contrasting forms in the design patterns. Collecting seeds from your garden or from the wild for a garden of native Southeastern herbs is the opening of a door you may not wish to close. Herbs can be multiplied for the garden or as gifts by propagating from seed, cuttings, divisions, layerings, runners, tubers, rhizomes, offsets, and bulb scales—and all with immense pleasure and satisfaction.

From Seed

A herb garden is distinguished from most other gardens by the preponderance of natural species among its plant inhabitants. Natural species have come into the garden from the wild without any intervention by man other than his having introduced them by intention or accident. Natural species, by definition, produce seed and breed true. Consequently, many herbs growing in the garden are a good source for seed. The seeds are viable, and the progeny can be expected to have the same characters as the parents.

Over and above the natural species in the herb garden have come, as natural growth through the centuries, an assortment of plant varieties. Not all varieties can be propagated from seed; from a selection of asexual or vegetative methods choices are made in order of best results.

An occasional disadvantage for beginning herbists is lack of information about the length of time a specific herb seed remains viable. Some herbal seeds, known to be viable only when fresh, are nevertheless harvested, packed, and readied for sale by seedsmen for the following season, by which time viability is seriously reduced and the seed is often worthless. Accordingly, not all the herb seed offered for sale can be expected to germinate, and, unfortunately, few herbs are included in the germination standards set by the Federal Seed Act.

By turning to the Descriptive Catalog you can determine which herbs are best started from seed and decide whether or not you will start them indoors.

When selecting nonnative herbs for propagation in the Southeast, note that the area includes climatic zones 6–11, according to the Plant Hardiness Map of the U.S. Department of Agriculture. Where temperatures decline at higher altitudes in climatic zones 7 and northward, special attention to winter hardiness is necessary. Plants with a reputation for winter hardiness in their native habitat—after generations of propagation in very warm climates, and as a result of natural selection—do not always produce winter-hardy plants in a cold climate. Southern gardeners who relocate and establish new gardens in colder climates experience the phenomenon when they transplant a favorite perennial herb whose roots are expected to remain alive through cold winter temperatures. When a herb like common sage, well-known for its winter hardiness, is propagated from seed through numbers of generations in a warm climate, it may lose progeny when it is transplanted to a colder climate. Likewise, winter-hardy perennials if propagated in nurseries in warm climates, cannot be guaranteed to survive a winter in a colder region.

Information on hardiness for specific herbs is given in the Descriptive Catalog.

The seeds of many shrubs, trees, and herbaceous varieties, before they will germinate, must undergo a period of dormancy that is necessary to complete certain physiological changes called afterripening. This dormancy must then be broken, which is done in cold climates by winter temperatures. To break dormancy in warm winter climates, seeds may be stored in wet sand or moist vermiculite and then put into a refrigerator at about 40 degrees F for two to six weeks. They are then removed and sown. The method is referred to as "stratification." A special treatment for seeds with hard, impermeable seed coats requires "scarification," the cutting, scratching, or chipping of the seed coat to allow water to enter. A second method to soften seed coats and commonly used for members of the legume family like *Baptisia* spp. is the hot water treatment. Boiling water is poured over hard-coated seeds and left to cool. After twelve to twenty-four hours of soaking, they begin to swell and are sown.

When collecting seeds of native species that grow over a broad range, consider the origins of the plants. They might not survive in your home region. Wide-ranging species can develop adaptations in order to survive various environmental conditions. They are described as forming "genetic ecotypes," a phenomenon also seen in nonnative herbal species introduced and cultivated in this country. Studies have shown the occurrence of ecotypic development when the natural distribution of plants cover a wide range of elevations from coastal areas to the mountains. Seed collected from a genetic ecotype growing in the warm coastal areas of Florida might not survive in the cool Blue Ridge, or its growth pattern may vary. Seed from a warmer climate may produce smaller plants in a cooler climate and bloom at a later date, or seed from a cool climate may produce smaller plants in a warm climate. If instead you collect seed from local sources or purchase young plants from nurseries that have been collected from local populations, you help preserve the integrity of the local gene pool, an important facet in conservation.

Large, well-known seed houses are satisfactory sources for common kitchen herbs, but be wary of the exceptions described.

When a herb is not well-known or confusion exists over the common name, seek a source that uses correct botanical or horticultural names. For example, "oregano" is a word signifying a specific aroma found in species of *Origanum* and other genera; among them variations in the "oregano" aroma exist. Many seed and plant suppliers attach the much used common name, oregano, to *O. vulgare*, a species which comes readily from seed, but when grown in most American climates is poor in "oregano" aroma. (For additional information see the *Origanum* spp. entry in the Descriptive Catalog.)

Look to your kitchen shelf for seeds of caraway, dill, fennel, anise, coriander, etc. It is less costly to use them for new plants than to purchase seeds from a seed supplier. Generally the seeds germinate well enough for the number of plants you require. Desirable cultivars become exceptions.

Keep in mind that many herbs, once seeded and permitted to mature in the garden, will self-sow. The cold dark earth provides perfect preservation, temperatures, and moisture conditions for breaking the dormancy of herb seeds. Though very small, some herbaceous herbal species have a hard outer seed coat: for example, the wormwoods, *Artemisia* spp., and the ambrosias, *Chenopodium* spp. In order to sprout, they must have moisture and low temperatures to soften the seed coats and make them permeable. Spring or indoor sowing can be a total failure with these species. Let them self-sow, and when they germinate in the spring, learn to identify the seedlings from their characteristic "seed leaves" (cotyledons). They are easily transplanted if you prefer to grow them in some other spot. There is considerably less effort when nature does the propagating.

For some gardeners self-sown seedlings may be a bit of a nuisance; numbers must be pulled up to let others grow. However, among them are the vigorous plants, superior by virtue of natural selection and more vigorous than those you started by sowing indoors or outdoors.

Herb seed known not to self-sow should be started indoors or outdoors the following season. Collect seeds from plants in your garden or from the wild when they have ripened and before they fall to the ground. Let the loose seeds and seeds held within ovary walls dry several days indoors. Loosen and shake seeds from the walls, clean away any impurities, place in labeled packets with the complete name, where collected, date of harvest, and store.

To retain viability, store seeds under cool (60–70 degrees F) and dry conditions, away from light. The length of time they remain capable of germinating varies; many can be stored for surprisingly long periods. Parsley is among the short-lived; by the second year germination percentages fall. Percentages of basils drop gradually; depend on good germination for five to six years after harvesting.

Throughout warm regions, there are good reasons to sow herb seeds outdoors in late summer and late fall (December).(1) Fresh seed matured in late summer gives a higher percentage of germination, higher than early spring outdoor sowings. Seeds of lavender, lovage, and angelica can be expected to germinate best upon reaching maturity (fresh); in a short time their germinating percentages fall to make spring sowing outdoors an almost total failure. (2) Late summer or late fall (through December) offers favorable circumstances for successful seed germination and growth by virtue of cooler temperatures and increased moisture. Fall-sown seeds will germinate at the first possible opportunity in early spring, earlier than you will be able to get them to grow if you wait for spring weather to begin your outdoor operations. (3) Certain annuals, biennials, and perennials produce sturdier plants if seeded in late summer or fall. The gradually cooling temperatures and the moisture are highly beneficial to herbs not acclimated to the fast-rising temperatures of spring in zones 8–11. In the early spring, when you are just getting started in the outdoor garden, you and your guests may be delighted to enjoy fresh dill, cilantro (coriander), chervil, borage, calendulas, fenugreek, and many more, either sown late in the year or self-sown. See the Descriptive Catalog for "time to sow" applicable to specific herbs and tables for propagation.

Starting seed indoors is not for everyone. But dealing with unpretentious, unsensational herb seeds, like working with most beginnings, can be sufficiently fascinating to hold one's interest till the herb matures. It leads to knowledge of a herb's complex behavior. Occasions for close observation bring to light the natural relationships of herbs into the families to which they belong. It becomes possible to identify a herb by its seed and seed leaves.

The following guidelines are provided for starting seeds indoors by methods to fit the average private garden.

Sowing Information for Common Herbs

Herb Common Name Botanical Name	Sow Indoors/ Outdoors	Time to Sow	Days to Germinate	Light/ Dark
		ANNUALS		
Basil *Ocimum basilicum*	indoors outdoors	early spring late spring	3–10	
Borage *Borago officinalis*	outdoors	fall*	5–10	
Calendula *Calendula officinalis*	indoors outdoors	early spring early spring or fall*	3–10	dark
Castor bean *Ricinus communis*	indoors outdoors	early spring late spring	5–20	
Chamomile *Matricaria recutita*	outdoors	early spring or fall*	4–10	light
Chervil *Anthriscus Cerefolium*	outdoors	fall*	7–14	
Coriander *Coriandrum sativum*	outdoors	early spring or fall*	6–10	
Dill *Anethum graveolens*	outdoors	fall*	5–10	
Nasturtium *Tropaeolum majus*	outdoors	late spring, zones 6–8; fall, zones 9–10	7–14	
Orach *Atriplex hortensis var. atrosanguinea*	outdoors	fall*		
Perilla *Perilla frutescens*	outdoors	fall*	10–15	light
Summer savory *Satureja hortensis*	outdoors	mid-spring or fall*	4–10	
Sweet wormwood *Artemisia annua*	outdoors	mid-spring or fall*	10–15	
		BIENNIALS		
Caraway *Carum carvi*	outdoors	fall*		

Optimum Temperatures (degrees F.)	Sowing Depths (inches)	Self-sowing Zones	Comments
warm 65°	1/16	zones 8–10	Tap seed firmly into warm soil.
cool 55°	1/8	zones 5–10	Sow where plants are to grow (in situ).
cool	1/4	zones 5–10	Excels in a cool situation.
warm	1/4	zones 8–10	Grows as a perennial to shrub or tree size in tropical regions.
cool 45°	S	zones 4–10	Not the perennial chamomile, *Chamaemelum nobile*.
cool 45°	1/8	zones 4–10	Seed viability reduced after 2 years. A cool weather herb.
cool 50°	1/8	zones 8–10	Sow where plants are to grow.
cool 50°	1/8	zones 4–10	Sow where plants are to grow.
warm	1/4		Sow where plants are to grow.
cool	1/16	zones 5–10	Sow where plants are to grow.
warm	S	zones 5–10	Fluctuating temperatures in winter and moisture break dormancy of Petilla seeds sown in the fall.
warm	S	zones 5–10	Sow in situ at intervals to keep a supply.
warm	S	zones 4–10	
cool	1/16	zones 3–10	Resists transplanting; sow where plants are to grow.

Sowing Information for Common Herbs (continued)

Herb Common Name Botanical Name	Sow Indoors/ Outdoors	Time to Sow	Days to Germinate	Light/ Dark
BIENNIALS (continued)				
Clary sage Salvia sclarea	indoors outdoors	early spring mid-spring, or fall*	4–6	
Foxglove Digitalis spp.	indoors outdoors	early spring mid-spring	10–20	light
Honesty Lunaria annua	indoors outdoors	early spring late summer, zones 6–7; fall, zones 8–10	10–20	
Leek Allium ampeloprasum Porrum group	indoors outdoors	early spring, zones 6–7; fall, zones 8–10	10–12	
Parsley Petroselinum spp.	indoors outdoors	early spring early spring or fall*	7–24	
Sweet angelica Angelica archangelica	outdoors	late summer or fall, zones 6–7 or cool, high elevations		
Teasel Dipsacus sativus	outdoors	late summer or fall*	5–10	
Woad Isates tinctoria	outdoors	late summer, zone 6 or fall*	4–10	
PERENNIALS				
English pennyroyal Mentha pulegium	indoors outdoors	early spring mid-spring		
Fennel Foeniculum vulgare	outdoors	early spring	5–15	
French sorrel Rumex scutatus	indoors outdoors	early spring mid-spring or fall*	3–5	
Hyssop Hyssopus officinalis	indoors outdoors	early spring mid-spring or early fall	4–8	
Lemon balm Melissa officinalis	indoors outdoors	early spring late summer*	7–10	light

Optimum Temperatures (degrees F.)	Sowing Depths (inches)	Self-sowing Zones	Comments
warm	1/16	zones 5–10	
cool 60°	S	zones 4–10	
cool	1/8	zones 5–10	
cool 60°	1/4		
cool 50°	1/8	zones 5–10	Germinate seeds in 7–12 days by leaving seeds in tepid water for 24 hours before sowing.
cool	1/8	zones 3–7	Sow seeds as soon as ripe or store in a freezer; viability decreases rapidly.
warm	1/4	zones 4–10	
cool	1/4	zones 5–8	
warm	1/16	zones 5–10	Likes a moist soil.
warm	1/8	zones 6–10	In cold climates fennel is treated as an annual.
cool 45°	1/16	zones 4–8	
cool 60°	1/16	zones 4–7	Find a cool microclimate for hyssop in zones 8–10.
cool 50°	1/16	zones 5–10	

Sowing Information for Common Herbs (continued)

Herb Common Name Botanical Name	Sow Indoors/ Outdoors	Time to Sow	Days to Germinate	Light/ Dark
PERENNIALS (continued)				
Lovage Levisticum officinale	outdoors	late summer or fall*	8–20	
Rue Ruta graveolens	indoors outdoors	early spring fall*	8–10	
Sage Salvia officinalis	indoors outdoors	early spring mid-spring	6–10	
Salad burnet Poterium sanguisorba	indoors outdoors	early spring mid-spring	5–10	
Sweet marjoram Origanum majoranum	indoors	early spring	5–10	
Common thyme Thymus vulgaris	indoors outdoors	early spring mid-spring	4–8	
Winter savory Satureja montana	indoors outdoors	early spring late summer	5–10	

Interpretation: early spring, a few weeks before the frost free date; mid-spring, immediately after the frost free date; late spring, when night temperatures are above 50 degrees; fall, September–December.
S—surface.
*—for more favorable germination and growth in warm areas.

Sow seeds indoors four to eight weeks (depending upon their growth rate) before they normally can be started outdoors. Seeds can vary enormously in the number of days they take to germinate under optimum conditions (anywhere from three days to months), so note the number of days given on the seed packet or check in the Descriptive Catalog. With a proper timing schedule, the young seedlings can then be set out in their final location.

Check well in advance in the Descriptive Catalog whether or not any of your selected seeds require special treatment for germination, then comply with them.

Select a container for seed sowing with a 2-inch depth and openings in

Optimum Temperatures (degrees F.)	Sowing Depths (inches)	Self-sowing Zones	Comments
cool	1/16	zones 4–7	
warm	1/8	zones 5–10	
cool 55°	1/16		
cool	1/8	zones 5–10	
warm	S		
warm	S		A scattering of sharp sand over the sown seed is beneficial.
warm	S	zones 5–10	

the bottom for drainage. For small to medium-sized seed, I prefer the small 5 x 3 1/2 inch plastic containers with six compartments and large drainage openings. They're suitable for stocking a collector's garden with more than enough plants plus some to share with friends. An ordinary household has space for the containers in trays; they are easily cleaned and stacked for storing. Larger seeds are sown in individual plastic pots.

Excellent mediums for germination and early growth are sterilized soilless prepared mixes. This lightweight porous blend of finely milled vermiculite and nutrients retains moisture and provides air spaces for aeration and drainage.

Arrange the containers in a tray to hold water, and fill them with the sterilized planting medium. Moisten the medium with water, and add water to the tray. By consistently watering from below, instead of wetting the surface where seedlings emerge, you need dread no loss from damping-off fungus infections. Because germination rates are usually high, spread the seed thinly by gently rubbing and dropping them from between a finger and thumb. Reserve a part of the seed in the packet for outdoor sowing.

Small seeds—and many are almost the size of dust particles—are left uncovered for necessary light or covered with 1/16 inch of the medium. I use a sprinkling of clean sharp sand over seeds belonging to the mint family. This has a threefold purpose: (1) sand is inorganic, cannot sustain life, and thus prevents damping-off fungus spores from developing and infecting emerging seedlings: (2) the weight of wet sand holds the seeds firmly in place; they cannot "float" with the accompanying danger of drying; (3) as the seeds absorb moisture, they expand, and the abrasive effect of sharp sand on the seed coats permits moisture to enter at an increased rate and hastens germination. Larger seeds are covered with the planting medium according to the rule "twice the diameter of the seed."

Each container requires a label, recording the name of the seed, its source, harvest year, date of sowing, and germination date. The value of information is obvious for record keeping. If you are a serious herbist, and prefer to avoid all confusion, use botanical names in all your record keeping. Using only common names can cause mistakes in distinguishing specific herb varieties, and the resulting misidentification can sometimes be serious. Since the *expected* germination date is known, keeping records of *actual* germination dates will tell you if your procedure is working properly.

Now slip the tray with water and containers into a plastic bag to retain moisture. For seeds requiring a warm temperature and darkness, the best spot for germination in most households is above the kitchen refrigerator. The waste heat from the motor gives an optimum temperature, and it is usually dark enough between the top of the refrigerator and the cupboards to protect the seedlings from light. Seeds that require light should be placed under a fluorescent tube mounted in a warm room. If they need a cool temperature, an unheated indoor space is best.

Some seed catalogs are generous with such pointers as days of germination to be expected, light or darkness required, temperatures, pretreatment, etc. Thompson & Morgan is an example; they provide a helpful booklet on request.

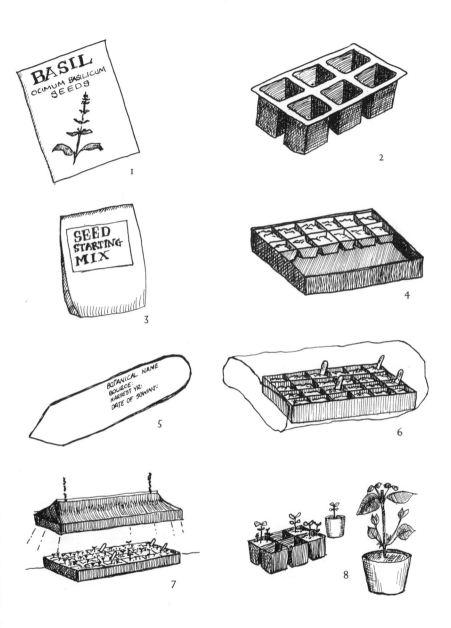

Fig. 14. Materials and steps for starting herbs from seed.

Check the trays each day for signs of germination. As soon as sprouts appear, remove the container from the tray to another tray of water and expose to good light. If a greenhouse is not available, an excellent source of light is an ordinary fluorescent light tube kept 4–6 inches from the tops of the seedlings. Keep the fluorescent tube energized for fourteen hours of a twenty-four-hour day, the equivalent of full summer daylight. It is unsatisfactory to rely on light entering through a window; during the winter when seedlings are grown, hours of daylight are not long enough, and cloudy days are common. Add water to the tray to keep the medium moist. Watering the surface of the medium washes soil away from delicate roots, exposing them to the air and drying, making seedlings more susceptible to diseases. If the germination rate is high, thin out seedlings to avoid spindly plants susceptible to disease.

When two pairs of true leaves have developed—that is, not cotyledons or seed leaves, which are the first to open—transplant seedlings to larger containers or individual pots with drainage openings. But don't employ pots too large for the seedlings; too-large containers hold too much moisture. My choice of a soil mixture for growing sturdy herbs in containers is the following: 7 parts sterilized potting soil, 3 parts sharp sand, and 1 part perlite with 3/4 cup bonemeal added to each bushel of mix. Select a sterilized potting soil developed from Northern peat, which tends to be less acid and is appreciated by alkaline-loving herbs. Bacto, a brand name, is available and very good. The potting soil developed from pine bark, although usually more available, is too acid. Settle each seedling into an opening deeper than it was growing in the germination medium, and firm the opening with soil. Do not hesitate to cover the seed leaves (cotyledons) with soil—for sturdy plants you can bury up to the first three leaves to prevent washouts that bare tender roots. Continue to water the young plants from below until they have adjusted, and keep them under good light. Pinching back stem tips as the herbs grow results in well-formed bushy plants.

Members of the parsley family, well represented in the herb garden, form tap roots but produce only a small amount of stem tissue at the root crown from which leaves arise. Transplant them when the first true leaf appears; like many biennials having tap roots, they resent transplanting. Because the modified stem tissue is not likely to produce leaves when covered with soil, take care to keep the root crown with stem tissue above the soil surface. When leaves arise from a root crown, there obviously can be no pinching back of a stem.

When vigorous root systems fill the containers, they need more room; keep your fingers crossed that weather will be suitable for transplanting them directly into the garden. If not, you will have to transplant to a larger container indoors. Transplanting to the outdoor garden comes only after the herbs have been hardened by gradual exposure to the cooler outdoor air conditions. Don't move herbs outdoors on a warm, breezy, sunny day; for best acclimatization a still, cloudy day is preferred for both the indoor coddled herbs and any large not reliably winter-hardy potted herbs you have protected indoors through the winter. (Protect all of them through cold night temperatures, below 50 degrees F.) Prepare your garden soil, water conditioned herbs well, then plant them out according to your garden plan on a warm, sunless day; and water in. If a hot sun appears in the sky, cover newly planted herbs until evening.

The success of starting annual seeds indoors is advantageous. Be wary of biennials through transplanting stages. Enjoy the savings realized by starting perennials.

Sowing special kinds of seed outdoors in spring begins when the prepared soil is dry, light, and loose, and when the last frost day has passed in your region. Last frost dates vary widely even within a region, so check your nearest agricultural extension office for local estimated dates.

In the garden, where seeds are dropped or scattered, use liberal amounts of sifted compost as a covering. Compost retains moisture and is fertile, both beneficial for the seed. Small seeds are barely covered; larger seeds are covered two to three times their diameter. Then tamp down with the back of a trowel or hoe. When seeds are sown on a gentle slope, top the soil with sharp sand. When the sand becomes moist, the seeds are held in place and less likely to wash out through a heavy rainfall. Each seed variety should be marked with a waterproof label giving relevant information.

Keeping soil moist but not soggy is essential to germination; drying is ruinous. A periodic sprinkling provides uniform moisture. A gentle rain is heaven's gift. If the temperature and moisture are right for germination, sprouts will appear according to the schedule for each species.

Thinning out seedlings is a regular procedure. When a garden cannot accommodate the fresh, flavorful, culinary herbs, use them as ingredients in a salad of greens.

Herbs that flourish when sown outdoors come from the ranks of annuals, biennials, perennials, shrubs, and trees. Sow them, give them a space to grow, move them if necessary, and permit them to self-sow as a recompense for your giving to them, with effort, a start.

For any of the steps in the process of growing herbs from seed, methods can be varied to fit equipment, area, and time schedule. The procedures described above are based on factual information and personal experience. Cloning, an advantageous method for large commercial propagation ventures, has been intentionally omitted. In modifying some of the procedures given, you may well improve them. In any seed-sowing operation, indoors or outdoors, methods for germination and growth in order of best results are documented and worth consulting.

Asexual or Vegetative Methods of Propagation

Marvelous as the process of seed germination is, a gardener is lucky that (when necessary or for convenience) nature has provided an alternative method to multiply herbs, asexual or vegetative reproduction. It is a process that gives most plants the ability to develop mature offspring, identical to the parent, from special cells found in plant organs other than the seed.

A gardener turns to vegetative methods of propagation when a natural species, natural or artificially created hybrid, variety, or cultivar does not produce viable seed, when the herb does not breed "true"—that is, desired characteristics are not transmitted through the seed—or when germination time is longer than a selected vegetative method or is irregular. Reproducing herbs vegetatively is accomplished by cutting stems or branches into segments, making divisions of roots, rhizomes, runners, and tubers, layering, using bulb scales—all based on the ability of such pieces to produce new plants identical to the parent. Practicability and possibilities will influence your choices; the Descriptive Catalog suggests some recommended methods.

From Cuttings
Both annual and perennial herbs with typical stem formation can be propagated from stem cuttings, which increase herbs or preserve herb stock through the winter. The best time to take stem cuttings for rooting is from late summer to early October. In August and September, herb gardeners in

climatic zones 6–7 note the great size of tender herbs and face the pinch of space indoors for keeping scented geraniums, toothed lavenders, African basil, pineapple sages, *Salvia dorisiana*, and other not-winter-hardy herbs. Taking stem cuttings is a solution. They have a good supply of food stored in their cells in late summer and early fall to keep them going until new roots form. Most herbs will root at other times, but the rooting process will be slower, and the longer time period invites decay.

From the herb you want to propagate, cut with a sharp knife healthy stems about 3–5 inches long and having about five nodes slightly below a node. The portion of a stem at which a leaf petiole joins the stem is called a node; it can give rise to root tissue when the leaf is removed and the area is kept moist. Free two lower nodes of leaves at the base of the cutting. To stimulate root production and prevent infection, dip the cut end straight into Rootone, a combination rooting hormone and fungicide. Tap off any excess powder. Have ready a moist rooting medium to support the development of roots and make an opening to the proper depth with a dibble; forcing cuttings into a medium may injure basal tissues. Then insert the cutting.

Practical and useful containers to hold the rooting medium and cuttings are 6–9 ounce styrofoam drinking cups. Propagators prefer a variety of mediums for rooting cuttings: sharp sand; vermiculite (mineral mica expanded by high heat, which holds water like a sponge), vermiculite with sharp sand or perlite (volcanic rock expanded by high heat, which permits drainage of water); plain perlite; or sterilized soil.

Prepare the styrofoam cups* in the following manner: With a heated ice pick or other sharp point make four holes equidistant around the sides at the bottom of the cups. One inch above these, make a second series of holes 1/4 inch apart all around the cup; the heated tines of a fork are faster than a single point. Now fill the cup with perlite to the top row of holes and add vermiculite above that. Place a collection of these cups in a pan of water and fertilizer mixture (1/4 teaspoon Miracle-Gro or similar commercial plant food dissolved in 1 gallon of water). Maintain the water level to just below the top row of holes.

The perlite is kept constantly moist by water entering through the four bottom holes, and the moisture is delivered by capillary action to the ver-

*This system is adopted from "Texas Pots," *The Avant Gardener*, June 1, 1977, page 126.

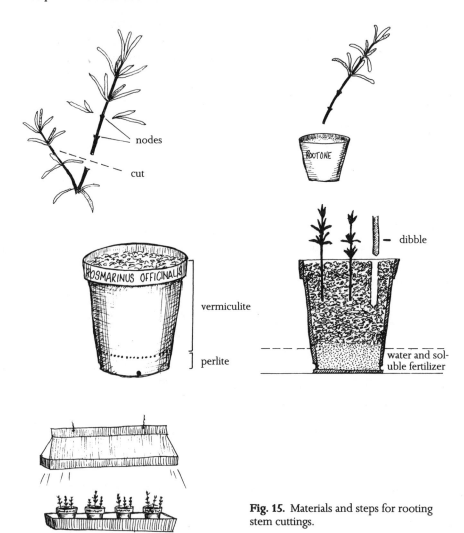

nodes

cut

ROOTONE

dibble

ROSMARINUS OFFICINALIS

vermiculite

perlite

water and soluble fertilizer

Fig. 15. Materials and steps for rooting stem cuttings.

miculite above. Because air is always available from the upper row of holes, cuttings do not drown in water, and roots never lack oxygen. The self-maintaining method of having water entering and rising from a bottom tray requires no daily watchful eye over a medium that may dry out.

When the vermiculite is moist from absorption of water, insert the cuttings prepared as described above. Keep each cup for a specific herb. The number of cuttings to a cup is dependent on the size of the cuttings; for ample growth and air circulation among them, limit the number. Attach the name of the herb to the side of the styrofoam cup with a laundry marker—before the vermiculite is moist, because a moist cup will resist the ink.

Place the pan containing the cups of cuttings in a good light. Fluorescent tubes kept energized for fourteen to sixteen hours daily give good results. Temperatures of 65–70 degrees F are satisfactory.

Most herb cuttings will root within three weeks, some in less time, and others in months. Warmer temperatures will hasten the rooting process for some; for others it introduces stem rot. Taking stem cuttings for rooting in the heat of summer is thwarting. Optimum time for rooting a specific herb is usually cyclic or seasonal. Keeping records of time periods, percentages of successful rooting, and seasonal dates will eventually prove invaluable.

To determine whether or not roots have formed, give a cutting a slight tug; if it feels tight, gently lift the cutting out of the medium and check the root development. Replace cuttings that are still without a healthy root system but transplant well-rooted cuttings into pots; use a sterilized potting soil mix, as described for seedlings. Settle the new plants firmly, and let the first watering be from the bottom. In good light after a day of rest, they will continue to grow and be on their way to the garden.

Leaving rooted cuttings in the medium until the time has arrived to take herbs outdoors saves a transplanting step. The eminent English gardener, Christopher Lloyd, regularly follows this procedure. Pay attention to rates of root and stem growth while the cutting is still in the medium and transplant when they look sturdy enough to survive outdoors.

The value of a propagation method is dependent on the modifications it can support to enlarge its range of function. Vermiculite, for example, is recommended as a rooting medium for a large number of herbs, but mixtures of vermiculite with sharp sand and/or perlite are better for cuttings requiring a long period for rooting or for cuttings with matted hair. The mixed mediums, holding less moisture, reduce the danger of stem rot. Run your fingers along the matted hair of a dry stem cutting before inserting it into the moist medium. The matted hairs are thereby removed, and the favorable host for supporting disease is diminished. For a still dryer medium, use perlite or sharp sand. Beneficiaries are bay, *Laurus nobilis*, Jerusalem sage,

Phlomis fruticosa, horehounds, *Marrubium vulgare* and *M. incanum*, peppermint-scented geranium, *Pelargonium tomentosum*, lemon-scented geranium, *P. crispum*, and *Artemisia arborescens*.

Cups that hold cuttings likely to drop leaves or slow to root should be covered with a transparent Plexiglas dome to reduce loss of moisture from leaves by transpiration and to retain humidity. Take cuttings of lemon verbena, *Aloysia triphylla*, where new green growth originates from the woody tissue. It drops it leaves under stress, and a stressed green cutting of a woody shrub needs protection. Cuttings of bay, old roses as a class, and very slow-rooting cuttings will be more successful in a domed chamber.

A short sprig, branching from a stem and broken off at its base—not cut—is called a "heel" and will root. The corky tissue at its base prevents infections, gives rise to root tissue, and makes it more favorable than a cutting for rooting. The technique is well-applied to the scented geraniums.

When you have only one long-sought cutting of a kind, minimize the risk of loss by transplanting it from the rooting medium to the potting mix by the following method: Place the sterilized potting mix in a 3-inch clay pot with drainage. Wet the soil from the bottom. When it is moist, scoop out at the top enough soil to equal 2/3 egg. Fill the hole with clean sharp sand. Make an opening in the sand with a dibble, and place the prepared cutting in the sand portion of the pot. Do not let the cutting reach into the soil. Cover the soil surface with a thin layer of sand to keep it clean. When roots form, they can reach into the soil with its nutrients. Until the plant outgrows the pot, transplanting is unnecessary.

Shun water as a medium for serious rooting of stem cuttings. Roots formed in water without a medium tend to be leggy and weak, inclined to mechanical injury and infection when transferred to the garden or pot of soil.

From Divisions

When spreading herbs crowd their neighbors or strangle themselves with entangled root systems, they should be divided. It keeps the garden trim and multiplies herb stock. Propagating from seed and cuttings can be better carried through indoors to have plants ready for early planting. But division takes place outside in the garden itself. It is naturally more successful than cuttings because the parent plant provides sustenance and moisture until new roots form.

The best time to make divisions is when the annual period of dormancy is shortly to begin: in late summer for climatic zones 6–7; into late fall and through the winter for parts of climatic zone 7 and throughout zones 8–10. This allows for vigorous growth before the dormant period begins. There are large areas in the Southeast where the ground remains warm and rarely freezes, temperatures are less stressful throughout, and rainfall is plentiful in winter. There is little or no dormant period. Growth occurs throughout most of the winter to give herbs a head start in early spring. The most difficult seasons for dividing are the late spring and long, hot, dry summer, which hinder the establishment of healthy root systems. In zone 6 and northward, where lower temperatures and winters arrive early, subtropical herbs cannot be expected to survive outdoors. Instead of dividing non-winter hardy herbs, multiply them by taking stem cuttings indoors to root, and set out new plants in the spring. Divide the marginally hardy herbs in zone 6 and northward in spring; this lets them establish new roots in the spring and summer when there is no risk of oncoming freezing temperatures.

To divide a herbaceous perennial, use a sharp shovel or trowel, dig down and around a large herb clump, and lift out the mass of earth with roots running through it. With your hands or trowel push aside the soil and have a look at the root system to decide where best to cut the divisions and the number of plants you can expect from the mother plant. You can divide it into as many sections as there are individual stems or crowns. Look for new root growth; try to separate roots as carefully as you can, keeping as many as possible attached to their original stem. Prune away all dead, straggly root and stem material. Plant each section in a prepared soil, and water it well. Spare yourself and the plant the heat of the sun; make divisions on a cloudy, misty day, which will be easier on the plants after the shock of being cut, bruised, and moved. Fertilize only after the divisions have adjusted, which they indicate by producing new growth.

From Layering
Herb gardeners regularly find a low branch of lavender, rosemary, sage, or thyme hugging the ground, to which it has fastened itself by forming roots

from the branch. The rooted branch can be severed from the plant and will then function as a new plant. You have witnessed natural layering. Select the herb you wish to propagate by layering. Choose a young branch, close to the ground, vigorous, and flexible; young branches are more inclined to root than old woody ones. The soil in which the plant grows should be soft enough to dig. Strip the leaves from a 3–4 inch length, and bend the near end into the loose soil with the far ends sticking out. Retain the leaves on the exposed growing tip. Some gardeners nick or scratch, moisten, and apply a rooting hormone on the underside of the branch to promote root production before placing it underground.

Cover the buried part of the branch with fine compost and secure it with a rock or pins. Keep the mounds moist. After several months remove the rock and tug at the branch. If it is tight and the tip is producing new growth, dig to see the viable roots. When the time is right for transplanting, cut the section from the parent plant and transplant the herb into its new home.

I like the layering technique for replacing old, straggly herbs. In the fall when I'm cleaning up the garden, I layer common sage and especially lavender cultivars known not to "come true" from seed, because it is a method with the least tending. I use sieved compost to cover the laid-down branches, and calcareous rocks to hold the alkaline-loving branches in place. Winter moisture nourishes them. By spring my stock has multiplied itself and is ready for transplanting, or the clumps of sage and lavender are larger and lovelier.

From Runners
Visualize the many mints that send slender stems horizontally along the ground surface and are disposed to developing roots at the nodes that penetrate into the soil. They need only to be cut into pieces and moved to a desired location.

From Tubers and Rhizomes
A tuber is a modified underground stem with buds or "eyes" and serves as a storage organ for a plant. Think of the American native, Jerusalem artichoke, *Helianthus tuberosum*, an important food source for the American Indian. To multiply tuberous herbs, divide the tuber into as many pieces as

there are eyes—actually, axillary buds from which new leaves and roots appear when planted.

A rhizome is an elongated, partially underground stem, distinguished from a root by the presence of nodes from which roots may arise. If a rhizome is cleanly cut into sections, each with a node, the sections will form new plants. Cover them lightly with a moist medium and transplant them into soil when the roots and leaves develop. Rhizomes are recognized among many well-known herbs: the Florentine iris, *Iris* x *germanica* var. *florentina*; sweet flag, *Acorus calamus*; Joe-pye-weed, *Eupatorium purpureum*; and many herbal ferns are examples.

From Offsets and Bulb Scales

Chive, shallots, lilies, and garlic all grow from bulbs, or offsets from which gardeners remove small new bulbs. (The term "offsets," in addition to being applied to bulbous plants, is used loosely for any side shoot from a parent plant that takes root and can be removed to start a new plant.) Borne on a small disk-shaped stem at the base of a bulb are fleshy scale leaves adapted as storage organs. Occasionally lateral buds develop in the axils of the scale leaves, and these become new bulbs or offsets. The bulbs or offsets can be separated from the subterranean larger bulb or cluster of bulbs and planted separately. Roots emerge on the lower side of the bulb, and a terminal bud develops into the aerial shoot.

Planting and Tending

Herb gardeners wait out the winter, yearning for the season to put in herbs. We have propagated and readied herbs for planting, bought herbs when we visited herb nurseries, and accepted deliveries from catalog orders. Now impatiently twiddling our green thumbs, we itch for the frost-free date of the area where we live—unless we live in zone 10 and are permanently frost-free. Suddenly, a moment of apprehension strikes us. That design for our garden, planned over a period of months—is it really suitable? Banish such anxious thoughts, and look forward to that first moment of plunging hands into soft soil.

At last the frost-free date arrives. Turn pots of herbs upside down, loosen and trim the root systems, and place the roots firmly into prepared holes, from which added water has drained. Remember to prepare cone-shaped mounds for herbs from arid climates for better air circulation at their base. You might add a teaspoon of bonemeal to the soil you removed in preparing an opening for a plant and set aside in a heap. Water in, firm the herb with soil from the side, and water again. For bushy growth, cut back any straggly stems now, or wait a day for roots to function normally.

If a soft spring rain showers down on the day you set herbs in the ground, be thankful. Moisture in the air and soil reduces the rate of water loss from the leaves and so prevents wilting. Once the herbs are settled in, roots take up water through tiny new root hairs and supply water to the root system, the stem, and the leaves. The gardener only needs to water the soil on rainless days. Protect the herbs from a strong sun, wind, or possible frost until they have adjusted to the environment.

Finding pockets for herbs in an established herb garden is less simple. Choosing a position for a new herb of distinctive color, leaf texture, or form is an exercise of aesthetic, fussy sensitivity, since it must blend in with and enhance the earlier settled herbs. Remember that herbs tolerate moves, and by constantly trying them here and there, you eventually achieve the desired effect. By the same thought, if a herb is not flourishing, move it until its success tells you where it wants to be.

Have a soil mixture for containers prepared (see Index) and plant herbs in assembled clay pots, troughs, and raised beds. If your plan includes bringing a herb indoors for the winter, grow the herb in a pot instead of planting it in the ground every spring and digging it up every fall. You profit by less work, and the herb is less damaged. For a single herb in a clay pot with drainage holes use a size large enough to allow an inch of soil around the root ball. Use a saucer to collect surplus water. Potted herbs like lemon verbena, bay, scented geraniums, or classic myrtle—taken indoors through the winter—may require transplanting. Trim the roots if rootbound, place them in a larger pot, and fill around it with fresh new soil. Press the soil in place to eliminate air pockets, and water well to settle the soil.

This is the time to clip and shape branches. Properly positioned potted herbs, shaped or trained as standards, add style to the garden. Rest pots without saucers and other containers on surfaces other than earth or plots of grass to minimize infection from harmful ground-related organisms, the tight bounds of a container invite attacks on the roots.

Light Requirements

Herbs make plain the light quality they prefer by their growth habits. The sun, as the source of light, introduces warming temperatures, sometimes too warm for a herb genetically adapted to a cooler climate. Herb gardeners of the Southeast observe herbs growing or languishing under different qualities of light. They draw conclusions and with persistence find methods of growing their favorite herbs in what might seem a limiting environment, especially when the required sunlight and temperatures are at odds. For example, many herbs prefer full sun, but the same herbs will do well with only six hours of it a day. High temperatures in full sun are detrimental to some herbs, and they will need partial shade to survive in zones 7–11.

To provide a cooler environment for herbs, line wire hanging baskets with soaking wet sheet-moss about 3/4 inch thick and lapped well over the rim to prevent its collapsing later. Add sterilized soil mixture for herbs to just below the rim and plant the herbs in it. The basket with its moist moss should then be hung in partial shade to keep the soil and roots cool.

Since light requirements are diverse, a herb garden planned to provide full sun, partial shade, and shade fulfills the needs of a large herb collection.

Too often we are inclined to forget that the shady corners of our gardens are the best places for herbs wanting protection from light and heat. Fill in shady patches with lungwort, *Pulmonaria officinalis*, lady's mantle, *Alchemilla vulgaris*, sweet woodruff, *Galium odoratum*, mints, *Mentha* spp., catnip, *Nepeta cataria*, and many more, in addition to a host of native American woodland species. Entries in the Descriptive Catalog state preferences in regard to quality of light or shade, temperature ranges, and recommendations for adaptive applications.

A growing number of herb gardeners go indoors in the wintertime to propagate and grow herbs; they depend for light on sets of two 48-inch long fluorescent tubes, one "cool white" and one "warm white." For herbs this supplies a broad enough spectrum of artificial light. The closer the plants are to the tubes, the more light they will receive. With an automatic timer, lights can be kept conveniently energized for fourteen to sixteen hours a day. Dust gathered on the tubes keeps light from your herbs, so dust them regularly. As a safety precaution remove the tubes from their sockets and wipe away the dust with a dry cloth, never a wet one.

For many years I have kept three sets of 48-inch fluorescent tubes in a basement room, where I have propagated thousands of herbs. By suspending three sets from the ceiling over benches set in a U formation and placing herbs needing less light in peripheral areas I can get a larger area of adequate light. In a warm kitchen, where close watch can be kept, I have appropriated a 20-inch fluorescent tube above a counter to give "just germinated" seedlings light.

Fluorescent tubes, asking only minimal attention, are an inexpensive and effective source of light for growing herbs. They decline in brightness and should be replaced once a year. If you are interested in indoor gardening, investigate the cost and weigh it against the pleasure you would derive from growing things in the gray depth of winter.

How Many Herbs of a Kind?

The kitchen needs only a few plants of each culinary herb. A very small supply goes a long way: in cooking you seek a delicate bouquet to titillate the senses of taste and smell, which are usually bound together as one.

Design enters into the numbers of herbs of each kind. Will there be an edging of salad burnet? Will a mass planting be used for an effect? You may need twelve or more herbs of a kind to light the garden decoratively; the design pattern needs to be satisfied.

Will you share your harvest, use herbs for gift giving? Do you wish to provide your friends, far and near, with a supply of several herb-flavored vinegars? You may want an extra herb plant from which to gather seed.

You may wish for great numbers of scented herbs, lending themselves to potpourri for their sweet, citric, spicy, and woodsy perfume.

You may want great quantities of the many *Artemisia* spp. and herbs for dried decorative arrangements or wreath making.

Whatever your want or need, the number of seeds in a packet is sufficient for the private herb gardener. Only you can decide how many herbs of a sort you wish to have in your herb garden without overcrowding. Like a child's appetite for candy, some of us are never satisfied.

Weeding

> I will root away
> The noisome weeds, which without profit suck
> The soil's fertility from wholesome flowers.
> —Shakespeare, *Richard II*

> And till I root out their accursed line
> And leave not one alive, I live in hell.
> —Shakespeare, *Henry VI*, Part III

Most gardeners react to weeds in their gardens with fury and rage or resigned acceptance. Herb gardeners, having a brushing acquaintance with the habits of plants, should take a contemplative look at each new or invasive plant and muse on its history: is it herbal or nonherbal, herb or weed? They may search through to identify it. Is it merely a plant in the wrong place or, in botanical terms, a plant genetically designed to take advantage of a disturbed environment? In the herb garden, soapwort, the garden mints, coltsfoot, scarlet pimpernel, or viper's bugloss can readily turn into aggressive weeds. Like invasive weeds, numbers of herbs carry to extremes their innate drive to reproduce, replicate themselves, and compete. Herb gardeners weed out portions of competitive herbs and eradicate all nonherbal plants that are disastrously aggressive.

Once we hired a good man to help us with garden work, who took the liberty of pulling weeds or—in his judgment and vocabulary—"hateful plants." Identification of a plant or its complete removal played no part in the task he assigned to himself. We had to part company, and ever since we have pleaded with county extension agents to arrange classes for identification of noxious weeds. Identifying the enemy sheds light on how to eradicate it—and how not to: for example, chopping it to bits and permitting pieces to remain are good methods of encouraging it to spread by vegetative propagation.

As soon as herb seedlings can be recognized, weeding begins. Weeding a herb garden is not tedious or mundane. As you weed, you brush up lightly against herbs and release volatile oils. As long as you are weeding, you should thin out crowded young herbs, which are bound to choke one another or develop into poorly headed plants.

You will find that early removal of weeds gives the herbs a chance to take over. Once herbs dominate a patch, little weeding is necessary. Weeding gives you the opportunity to get close to the herbs; often you see what you haven't seen before, and you may begin to unravel a long, puzzling problem.

Mulches, used in gardens to retain moisture, decrease the growth and germination of weed seeds by blocking out light. For herbs not requiring aridity, mulches of chopped leaves are helpful. But when a mulch retains abundant moisture through rainy or humid weather, fungus spores are supported, a bane to a great number of herbs.

Chemical weed killers (herbicides) are discouraged for use in private herb gardens.

The Dutch hand weeder with its thin, sharp, and angled blade remains my favorite weed eradicator. It comes for right-handed or left-handed herb gardeners. When I am fretful at finding the garden faulty with weeds, I transform my spirit with a whiff of toothed lavender leaves and proceed to root out weeds.

Watering

Watering a herb garden is an art, not unlike cooking, where amounts of the same ingredients may vary with the particular dish in preparation. As cooking is an act of love for those who sit at the cook's table, so watering is an expression of attentiveness to the herbs in the garden. In our devotion to herbs, we have a natural tendency to overwater. One must recognize that the amount of water herbs need varies according to their origins and stage of development. Soil surrounding a seed should not dry out during the germination period, so water the soil gently after sowing seed and through the seedling stage. For large areas a water computer can be installed to program a sprinkler, soaker, or drip irrigation system for effective early morning watering. Watering in the evening keeps herbs too wet through the night, and that promotes plant diseases.

Most established herbs can withstand drought better than wet weather or overwatering. In the parched earth and under a hot sun, xeric herbs will temporarily wilt enough to frighten you into dousing them with water. Give them a little drink and stand back; wait for evening to come and watch them regain normal turgor. High humidity, prevalent during a summer in warm regions, in combination with excessive watering seriously damages these herbs. Herb gardeners are kind by keeping them high, dry, and in a less than moist soil.

In place of marking watering dates on a calendar, decide whether watering is necessary by rubbing soil between fingers to sense dryness or moisture, and consider the humidity. Water herbs that thrive under moist conditions more frequently than herbs preferring aridity.

Unlike herbs planted directly in the garden soil, herbs in pots or containers absorb heat from a hot sun and need watering in the morning to hold lower root temperatures; see Index about watering potted herbs. The chore of filling and toting a watering can to individual pots and containers can be minimized by using a watering wand attached to the hose. With a wand it is easy to reach the soil around herbs that want water, keep the foliage dry, and stay away from herbs preferring to be kept dry.

If heavy summer rains are suspected of having leached out nitrogen, give the herbs additional fertilizer for the late summer spurt of growth.

One cannot state the exact amounts of water to apply to the herb garden for several reasons: (1) the wide differences in soil drainage and humic content in relation to water absorption in prepared garden soils, (2) variation in weather conditions that affect soil moisture, and (3) the differences of water requirements among herbs.

Herb Rotation

Rotating herbs in the garden is using the soil to its optimum. Herbs gain from the nutrients provided, and you can control infestations of organisms in the soil that thrive in company with specific herbs. A good time to rotate herbs is when you divide them in late summer or fall. Exchange chive, leek, and garlic with mints after several years in the same space. Add fertilizers to the soils; keep an eye open with rotating in mind. Mints are notorious for de-pleting soil.

Mulching

Mulching is a heavily debated subject among herbists. Which mulching material to use or whether to mulch at all are serious matters. Chicken grit (chopped oyster shells) or pea-sized gravel are well-suited inorganic mulches for beds of xerophytes. The Tullie Smith House herb garden—a restoration on the grounds of the Atlanta Historical Society and among the loveliest of the Southeast's herb gardens open to the public—demonstrates the good effect that pea gravel provides in a Southeast herb garden. When we visited there during hot, rainy, humid summer weather, not a single Mediterranean herb appeared distressed; one particular rosemary, well-formed and important, was packed with gravel around its base and thriving unforgettably.

Mediterranean herbs in our garden, well-spaced and mounded, do well with a chopped oyster shell mulch at the base. With this protection, they tolerate an average rainfall of 60 inches per year and spells of high humidity.

A summer mulch of organic materials like aged chopped tree bark or shredded leaves help a soil to retain moisture and retard water runoff through dry periods. Thick 5-inch layers of unshredded leaves keep down weeds in a woodland garden. A mulch presents a semblance of tidiness. Unfortunately, in wet weather, which is unpredictable, and under humid conditions, a mulch of moisture-retaining material contributes an attractive environment for disease organisms and soddens some herbs to death. Fresh wood chips or sawdust can upset the nutrient balance of a soil. Bacteria utilize nitrogen in the soil to make available necessary nutrients from the fresh wood, and deprive herbs of nutrients in the process. As a mulch that contributes acidity to the soil, pine needles and pine bark are best left for rhododendrons and rejected for herbs preferring alkalinity. Before applying a mulch, cultivate a soil to its best possible condition.

A winter mulch helps to hold moisture through a dry winter. Leaves that the wind blows in around herbs not cut back protect herbs from freezing temperatures and aid in moisture retention. In the colder areas of climatic zones 6–7, a covering of hay, free of weed seeds, keeps soil at a uniform temperature. Hold off laying down a winter mulch until the first light frost sticks to the soil. This will prevent small animals from nesting in your mulch. Repeated thawing and freezing of moisture in the soil and in tissues of perennial and biennial roots is injurious and results in plant losses, hence the virtues of a hay mulch.

Lurking Liabilities

Weaving spiders, come not here;
Hence, you long legg'd spinner, hence!
Beetles black, approach not near;
Worm nor snail, do no offense.
—Shakespeare, *A Midsummer-Night's Dream*

Insect pests need not be a serious problem in a herb garden when the plants are sturdy enough to resist. Make available the necessary macro- and micronutrients from a well-prepared soil, not overfertilized, and when the plants' cultural needs are met, according to their genetic makeup, they will develop mechanical and chemical inhibitors—as well as attractants when insects are needed for pollination.

There is little reason to use insecticidal sprays in the outdoor herb garden. A limited number of old roses are sprayed for infestations of Japanese beetles or aphids when and if they attack. High temperature and dry weather invite red spider mites on bay trees, and other types of mites thrive on the classic myrtles, junipers, and an assortment of herbs in the hot sun. During dry periods, regular sprays of cold water on the herbs mitigate mite infestation.

Certain insects are one of the delights of a garden: bright butterflies hovering, busy, humming honeybees crowding carpets of thyme and lavender spikes. These more than make up for the vexing insects. The sights, sounds, and fragrances bring to mind a day we spent herb collecting on the slopes of Mount Hymettus and a dessert we later enjoyed in an Athens restaurant: yogurt covered with English walnuts and Greek honey made by bees from thyme and lavender growing on the mountain slopes.

Indoors, where the balance of nature is missing, some herbs are attractive to whiteflies. Among them are the scented geraniums, lemon verbena, basil, oreganos. Precautions can be taken. Before bringing susceptible herbs indoors in the fall, flush them off with effective sprays of cold water that reach all sides of the leaves. Once indoors, spray immediately with an insecticidal soap, and repeat every five days three times. The objective of close-interval sprayings is to annihilate newly hatched whiteflies from eggs not killed by the insecticide, and so interrupt the life cycle. Reasonably, the enemy is crushed until a mature female whitefly enters the domain and lays eggs. Then a repeat of the first procedure is necessary to stop what otherwise might become a monstrous infestation.

In early spring when sorrel leaves are fast-growing, they almost regularly become infested with leaf-miner flies. The little flies, less than 3/16-inch long, insert their eggs singly into the tissue of a leaf and then drink the sap exuded from the puncture. The shapes of the mines or tunnels—linear, serpentine, blotch, etc.—left by juvenile miners are characteristic of the species. The mines are unsightly, but seldom seriously injure the sorrel or other herbs infected. Infected leaves should simply be removed and uninfected leaves collected for a fine French sorrel soup or sauce. When summer arrives with dry spells, leaf-miner damage is negligible. But snails and slugs find the dark, moist surface under the sorrel plants a favorable environment to reach the tasty green leaves and feed. Spread wood ashes around and about the base of sorrel plants as a deterrent; snails and slugs dislike crawling over the ashes.

Small animals can be a problem. Baffling rabbits, which enjoy young, tender herbs, is difficult. Enclosing a garden within a solid wall is hardly feasible, but a tall wattle fence, as used by medieval European peasants, is attractive and lets air circulate. But walls and fences are no protection against moles, which tunnel underground and feed on grubs or against voles, which use mole tunnels and chew through roots just below the surface of the soil, especially those of scented geraniums and roses. We are told voles can be trapped by setting a mousetrap baited with apple and kept covered, but trapping is likely to succeed chiefly in fall and winter. Our traps have not been successful. Many plausible solutions for mole and vole eradication spread among gardeners by word of mouth. All give credence to the problem but no absolute solution, and most are abandoned as unsuccessful after they are tried for a year or more. Some gardeners do credit a hungry hunting cat, though others can only credit voles with the good taste to chew through scented geraniums and rose roots.

Nematodes, microscopic parasites that infest soil (usually acidic), do damage to specific herbs by infecting roots. Infected roots are more susceptible to fungal and bacterial diseases. There are many ways of combating nematodes, among them crop rotation. A new method treats infected soil with Clandosan, developed at Auburn University. Clandosan is a biological control agent composed of a blended crustacean chitin-protein complex with agricultural urea and an organic buffer. Ask your county agent if it is advisable to try it in your area.

Herbs that like a dry climate are susceptible to stem rots and blights (fungus diseases) in humid summer environments. Stems and leaves should not come in direct contact with a soil where fungus spores live.

The goal of all gardeners is to use no harmful pesticides or fungicides. Investigations on cumulative effects of systemic fungicides are incomplete. In recognized guides for fungicide use, "caution," the word applied to the least dangerous fungicide, is assigned to benomyl. The decision to use an effective systemic fungicide as benomyl rests with informed gardeners. Damage from fungus and insect diseases can be minimized by (1) having a well-drained, slightly alkaline soil with proper fertility, (2) properly spacing herbs from dry regions, (3) keeping herbs raised for improved air circulation, and (4) banning moisture-retaining mulches. Rainfall cannot be controlled, but watering a dry soil carefully in minimal amounts and early in the day, in addition to recommendations given above, can substantially reduce fungus diseases in a garden of xeric herbs.

Pinching and Pruning

> Superfluous branches
> We lop away, that bearing boughs may live.
> —Shakespeare, *Richard II*

Cutting out dead wood from shrubby herbs like thyme, sage, or rosemary begins early in the Southeast, January in zones 9–11; by February and March the entire Southeast has finished the task, including pruning back. For sizable, good-looking, low-growing clumps, sage is pruned to the ground. (See plate 17.) After pruning, new growth rises immediately from the base, and before summer comes, the herb looks vigorous, full, and bushy. If you prefer the natural form of a herb, leave it alone; if formality is your aim, trim and shape by pinching and pruning as a herb grows.

As plant-loving people, beginning herb gardeners are timid and uneasy about pinching the tip from a healthy, growing seedling. Once the fear is overcome, positive results create enthusiasm. Pinching, or tip-pruning, is the removal of a growing stem tip just above the origin of a leaf or bud to encourage branching. A young seedling not tip-pruned becomes a leggy herb drooping over onto the soil A seedling tip-pruned at its stem tip as soon as two pairs of leaves have formed and tip-pruned repeatedly at the tips of newly formed branches stands erect and becomes an attractive bushy plant. A herb with leaves opposite on the stem like basil (and all other herbs of the mint family) will give rise to two opposite branches when you tip-prune; a stem with alternate leaves gives rise to one branch. As a matter of fact, tip-pruning can stimulate branching at more than one node on a stem below the cut point. Branching and a herb's entire direction of growth can be redirected by removing tips above a leaf or bud pointing in a desired direction; it is a favorite pruning technique for training herbs. Roses and dwarf fruit trees are espaliered by judiciously planning and executing branching with tip-pruning. Classic myrtles, boxwoods, scented geraniums, rosemarys, heliotropes, and bays become handsome topiaries or standards.

Forming bonsai with herbs gives immense pleasure and adds decorative notes to a herb garden and the house. People who follow the art of genuine Japanese bonsai, in which true dwarfing occurs, refer to herb bonsai as "American bonsai." Small-leaved woody herbs like classic myrtle, thyme, lemon-scented geranium, prostrate rosemary, santolina, and bush basil lend themselves to the practice. Miniature topiaries and standards are created by the same procedures involved in shaping taller and larger herbs, simple tip-pruning being the essential factor. Thyme, prostrate rosemary, and santolina are more suitable for a combination of directional tip-pruning and simple tip-pruning. Natural growth habits lend themselves to informal upright styles with slanting straight or curved branches and cascades. Alter the usual practice of placing a woody main stem in the center of a pot in the usual vertical position. Instead, place the roots of your selected herb off center in a bonsai pot, slanting the stem at a 30 degree angle with the horizontal soil surface. By doing this, one of the many Japanese bonsai styles is mimicked. Admittedly, herb bonsai will not reach the venerable age of Japanese bonsai, but tip-pruning them at intervals to keep the style you have set is a relaxing pastime. Check their root growth at least once a year; if the roots fill the pot, lift out the herb, loosen the roots gently with your fingers, prune two or more inches off the ends and repot with fresh soil in the same pot to keep the herb in proportion to the pot. When roots and leaves are both kept in balance by pruning, the herb will be healthier.

Large herbs shaped by tip-pruning at their beginning are sheared as they grow larger. It is easier to maintain a neat and thick sheared edge with a battery-operated clipper than with a tip-pruner.

Incorrect early pruning, or natural growth that has produced crossed branches, can be corrected by pruning out the branch. To eliminate the branch entirely, prune it at its point of origin, leaving just enough tissue to develop protective scar tissue. If you wish it to branch in another direction, have a look at the dormant buds at the base of every leaf, and prune just above a leaf that points in the desired direction. To broaden a plant, prune above a bud that points away from the center as you do in pruning roses.

Remember to do your last pruning or shearing of herbs that remain outdoors at least four to six weeks before the first expected frost date. Later pruning of herbs, whether evergreen or deciduous, stimulates new tender growth that may be killed by frost.

For best times to prune large herbal trees and shrubs check with county extension agents or a good book on the subject. Felder Rushing's *Gardening, Southern Style* covers the subject very well.

In veiled legends and folklore—now and then associated with superstition or "the magic of herbs"—are historical approaches to planting and tending a herb garden. But when it is time to plant and tend our own gardens, we look for factual information and sift out misinformation that has come down through the centuries. We are inclined to follow procedures based on tangible evidence. Curiously, the explanations that are brought to our attention also shed light on folkloric directions. For example, folklore's advice for sowing basil seed—"stamp it and curse it"—becomes, "place it firmly in the soil because wet seed coats become gelatinous, which causes the seeds to rise and float on the soil surface where they dry out and so reduce germination percentages." And then too:

Sweet are the uses of adversity,
Which like the toad, ugly and venomous,
Wears yet a precious jewel in his head;
And this our life exempt from public haunt,
Finds tongues in trees, books in the running brooks,
Sermons in stones and good in everything.
—Shakespeare, *As You Like It*

Smells are surer than sounds or sights
To make your heart-strings crack.
—Rudyard Kipling, "Lichtenberg"

7 ❧ A Time to Pluck Herbs

A herb garden is never static; there is hardly a moment when the lovely area is not at least in gentle motion, is not growing, and changing in composition. Through the seasons herbs pass from one stage of development to another. There is no tiresome sameness. In early spring the sight of green herbs captivates and bonds you to the garden. As temperatures rise and the air in your garden becomes heavy with the perfume of myriad herbs, you reflect on the sense of smell as the most remarkable of senses. It possesses greater associative powers than any other sense. Sight functions only in light, taste when you eat—and there are only four basic types, sour, salt, sweet, and bitter, and then mixed sensitivities of these. Hearing may be nonactive, and touch requires contact through movement. But a sensitive nose functions day and night, in light and dark, without effort. It starts working at the moment of birth, and this perhaps explains its most extraordinary power—it is why a smell can take us so far back into our dimmest recollections and stir the unconscious so profoundly. Memory is more easily evoked by our sense of smell than by any other sense.

A herb garden is perhaps the source of more scents that become familiar to us in our lives than any other place. We become aware of odors because our olfactory sense is stimulated by the complex system of molecules. These molecules reach the receptor ends of the olfactory cells, and the message is relayed to the brain centers associated with emotions, hormone secretions, pleasure, and appetite. No wonder a herb garden fulfills expectations.

In a singular manner, plucking sprigs in a herb garden gives pleasure, because it appeals to all the senses. In the process the eyes see; the nose smells; the tongue tastes; the fingers touch; and the ears hear the humming bees as they gather nectar. Five senses possibly active at the same time create an intensely rapturous and sensuous spirit.

When to Pluck Herbs

One of the joys of growing herbs is that there is no need to wait for a particular time to harvest. You can have fresh, tender sprigs of herbs in the salad or cooking pot as soon as you thin seedlings or pinch their tips to encourage branching. Evergreen leaves of the woody herbs, rosemary, thyme, and bay are available from the garden at any season, and in warm regions will produce essential oils throughout the year.

Some herbs are ready for plucking earlier than others, and the foods they flavor are often seasonally available at the same time. Therein lies the origin of culinary combinations: fresh herb with fresh nutritious food. The delight of savoring fresh herbs begins in February or March when fines herbes— finely chopped fresh chive, parsley, chervil, and French tarragon—season spring egg and fish dishes. European countries have for centuries added this historic spring quartet to springtime dishes. Strew it over the omelet just before folding; sprinkle it on any egg, fish, or cheese with grits soufflé. The fresh green color and aroma are welcome tokens of spring.

If you are harvesting more than the daily handful, the timing is critical because the production of essential oils in leaves has daily ups and downs. Herb leaves have their highest oil content (flavors and aromas) on clear days, after the dew has lifted and before the sun brings the highest temperature of the day—when the oil dissipates. Once buds are set and permitted to bloom, a herb's energy is directed to flower and seed production; vegetative leaf growth and oil production decrease. To maintain leafy growth rich in oil, snip off buds before they come to full bloom. For flowers in the garden, which you may wish to preserve at a later date or from which you may collect the seed, withhold debudding.

Plucking herbs is interaction, involvement, and therapy. You catch perfume from one and bite another. Some herbs taste delightful, whereas others are unpleasantly bitter. Anyone who has read or heard of the disagreeable taste of bitter wormwood, *Artemisia absinthium*, is unlikely to bite into a leaf. A number of herbs lose their aroma within a short time when dried. Fresh sprigs of pineapple sage, *Salvia elegans*, have a delicious aroma, flawless for adorning a fruit platter, but their dried leaves quickly lose potency. Fresh French tarragon bites the tongue in a tantalizing manner; drying diminishes the sensation. Unpredictable events and constant changes occur through the growing season, while hummingbirds hover near into the monarda flowers.

All dried herbs lose their potency when stored for a long time. Instead of saving your old herbs, renew your herb supply each year. Strew old herbs across the floor and then sweep them up with the vacuum cleaner. The fragrance lingering in the air makes the vacuuming less of a chore.

In climatic zones 9–10 it is possible to harvest a fresh herb supply throughout the year. The stratagem for success involves time of planting. In this region, high winter temperatures provide a longer growing season and keep herbs from dying out over the winter. Accordingly, young plants are put in the ground around the first of November or December. Top growth during the first year is not spectacular, but deep roots are put down for survival through hot weather. (By contrast, herbs planted in early spring quickly produce foliage and have little time to establish a good root system before hot weather arrives.) Likewise raised containers or hanging baskets holding the proper soil mixes for moisture, drainage, and fertility are equally successful in maintaining a year-long harvest. Mediterranean herbs excepted, all herb gardeners of zones 9–10 agree that herbs like shade by three o'clock in the afternoon and partial shade throughout the day during the hot summer.

Preserving and Storing Herbs

June is a time to put by great bunches of aromatic plant parts for culinary use, for potpourri, and for decorative arrangements. Herbs are to be utilized. In gathering you shrewdly control the tendency of one or more herbs to smother other herbs by their rapid growth rate. The garden is kept properly groomed by cutting and trimming, new growth is encouraged, and you carry as much to the compost heap as you do to the kitchen.

Methods of storing herbs for the winter depend upon the specific herb,

its intended use, the variant methods available for optimum quality, and fa-
cilities for storage. Our foreparents' attics were redolent with bunches of
herbs hanging from the rafters; their larders contained herbs laid down in
crocks of salt, bottled in oil, vinegar, or wine. Today we continue to follow
established herb storage procedures that satisfy us and add methods not
formerly available.

Freezing Herbs

Many herbs keep their color and potency better in a frozen state than when
dried. Freeze chive, parsley, basil, dill, French tarragon, and fennel. Cut
clumps of chive close to the ground to renew growth; rinse and dry between
towels; finely snip, then package and store in the freezer.

Cut parsley, both curled and flat-leaved, to include stems. (All good chefs
know that the strongest parsley flavor resides in the stems and keep them
aside for the soup stocks.) A good dousing in fresh water is necessary to
wash away sand and extraneous material from the tightly curled leaves; dry
between towels; then with scissors or food processor, finely cut the leaves,
package, and freeze. Though frozen, chopped parsley is readily scraped from
a plastic box at a last minute.

When freezing basil, do not chop; chopped basil leaves turn black as a
result of oxidation, and black basil is not accepted by most cooks. Instead,
drop loose sprigs or whole leaves into a plastic box.

Sprigs of leafy dill are superlative frozen; snip dill leaves while frozen just
before adding them to a butter or stew. Freeze the stalks separately for a
Swedish lamb stew or for pickling small cucumbers.

A branch of frozen fennel laid below the fish to be baked or broiled becomes the embellishment when the fish is turned over onto a platter.

Early spring is the time to enjoy the tender leaves of French sorrel in a
soup, called by the French, who are fond of it, *potage crème d'oseille*. If the
acetous taste, which comes from small amounts of oxalic acid present in the
leaves, is a favorite, you can prepare and freeze a base for sorrel soup to be
served year-round. Cut, wash, remove stems, and towel-dry two handfuls of
French sorrel leaves. In 4 tablespoons butter or margarine, sauté the coarsely
cut leaves until they become a pulp. Sprinkle 1 tablespoon of flour over the
pulp, blend, and freeze the mixture. If the demand for sorrel is high in your
family, you can repeat this operation as the plant's leaves are replenished.

When you are ready to serve the soup, add 2 cups of chicken stock to the frozen base, simmer in a covered pot for 20 minutes, blend in a blender, and strain to remove fibrous matter. Just before serving, add 1 cup of cream blended with two beaten egg yolks, reheat—gently to avoid curdling—and serve. Or serve cold. Cold French sorrel soup is delicious on a hot summer day. The base can also be utilized as a sorrel sauce to serve with fish or lamb.

If your local temperature is predicted to drop to 45 degrees F, gather any remaining Italian basil in the garden and make a base for pesto. Wash, towel-dry, and place in a blender 5 cups of basil leaves with 1/2 cup of olive oil and salt to taste. Blend thoroughly and uniformly, then pour into ice cube trays to freeze; when the mixture is frozen, remove it to plastic bags and keep frozen. Use the frozen cubes in your favorite pesto sauce, or thaw and spread on a crusty Italian bread.

Air-drying Herbs

Air-drying, as a traditional method for storing herbs, is satisfactory for a large number of herbs if a dry spell remains uninterrupted by humid days. Air-dry summer savory, sage, spearmint, oreganos, lovage, sweet marjoram, and bay for cooking. For teas, air-dry chamomile blossoms, *Matricaria recutita*, the blossoms with accompanying bracts of American basswood and European linden, *Tilia* spp., peppermint, and wintergreen, *Gaultheria procumbens*. For decorative arrangements and potpourri ingredients, the list is endless. In addition to taking lavender flowers on long spikes, scented geranium leaves, or petals of the old roses from your garden, scuffle along a weedy roadside or explore an exciting patch of woods for native or naturalized herbs in flower or fruit to dry and enhance a herbal wreath. Sometimes your nose remembers what your other senses have forgotten and leads you to leafy flowering herbs to pluck, dry, and put into a mixed bouquet or potpourri with memories. As a precaution always know or identify before you pick.

Take leaves or flowers when they are at their best in aroma and form; for highest content of oil, cut leafy stalks when buds begin to form but before they open. Avoid gathering after a heavy rain or when they are covered with dew. Check all gathered plant material for insect infestation or extraneous matter; rinse herbs for tea and cooking if necessary and dry between towels without bruising the leaves. To dry herbs with their stems, arrange stalks in small bunches, and tie each bunch securely; leave a loop on the end by which to hang it. Use an added plastic-coated wire tie that can be twisted tighter as the bunches dry and shrink; this will keep them from slipping out of their string noose. You want small bunches, because large ones decrease air circulation in the center and thereby invite mold growth. Also, crowding can press the blossoms out of shape. Find a well-ventilated hot, dark space, preferably with temperatures between 80 and 100 degrees. The heat dehydrates, circulating air carries away moisture, and darkness minimizes color loss. Hang bunches upside down on lines, from pegs, or on a clothes-drying rack.

Air drying is also achieved by laying flower petals or leaves, separated from stems, in a single layer on a nonmetal screen, set so air can circulate under and over them. In a warm, not humid, dark unoccupied room a sweater-drying screen, a cheesecloth screen laid over an open luggage rack, or one of the drying devices found advertised in gardening catalogs can be used.

For good quality leafy herbs, one wishes them to be "chip-dry" in a few days. Flowers hanging by their stems may take two or three weeks. Strip chip-dry leaves from the stalks onto a clean, smooth paper from which they can be slid into a container for storage.

Drying Herbs with Microwave Ovens and Silica Gel

Obviously, some herbs, depending on size or moisture-holding capacity, dry more successfully than others. Enemies of the air-drying process are humidity and strong sunlight. Light can be controlled more easily than humidity, but humid air can be circumvented by drying herbs in a microwave oven or with silica gel.

Herbs dried in a microwave oven, especially under the watchful scrutiny of a cook with a sensitive nose, produce herbs of good color and potency. You may have to experiment with each kind of herb before you become proficient at this technique.

For common culinary herbs, separate the leaves from the stems and spread the leaves on a paper towel laid over a paper plate; cover the leaves with another paper towel and place in the microwave oven on a medium setting. Heat for 10–15 seconds, then test by touching the leaves; if they are not chip dry, add another few seconds, and continue with diminishing time periods. Cool and jar the leaves once they have dried to your satisfaction.

Time is crucial in microwaving; slight overdrying can reduce the quality of the essential oils and affect flavor—noticeable when you compare leaves microwaved with air-dried leaves collected at the same time. Favorable results may vary widely for different herbs; we find that microwaved French tarragon leaves and stalks remain marvelously aromatic. The different textures, shapes, and moisture-holding capacities of herb leaves explain why no absolutely exact time fits them all—just as in air-drying. Dried flower devotees are usually enthusiastic microwavers, because flowers dried in a short time retain their fresh natural colors and shapes. As with leaves, the process is done very quickly and takes practice.

When acceptable drying seems doubtful because the weather is humid, turn to silica gel (anhydrous sand), a drying agent. By using silica gel to absorb moisture, you can get herb leaves chip dry within twenty-four to thirty-six hours; color and potency are as good as when the herbs were gathered in the garden. Chervil, for example, which dries to yellow, odorless straw by other means, retains much of its fresh quality. French tarragon is also successful. Use a circular metal cookie container filled one third with silica gel. Lay over the edges of the container a piece of muslin or cheesecloth, retain it in place with a rubber band, and lay the leaves on it, with stems removed; avoid overcrowding. The suspended cloth keeps the leaves from contacting the silica gel. Add the container's lid, fitting it down tightly over the overlapping cloth. After two days, raise the lid, and check. Moisture from the leaves should have been absorbed by the silica gel. If not, restore the lid for another day. If the leaves are dry, remove them into jars.

Bright blue crystals scattered in silica gel indicate aridity. When their color pales with absorption of moisture, place the opened container in a moderately warm oven until the crystals regain their bright blue color. The silica gel, covered and cooled, is then ready for reuse.

For decorative (not culinary) purposes, you can imbed flowers or portions of herbs right in silica gel and thus preserve much of their beautiful colors and forms. Half-fill a container with silica gel, set the plant material in it, then pour more silica gel slowly and gently between, around, and finally over the top of the flowers and leaves. Cover to make an airtight seal. Drying time varies with the material; after a week, test by withdrawing a sprig carefully. As sprigs dry, remove them with small forceps or tweezers and needles; any silica gel remaining on sprigs can be removed by dusting with a soft watercolor brush.

Sprigs of tiny, exquisite blossoms of thyme, opal basil, rosemary, sweet marigold, or peppermint find places in well-designed dried arrangements. Set them in crystal salt cellars filled with sharp sand for support or collect miniature vases to hold your treasures. I began to use flower sprigs dried in silica gel in herb classes to demonstrate botanical details of flower structure and their arrangements on stalks; it was a practical method for participants wanting to know identifying characteristics of plant families. Unexpectedly, a movement began; class members applied the method and made lovely miniature herbal arrangements.

Containers for Storing Herbs
Dried herbs used in food should be stored in a cool, dark place and in air-tight opaque glass or Plexiglas containers. Metal containers can taint the oils. Open shelves displaying transparent glass bottles of herbs or dried herbs hanging in bunches may be attractive, but it works against the usefulness of culinary herbs. Light reaching dried herbs rapidly reduces their potency and color.

Frozen herbs are best stored in plastic containers, labeled with a water-proof marker, and placed in a designated section of the freezer. Because plastic containers absorb aromatic oils, they are not reusable. The disadvantage of glass is the danger of having it slip from your fingers. Cleaning up broken glass mingled with snipped herbs, while cooking an exacting meal for guests, is unnerving for any hostess.

Gathering and Preserving Herb Seeds
Collect seeds of caraway, coriander, dill, or fennel by cutting the stalks with seeds just when they begin losing their green color. Tie the stalks in bunches, and hang them upside down in a well-ventilated room. Place a large sheet of paper or cloth below to catch seeds as they ripen and fall. An occasional tapping helps to loosen them. Gather the seeds from the cloth into a container. If insect infestation is suspected, place seeds in a fine sieve, pour boiling water over them, and spread them out to dry thoroughly. Boiling water kills any eggs or larvae in the seed.

Gathering and Preserving Herb Roots and Rhizomes
Tap roots or rhizomes of herbs used in the kitchen or for perfume are dug, thoroughly scrubbed, and air-dried. Drying can be finished off by placing roots on a cookie sheet in a low oven until they break without effort.

Hamburg parsley and lovage roots are classic, flavorful ingredients in the winter stock pot. Angelica and vetiver roots enter into a potpourri. Harvest vetiver roots about every third year when you dig up the clump to make divisions. Chicory roots, dried, roasted, and ground, contribute the bitterness to renowned New Orleans coffee or give a coffeelike flavor to roasted, ground barley used as an inexpensive, caffeine-free coffee substitute.

Herbal Teas

Herbal teas make us conscious of variations in fragrance. They are delightful to the senses, can be drunk for pleasure, religious rites, or ceremonies. The steeping or brewing of a tea or tisane (an infusion of leaves or blossoms) is centuries old. Tisanes are described as having soothing and stimulating qualities. Therapeutic qualities of herbal teas are seldom medically proved and, in many cases, are reported to be harmful when used in quantity. Caution is advised. Nevertheless, the fragrance of a herbal tea, like a perfume, taps the endocrine system, which is important to the psyche.

A tisane prepared from herbs follows the same procedure used for China tea. The dried leaves or blossoms are steeped in boiling water and then sweetened, usually with honey.

The words "linden blossoms" or "basswood blossoms" (*tilleul* in French) call to my mind the avenue on which I lived as a child, beautifully bordered with European linden trees; their blossoms and bracts scented the air in late June and early July. When the school term came to a close, just as the trees blossomed yellow, I was transported with my brothers and sisters to spend the summer with grandparents in the country. There, the magnificent American basswood trees were equally fragrant, waiting to have their blossoms plucked. As the bees flew into the trees to gather nectar, we climbed them and returned to the ground with muslin sacks filled. These were then hung to dry in a spacious attic. Each morning the breakfast table offered a fresh comb of basswood honey and at every evening meal basswood or linden tea was served. I did not encounter China tea until my first year at college. The sight and scent of blossoming lindens and basswoods trigger a poignant memory of my childhood.

Herb Jellies

July and August are the months to prepare subtle herb jellies—not just mint for the joint of lamb, but rosemary as well, sage for the loin of pork, French tarragon for poultry. These are embarrassingly simple to make and may be used in cooking as well as on-the-side embellishments.

Follow the directions for mint jelly that come wrapped around the Certo (pectin) container, substituting fresh herbs of your choice. Lemon juice, sherry, or a dry wine add flavor or emphasize a herbal fragrance. Of course, if you are a purist, start from scratch, making your pectin with apples according to an apple jelly recipe. After funneling the prepared pure apple jelly into jars, place a fresh rose-scented geranium leaf on the top before covering with paraffin as our grandmothers did. This is an appetizing way of preserving the bounty for future pleasure or laying up a supply of Christmas and hostess presents.

Herb Brandies

Follow another extraordinary direction by gathering fresh herb leaves for making herb-brandy flavorings. Put into a crock or jar 1 cup of washed and patted-dry herbs bruised in a mortar. Cover with 2 cups of brandy. Let the infusion steep for a week; then strain the herbed brandy into a bottle. Use the concoction for flaming seared poultry or meat, splash onto broiled steaks or chops, add to sauces and soups just before serving in place of sherry. Have a mint brandy for lamb, a French tarragon for fish, a basil bottle for tomato dishes, a blend of rosemary, thyme, and sweet marjoram for stews.

Herb Vinegars

Vinegars can become the vehicles that transport aromas from the herb garden to the table. Vinegar—white, wine, malt, or cider—if carefully steeped with fresh herbs, can convert a throat rasping dish to a mellow delight. French tarragon vinegar used for dressing a salad is piquant yet delicate. Its flavor subtly enhances sauces used in egg dishes or in a court bouillon prepared for poaching the less expensive fish. Basil, blended with other herbs in a vinegar, marries well with the tomato, marinates a piece of beef before roasting, and introduces warmth in a beef or tomato salad vinaigrette. A blended dill vinegar excels in a green or yellow wax bean salad, cabbage slaw, cucumber salad, cold fish dishes, or in an aspic. Do you wish to cool a green salad almost magically? Use a vinegar that has been steeped with leaves of salad burnet. Employ a Greek mushroom marinade for vegetables, to introduce tantalizing herb flavors through a herb vinegar.

Select herbs for flavoring vinegar just before blossoming and pick them on a dry, sunny day after the dew has lifted.

For a basil-blended vinegar, start with 1 gallon cider vinegar in a glass jar; remove and set aside (for other use) 1½ cups. (1) Combine 2 cups sweet Italian basil sprigs, 6 purple basil sprigs, 8 thyme sprigs, 4 lemon basil or lemon balm sprigs, and 4 rosemary or sweet marjoram sprigs, ¾ cup pickling (noniodized) salt, and 2 scant cups of sugar. (2) Add these ingredients to the glass vinegar jug, and store in a dark cupboard for two to three weeks, shaking occasionally. Strain the herb vinegar through a paper coffee filter. (3) Add 1½ cups of claret or burgundy wine to the filtered herb vinegar, and (4) store in clean bottles with nonmetal screw caps or new corks.

For a dill-blended vinegar, start with 1 gallon cider vinegar less 1½ cups as above. (1) Combine 3 cups chopped dill (include leaves and stalks), 6 French tarragon, chervil, or sweet marjoram sprigs, 8 parsley sprigs, 4 lemon balm sprigs, ¾ cup pickling (noniodized) salt, and 2 scant cups of sugar. Follow steps (2) and (4) given for the basil-blended vinegar.

For a French tarragon vinegar: Add twelve 10-inch French tarragon sprigs to a 1 gallon glass jug of white vinegar. Store in a dark cupboard for two to three weeks. Filter the herb vinegar, and add 1½ to 2 cups dry white wine.

Purchase vinegars in glass bottles or jugs, and store all herb vinegars in glass containers to avoid possible bacterial contamination, which is possible with plastic containers. A number of state food and drug laws require that food or drug products to be sold must be bottled in new containers.

Wine is added to reduce the sharp character of common white and cider vinegars. Some Italian cooks, well-known for not stinting in the kitchen, have taken exception to my preserving herbs in ordinary vinegars rather than in high quality wine vinegars. But for most people—and their pocketbooks—the above method has been eminently satisfactory.

Light Tips for Fresh Herbs in Summer

All through the summertime snip fresh leaves of lemon verbena, peppermint, spearmint, citrus mint, and rose, lime, lemon, or cinnamon-scented geraniums. Combine one or the other with tea leaves you are steeping for a hot or cold tea with lemon slices, and perhaps a sweetener. Or, place a few leaves of a single herb in the amount of sugar specified for a cake, icing, or sweet biscuit batter twenty-four hours before preparation, allowing its scent to be imparted to the icing or baked product.

Perfume and Potpourri

A social convention that has lost its original purpose in our time is the giving of a nosegay called a tussie-mussie. The tussie-mussie, made of fresh, fragrant leafy sprigs and flowers, was handed to a personage who had to enter unsavory buildings or pass through crowds of people in malodorous streets. Herb gardeners, enchanted by summertime scents in their gardens and by the language of flowers, give tussie-mussies to friends or carry them to sick beds. The sight and scent induce a desirable frame of mind.

A winter counterpart for the summer tussie-mussies is potpourri. Throughout the growing season, a creator of potpourri collects parts of herbal plants bearing fragrant essential oils. These are blended into a perfume to freshen indoor spaces. Scents used to make potpourri are in effect the same as those used by the perfumer, who blends essential oils—extracted, distilled, or expressed from leaves, stems, flowers, fruits, roots, bark, wood, or seeds—into a special scent.

Different species concentrate oils in different parts of the plant. Pure rose oil, called attar or otto of rose, is concentrated in petals of such old roses as the apothecary rose, damask rose, or cabbage rose. Two of the constituents of rose oil are geraniol and citronellal, chief oils in the leaves and stems of scented geraniums. Ever since scented geraniums were introduced into Europe from South Africa, they have been grown and cultivated in southern France and Turkey and used as an adulterant of costly attar of rose and as a supporting scent in many rose perfumes and potpourri.

Purple flowers of heliotrope, *Heliotropium arborescens*, yield a sweet floral oil for perfume, but because the oil dissipates rapidly on drying, heliotrope is useless for potpourri except for the purple color it contributes. Many perfume plants like rosemary, thyme, mints, and lavender possess oil in leaves, stems, and flowers; cinnamon and cassia from the tropics concentrate oil in their bark, and cedar and sandalwood contribute scented wood. The spicy nutmeg is a nutty fruit, and citrus fruits contribute oils from their leathery rinds. Roots of sassafras, ginger, vetiver, and sweet angelica are sources of scents, and rhizomes of orris and calamus are gathered as fixatives. Bitter almonds, anise, and coriander are a few of the seeds used in perfume.

Those perfume plants that do retain their fragrance after drying are collected when the oil production is at its peak. Taking scented leaves hardly affects the look of the garden; but can you bear to cut off roses just as they are unfolding their exquisite petals or take lavender spikes before the flowers are fully open—the recommended procedure for potpourri? Unless you keep a great many old rose bushes and lavenders, it is understandable to hesitate. Instead, pick a few buds and a number of not fully opened roses, and cull dead heads earlier than usual. Quite regularly new lavender stalks bloom after a first cutting for potpourri. Pull the taproot of sweet angelica after the second or third year and after it has produced seed. Vetiver roots are taken when the plant is dug for dividing.

Dry what you collect through the entire season by whatever method is best to retain fragrance. Spread flower petals on a nonmetal screen in a well-ventilated dark, warm room. When they are dried, check for the eggs and larvae of small insects like weevils. Eaten away patches or small round holes in petals, and the hatched small beetles often turn up in the blended potpourri. Juanita Lykins, a grower of old roses and a blender of exquisite potpourri, suggests this simple method for overcoming troublesome infestations.

After air-drying rose petals, Juanita places a cookie sheet covered with a single layer of petals in a 150 degree F oven with the door ajar for 5 minutes, stirs the petals, and repeats for another 5 minutes. After cooling to room temperature, the material is jarred and ready for blending minus insects.

Use silica gel to preserve whole buds and minimize leaf and flower crinkling. Include flower petals that, though scentless, convey by their color the idea of a specific fragrance; lemon-colored flowers mingled with green lemon verbena leaves project a lemon aroma. By the end of summer containers will be filled with different dried materials, and when the garden closes for the season, the dried materials can be blended to become homogeneous mixtures, beautiful to look at and beautiful to smell.

Creating pleasant fragrances by combining scents follows the basic guidelines of the perfumer. One scent does not make a perfume or a potpourri, nor will a single scent hold its power. When two different odors are presented at the same time, they may both be readily identified. A skilled scent chemist is usually able to discriminate component notes of a successfully blended perfume. The more the odors resemble each other, the greater will be the tendency for them to blend. When the intensity of one odor is substantially greater than that of a second, a masking often occurs. Odor blending and compounding for perfume is in good measure an art and not a science.

The large number of pure basic odors that man can smell is too large to be definitively classified. But grouping of odorants used in perfume, potpourri, and incense into different classes is to a degree possible. There are four classes or "scent personalities" in perfumery: (1) *Floral:* a single flower aroma like rose, lavender, sweet violet, or carnation, or a bouquet of several floral notes. Some scent chemists describe the floral attribute as a narcotic or intoxicating scent. (2) *Woodsy, mossy, leafy, green:* the fragrance of a foresty area of ferns and leafy herbs. An "eau de Cologne" with its base of citrus oils is a good example. Attached to these fragrances are good health, clean feeling, refreshment: the vanilla and new-mown-hay aroma of sweet woodruff, the resinous odors of pine, camphors, rosemary, bay, sweet wormwood, bee balm, thyme, lemon thyme, sweet marjoram, and some mints, plus sandalwood and vetiver. Seeds of crushed dill, coriander, or caraway may be additions. (3) *Spicy:* as the word implies, cinnamon, clove, nutmeg, mace, vanilla, allspice, basil, and all pungent scents. The effect of a perfume in this category would be invigorating. Often they are combined with the floral notes as overtones. (4) *Fruity:* chamomile flowers, leaves of *Salvia dorisiana,* apple-scented and lemon-scented geranium leaves, lemongrass, lemon verbena leaves, and bergamot oil. The citrus notes contribute freshness and bergamot introduces a woodsy personality.

Choosing a main scent for a potpourri is a very personal choice. For a bedroom or dressing room, blend toward an exotic combination that is strictly personal in its appeal. In spaces you share with others, the most welcome scents are herbs, citrus, woodsy, or simple floral fragrances readily recognized and supportive of the outdoors.

Once the main scent has been selected, the secondary odors or blenders can be chosen. The second odor may resemble the main scent or be almost anything that will enhance the first odor. Use dried lemon zest with woodsy scents or small amounts of essential oils not available from plants in your garden. Add small amounts of crushed or broken bits of cinnamon, nutmeg, or cloves to a floral-scented potpourri of chiefly rose petals or crushed spearmint leaves. Sandalwood complements rose petals perfectly. The blend is successful when no single ingredient dominates; aim for a subtle masking of fragrances.

The final element in the preparing of a perfume substance is the addition of a fixative. The fixative retards evaporation of the volatile oils and locks them into the blend. The fixative may or may not add its own note to the main fragrance, and certain fixatives work better than others with specific scents.

Fixatives are of both animal (musk and ambergis) and vegetable origin. Dried, powdered rhizomes of orris, *Iris* x *germanica* var. *florentina*, or *I. pallida* and sweet flag, *Acorus calamus*, are fixatives with a delicate violet odor and have a natural affinity with lavender and rose-scented geranium leaves. The violet odor of sweet flag is not as strong as orris. Benzoin, a gum or resin from the bark of a species of *Styrax* grown in southeastern Asia, needs to be purchased from a supplier of perfume materials. It is odorless and thus can be used to avoid the introduction of a discordant note.

Many fragrant flowers or scents from different plant parts lose or change their aroma when dried, or the amount of material required for an effect is not practical. In such instances the scents can be supplied or supplemented by adding small amounts of pure oils available from perfume suppliers. This should not discourage you from collecting scented flowers; often they surprise you with a marvelous scent for blending or contribute color and bulk to potpourri.

Recipes for potpourri vary. Some are reliable; others are complicated and present problems in finding the recommended essences, extracts, gums, and resins. If you have a herb garden, it is fitting to gather from the garden and kitchen shelves; buy powdered fixatives and small vials of pure essential oil; follow your nose, and respect scent perfume categories. This is being inventive and provides many delightful discoveries. Herbists who have a special gift for smelling—like perfumers, tea tasters, and whiskey blenders—can develop the skill by practicing.

A few recipes may be helpful:

Floral: Rose Mint:
1 cup rose petals
10 mint leaves, crushed
½ teaspoon powdered orris
¼ teaspoon each of ground cinnamon, ground allspice, grated nutmeg
Blend.

Fruity:

½ ounce apple-scented geranium leaves
½ ounce bergamot mint leaves
.4 ounces ground coriander seed
.2 ounces whole coriander, pounded
½ ounce vetiver root, chopped
.3 ounce powdered benzoin
1 teaspoon powdered orris
2 drops bergamot oil
Blend.

Floral Bouquet

2 cups rose petals
½ cup lavender flowers
1 cup rose-scented geranium leaves
Crush and add 2 tablespoons patchouli leaves, 1 tablespoon rosemary
    leaves, ½ teaspoon anise seed, 1½ teaspoon cloves, 1½ teaspoon
    cinnamon
1½ teaspoon grated nutmeg
3 drops pure jasmine oil
¼ ounce powdered orris
1½ teaspoon powdered benzoin
Blend.

Woodsy: Herbal Green

1 cup sweet marjoram leaves
1½ cups rosemary leaves
½ cup sage leaves
¼ cup summer savory leaves
1–2 crushed bay leaves
¼ cup dried lemon peel
¼ cup dried orange peel
¼ cup dried lime peel
Blend and crush the mixture very fine or put it through a coarse setting of
    a meat grinder.
Add and mix thoroughly with the above 1 tablespoon powdered benzoin
Put mixture in a tightly closed jar to blend for several weeks.

Above: An uncultivated rosemary thriving in its native habitat of thin, dry, calcareous soil of Andalusia in Spain. *Right:* Interlocking rectangular planters, 22 inches high, within the author's paved garden facing south-east. Evergreen and evergray plant-ings provide a year-round scene from windows of the house which shields the close from northwest winds.

A contrived design within the garden at Barnsley House in the English Cots-wolds. The arrangement in a shaded area with cool water can be adapted as a cool microclimate for growing herbs from cool climates in a warm region.

Interspersed potted herbs with herbs planted in openings of a paved garden bring into view an agreeable scene from a bench or window.

Posted and fragrant standardized, shaped, and clipped classic myrtles, *Myrtus communis*, in classic clay pots identify a home where herbs are grown.

A herb garden divided into squares at Sissinghurst in Kent, England

Creeping thymes and a sundial in the herb garden of the Missouri Botanical Garden in St. Louis, Missouri

The easy-to-establish creeping thyme patch, convenient on a slope among rocks, is in the historical restoration of Old Salem in Winston-Salem, North Carolina.

Above: Vetiver in the author's garden.
Right: A setting for native American herbs in the author's garden that includes a fabricated bog

In an assemblage of plants from arid regions at the Atlanta Botanical Garden in Atlanta, Georgia visitors can find *Origanum* spp. and *Thymus* spp. growing vigorously in a habitat copied from their native environment.

An apothecary rose in the author's garden

Traditional, protected bee skeps

A natural landscape site for native plants of the Sandhills at Sandhills Community College in Pinehurst, North Carolina

A skillfully devised berm, adjoining woodland, and meadow succeed as natural landscapes for native American herbs.

A garden of satisfied herbs on a mound of introduced soil. University of Minnesota Landscape Arboretum.

Common sage after early spring pruning is lovely and well-placed with spring-blooming chive and large, rough-leaves of horseradish in the background.

Black cohosh, *Cimicifuga racemosa*

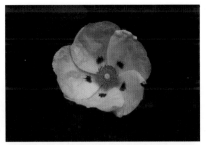

Flower of the rock rose, *Cistus ladaniferus*

Flowering prickly pear cactus, *Opuntia humifusa*

Hen-and-chickens, *Sempervivum tectorum*, in a hen-shaped clay pot

Globular flower heads of salad burnet, *Poterium sanguisorba*

Hen-and-chickens, *Sempervivum tectorum*, on a Cotswold cottage roof in Greenfield Village, Dearborn, Michigan

Floral with Citrus and Spicy Overtones
1 quart rose petals
1 pint lemon verbena leaves
1 pint rose geranium leaves
¼ cup rosemary leaves
1 tablespoon orange peel, ground with 1 teaspoon cloves
6 drops each of bergamot oil, rosemary oil, lemon verbena oil
1½ teaspoon of each, crushed cinnamon sticks, cloves, mace, nutmeg, all-
    spice, cardamom seeds, ginger root
1 tablespoon finely cut vetiver
2 tablespoons each of powdered benzoin, powdered orris
Blend.

Lavender with Woodsy Overtones
1 cup lavender flowers
¾ cup sweet woodruff leaves
½ cup rosemary leaves
½ cup lemon verbena leaves
½ cup thyme leaves
½ cup rose geranium leaves
½ cup orange peel
Mix and put through a coarse meat grinder.
Add and mix well with ⅛ cup powdered benzoin.

A potpourri needs five or six weeks in a closed container to blend thoroughly or marry; stir the mixture every few days. One whiff of a fine mel-
lowed potpourri transports you to the garden from whence it came; floral
scents should have the smell of the rose garden after a fresh rain. When you
have revived a bowl of potpourri by loosening it with your fingers, set it out
in a guest room, an entrance hall, or on a shelf among the books. By adding
a few drops of a complementing pure oil from time to time, you can keep it
pleasurable for as long as you wish. Do not be surprised when a potpourri
scent plays subtle effects on your memory no different from a costly perfume.

Sundry Uses for Dried Herbs

Your herb garden helps you to live plain and live well, to have more with
less. Make a scented bouquet garni or lavender bundles with fresh material,

dry, and slip them between the bed linens. For friends of cats, stuff mice and fish shapes of strong fabric with dried catnip. Herb pillows of dried rosemary or camphoraceous leaves of African basil help alleviate the discomfort of a stuffed-up nose. Add a band to hold the pillow to your warm cheek while reading a book near the fire. Dried, ripe cones of female hop flowers, lavender flowers, or rose-scented geranium leaves enclosed as sachets are comforting near the bed of a convalescent. Wormwood, santolina, southernwood, and tansy are insect repellents; bagged and distributed in closets and drawers, their dried leaves ward off harmful insect invasions.

Dried Decorative Arrangements

Next most appealing to fresh herbs in the house are charming dried winter arrangements. A large vase holding great stalks of silver honesty, *Lunaria annua*, brightens winter days. With your fingers, slip off the valves and seeds when the flat capsules are ripe, to expose the clear center film, which Gerard describes as "shining like a shred of white Sattin newly cut from the peece." A small narrow vase with one to three clownish stalks of rocambole, or serpentine garlic, is jocular herbal entertainment.

Three globular skyrocketlike flower heads of leek with stalks of different heights in a low, broad, flat porcelain dish are striking. If a tussie-mussie is brought to your door, you may wish to preserve it by air-drying or using silica gel. When you start looking for native American herbal plants suitable for dried arrangements, seek out the woody herbal vine, bittersweet, *Celastrus scandens*, for its yellow to orange to red fruits that announce the autumn season.

Perhaps you will follow directions for drying herbs with silica gel and make diminutive arrangements. With or without the aid of a magnifier, there will be reason to marvel over the elaborate details and colors of dried herbs. Remember, the enemies of the drying process, humidity and strong sunlight, are also enemies of dried flowers. Keep that in mind when picking a location for an arrangement.

You may discover that by using only one to three different kinds of dried herbs and keeping the stems, with or without flowers, well-separated from one another, a refined charm presents itself—often unnoticed when herbs are juxtaposed in the garden. More often than not, in the justifiable, concen-

trated effort to match or contrast herbs for beauty in the garden, we sometimes miss their singular exquisite qualities. Airier, see-through arrangements introduce a quality of openness in indoor space through the winter.
A case of much with less.

Herb Wreaths

In putting together the house for Christmas, we make wreaths from summer's herbal bounty and the spice cupboard. Two purchased wreaths of
straw are wrapped with silver king artemisia branches. The wrappings are
held in place with extra-strong button or carpet thread, color-matched to
the artemisia, and hidden under the overlapping branches. When the artemisia completely covers the wreath, leaving no straw exposed, we decorate
one of the wreaths with herbs while the other is placed to the side.

For this first wreath small bundles and sprigs of miscellaneous dried herbs
from the garden are arranged on the wreath and pinned to it with florist
pins. Bundles and sprigs flow in the same direction and overlap to cover
pins of an adjoining bundle. There is no planned symmetry. Clusters of rose
hips or small rose buds, spikes of lavender or anise-hyssop, dark red cayenne
peppers, teasel heads, long sprigs of evergreen rosemary, sprigs of lady's
mantle with flowers, umbels of yellow fennel, flower heads of pink chive, a
split yucca capsule attached to a trio of bay leaves with glue—any and all
become accents. The background of silver artemisia shows off both subtle
and strong colors of the dried herbs. The wreath is planned to lie flat, but
with a wire loop at the back it can hang on a wall.

Then the second wreath, put aside while the first was being decorated, is
adorned. This wreath is planned to hold cinnamon sticks, marzipan, and
pomander balls made of crab apples stuck with cloves and rolled in a spice
mixture. All are fastened to the wreath base with strong toothpicks partially
imbedded in the pomander balls, marzipan, and cinnamon sticks; the remaining toothpick is pierced into the wreath.

The wreath of herbs is placed on a table with candles through the four
weeks marked for Christmas preparation. At midnight on Christmas Eve the
spice wreath replaces the herb wreath. Our two wreaths typify a time in
history when costly spices were reserved for festal fare while herbs seasoned
daily fare. The convention remains in Christmas cakes and cookies. Hinging

festive customs to a manner of wreath making indicates, like a herb garden, that herb and spice wreaths are more than decorative things.

Pressing Herbs

From ancient times and onward, plants have been dried by pressing them between absorbent sheets under pressure. This method of preservation makes possible taxonomic as well as other botanical study for an indefinite time period. A well-collected plant specimen contains the vital parts—flowers and fruits—plus some leaves attached to the stem. Dried pressed plants are glued onto standard-sized sheets of heavy mounting paper, 16½ x 10½ inches, together with labels, before being filed away in systematic order on the shelves of herbarium cabinets. The label is essential; it carries field notes, the collector's name, date of collection, the botanical name when identified. More and more herbists are collecting dried, pressed herbal specimens as an adjunct to a library and herb garden. Mounted and labeled, they offer opportunity for close scrutiny and exact botanical identification of puzzling species as in the genera *Origanum, Thymus,* and more.

Herbists and artists, fascinated by the different shapes and colors of herb leaves and flowers, carefully mount dried, pressed herbs on selected papers or between transparent rice papers, or imbed them in clear plastic. A collage of pressed herbs becomes a realistic or impressionistic scene.

A standard plant press consists of two latticed wooden frames, 18 x 12 inches. A doubled sheet of newspaper is laid on one of the frames and, on top of that, heavy absorbent papers (blotterlike). Herbs to be pressed are placed between two additional newspaper sheets with pertinent information on a separate paper; an effort is made to keep all herb parts in a single layer and to display identifying characteristics of the flower parts. The pressed specimen in newspaper is laid on top of the blotter, then another blotter, another specimen between newspaper layers, then a third blotter and so on. Top the stack with newspapers and the remaining frame.

Wrap two strong canvas bands with locking fasteners (commonly used for snugging camping equipment or luggage) tightly around the two frames to press. After several days, open the press, exchange moist blotters for dry ones, and rewrap. Store the press in a well-ventilated dry room or attic. Herbs are mounted and labeled when completely dry. Many ardent collectors make their frames using the measurements given.

Herbs for Medicine

Herbs were, from the dawn of history, the source of help for the sick. By the eighteenth century the immense success of experimental methods introduced to chemistry induced their application to biology. Since the nineteenth century organic chemistry has developed with broad benefits that include investigations of organic chemical compounds in plants. Scientific research on the therapeutic properties of botanicals continues to yield valid organic compounds for medicinal use. Frequently toxic organic compounds are among the numberless organic molecules found in plants. On this account, suggestions for gathering medicinal plant material with complex organic chemical compounds in unknown amount, possibly comprising toxic molecules with questionable effects, are responsibly not in the directives of the present book.

On the other side, hortitherapists affirm the positive effects that herbs have on handicapped and bedridden patients. Handling herbs, dried or fresh, raises spirits, generates smiles, and creates optimism. For a time I was privileged to serve in a herb hortitherapy program for paralyzed stroke victims suffering from negative attitudes. They were unhappily and physically forced to insert cuttings of scented geraniums into a planting medium. Three weeks later, when they discovered the cuttings had developed roots, they almost instantly turned positive, cooperative, and joyous. Each herb was eagerly potted, and one owner declared excitedly, "I want to root all the different kinds you have, please."

Planting, tending, and harvesting herbs are mentally and emotionally invigorating for handicapped children or adults. Being among the elderly making lavender bundles, crumbling dried herbs for kitchens or sachets, speaking of herb connections, and hearing their plans for giving herbal gifts was ample reward for having helped them make a herb garden.

Living with aromatic herbs in a house or in a garden is living with extraordinary visual serenity and olfactory gratification. Herb gardens bear the mark of simplicity and frugality, which has had more purpose through the centuries than gardens exclusively for decorative plantings.

8 ❦ Descriptive Catalog of Herbs

Abbreviations and Symbols used in the Descriptive Catalog are as follows:

Δ	native American herb in the Southeast	c.p.	coastal plain, plains	
☠	poisonous	cv.	cultivar	
☉	annual	ft.	foot, feet	
☉	biennial	in.	inch, inches	
♃	perennial	mts.	mountains	
[ ]	encloses a former, no longer valid botanical name	pied.	piedmont	
		sp.	species (singular)	
		spp.	species (plural)	
		subsp.	subspecies	
x	sign for a hybrid	var.	variety	

Acanthus mollis L. ♃   Acanthus family
   Bear's-breech
Native on dry, rocky, well-drained soil in the Mediterranean region. A handsome perennial with large, deeply cut, not spiny, dark green basal leaves rising from a deeply rooted crown. Flowers are white to pink on erect spikes to 4 ft.; blooms from May to July. *A. spinosissimus* Pers. of dry, waste places in southeast Europe has stiff white spines on deeply cut leaves.
CULTURE   Sow seed or divide roots. Grow in full sun or partial shade. Not reliably winter hardy north of zone 8.
VIRTUE   The bold leaves inspired the motif for the capitals on Corinthian columns. Dioscorides recorded medicinal uses.

Achillea millefolium L. ♃   Composite family
   Yarrow, milfoil, woundwort
Native in Europe and western Asia; widely naturalized in North America; weedy. A hardy, aromatic perennial to 3 ft. with dark green, alternate, feathery leaves. White to pink-tinged flowers massed on a head in flat-topped clusters bloom throughout the summer. Cultivars are based on flower colors.
CULTURE   Divide rhizomes or sow seed; self-sows. Prefers sun, but will grow in partial shade and tolerates most soils; a good plant to fill a difficult situation.
VIRTUES   A tea or poultice made of steeped dried leaves and flowers is deeply entrenched in ethno-medicine.

Aconitum napellus L. ♃☠   Crowfoot family
   Monkshood, wolfsbane
Native in shady places of northern Europe. A hardy perennial to 3 ft. with dark green, deeply divided leaves. Clear blue, hood-shaped flowers in erect clusters form on tall, imposing spikes in late summer.
CULTURE   Sow seed, moist-chilled below 40°F: for six weeks to break dormancy, or divide roots; self-sows. As a plant of cool climates, grow monkshood in a cool, moist, and shaded spot.
VIRTUES   Medicinal. Yields aconitine, a formidable poison. Root was formerly used to kill animal pests.
    A. fischeri ☠ from East Asia is similar to *A. napellus* ☠ in appearance and was used in ancient time as an arrow poison. It is commonly confused with *A. carmichaelii* ☠ having deep blue-purple flowers and growing to 6 ft.

Acorus calamus L. ♃   Arum family
   Sweet flag
A bog plant of the Northern Hemisphere, naturalized as far south as Florida and
Texas in shallow water and marshy places. The perennial with aromatic rhi-
zomes grows to 6 ft. Erect leaves are sword-shaped with crinkly margins. Minute
flowers are borne on a dense finger-like spike rising on the side of a leaf-like
stalk.
CULTURE   Divide rhizomes. Grow in wet soil and full sun or partial shade.
Sweet flag fits congenially as a water-edge subject to the water garden that provides a microclimate for herbs from cool climates.
VIRTUES   Rhizomes are used as a fixative and for a delicate, gingery fragrance
in perfumes; were used medicinally, and as a liqueur flavoring. Leaves, fragrant
when bruised, were used as strewing herbs.

Actaea pachipoda Elliott ♃ ▲ ☠   Crowfoot family
   White baneberry, white cohosh, doll's eyes
An erect perennial to 2 ft., native in rich woods from Nova Scotia to cooler
upland woods southward into Georgia. Leaves are divided into three segments,
each similarly divided into sharply toothed leaflets. Stalked, small white flowers
are in a cluster along an elongated common stem in spring. Fruit is a pea-sized
white berry set on a red stalk. Clusters of poisonous berries are attractive, attention receiving accents in the woodland.
CULTURE   Sow seeds in late autumn or divide roots in spring. Prefers woodland shade.
VIRTUES   Cherokee Indians used the root medicinally.

Aesculus pavia L. ▲   Horse chestnut family
   Red buckeye
A deciduous shrub or small tree to 12 ft.; native to low pine-deciduous woods
and along stream banks in the Southeast; hardy to zone 5. Leaves are opposite,
palmately compound, with 5–7 leaflets. Bright red flowers in 1 ft. long upright
branched clusters bloom in spring. Rounded fruits split in three parts and contain 1–3 shiny seeds.
CULTURE   Sow seed in autumn or treat seed indoors to stratify; or layer low
branches. Grow in sun or shade; full sun results in more compact plants that
flower profusely, but open woodland suits them well. Neutral or alkaline soils
require amendments to increase acidity.
VIRTUES   Cherokee Indians used pounded nuts and bark medicinally and as
food after leaching the meal with water for several days. Toxicity of all parts is

harmful; Indians of the Southeast spilled slurries of the leaves into streams to stupefy fish; a paste made of buckeye starch is toxic to insects.

Agastache foeniculum (Pursh.) O. Kuntze ♃ Δ   Mint family
  Anise hyssop, giant hyssop
Native on plains and borders of woods in north central North America. A pleasantly aromatic, erect, branched perennial to 3 ft. Leaves are dark green, ovate, sharply toothed with a gray down on the underside. From July to October an open woodland or sunny border is embellished with bluish-lavender flowers arranged in dense spikes, 3–8 in. long. Unconventionally, anise-hyssop does not bend towards the source of light, but remains erect with branches well-arranged on all sides; the characteristic is appreciated when plants hug a west-facing wall, freely branch, do not lean—and all with out staking. *A. rugosa*, introduced into the United States from Korea in 1947, is distinguished from *A. foeniculum* by its ovate-cordate leaf shape and differences in flower parts, criteria of interest to a serious collector of native American herbs.
CULTURE Sow seed or divide roots in fall; seeds germinate indoors in 5–8 days; self-sows. Thrives in sun or partial shade.
VIRTUES American Indians used scented leaves for a tea and medicine. Beekeepers recognize anise-hyssop as a bee plant, flowers yielding nectar throughout the day. Dried flower stalks are decorative.

Agave americana L. ☉ or ♃   Amaryllis family
  Century plant, American aloe
Native annual in warm, arid regions of Mexico; sometimes found naturalized in southern parts of the United States. Immense cactus-like leaves, gray, curved, or reflexed at the tip, rise from a basal rosette; rarely a perennial, for it is after decades that a tall stalk appears and bursts into bloom which by exaggeration has contributed the common name, "century plant." The plant's demise follows the production of seed in the pale yellow flowers.
CULTURE Propagate from suckers at the base taken before the plant blooms. Requires full sun, a well-drained soil, warm temperature, and controlled moisture. Gardeners appreciative of the architectural features treat *Agave* as a tub plant, grow it in a sterilized soil with added sand, avoid excessive watering to prevent root rot wilt, and take it indoors through the winter.
VIRTUES In Mexico the traditional beverage "pulque" is produced from the fermented sap; distilled sap is "tequila." A juice, extracted from the succulent leaves, is made into a soap with wood ash. The vicious spine at the end of the leaf functions as a threaded needle with leaf fibers attached as the thread. Fibers

are spun into a strong thread and woven into cloth. Recent investigated agaves have led to the discovery of a new cortisone compound of possible value in medicine.

Agrimonia eupatoria L. ♃   Rose family
  Agrimony
The erect, slightly branched perennial to 5 ft. with hairy stems grows in open fields and hillsides of Europe, west Asia, and North Africa. Leaves are pinnately compound with 7–13 rough-textured, toothed leaflets. Small golden-yellow flowers along an erect stalk bloom from June to August. Fruit with seed is a bristly burr.
CULTURE Sow seed in late summer or divide roots in spring; self-sows. Once started in the sun, agrimony flourishes to become weedy in sun or partial shade.
VIRTUES Leaves and stalks yield a yellow dye. Medicinal uses, known to the ancient Greeks, remain in folklore.

Alchemilla vulgaris L. ♃   Rose family
  Lady's mantle
A perennial, 8–12 in. high, of grassy meadows in north temperate Europe, forms attractive clumps. Rounded, slightly lobed, and toothed leaves are pleated like the folds of a cape (mantle). The modest beauty of the funnel-shaped leaves is enhanced by drops of dew they collect. Small, yellow-green flowers borne in clusters bloom from May to August.
CULTURE Divide roots in fall or spring; self-sows. In warm regions grow lady's mantle in partial shade. In sun or light shade it may turn drab in July and August, but revives in September to remain almost evergreen.
VIRTUES In ethno-medicine. In Norway the leaves and stalks are used to yield a yellow color. Flower clusters contribute an ethereal quality to a bouquet.
    A. alpina from grassy mountain meadows of Europe and a favorite in the rock garden is petite compared to *A. vulgaris*, but equal in herbal documentation.

Allium spp.   Amaryllis family
  In "The Canterbury Tales," Chaucer wrote of a trencherman: "Wel loved he
  garleek, onions, and eek leekes."
A genus of strongly odorous, mostly perennial, bulbous herbs; native to the Northern Hemisphere. Leeks, shallots, onions, garlic, and chive are important members of a herb garden or potager, have been cultivated since prehistoric time, and are native to middle Asia, with secondary development centers in western Asia and the Mediterranean region. Welsh onions and "garlic" or Chi-

nese chive are from the Far East; American Indians and early French missionaries in North America were nourished in early spring by native wild onions and wild leeks. Visually, the linear stalks of *Allium* spp. with round flowering heads as large as grapefruits, or as small as grapes, are striking features among bushier, leafy herbs in a herb garden. Plant twice as many Alliums as you need; remove developing flower stalks from half of the plants to encourage bulb and leaf growth for kitchen use. Leave remaining flower stalks to mature and decorate the garden.

A. ampeloprasum L. Porrum group ⊙
Leek

The bulb of biennial leek is long, thick, and soft, not rounded as an onion bulb. Flat and keeled leaves to 2½ ft. form a sheath about the bulb. In the summer of the second year a flower stalk to 3 ft. is terminated with greenish-white flowers in a round head.

CULTURE Sow seed outdoors as soon as soil is workable or indoors two months before spring planting; seeds germinate in about 12 days. Thin and transplant to a sunny position in a trench of well-prepared rich soil, 6 in. apart. As the leeks grow hill with soil or mulch to blanch. Harvest through the season and in warm climates through the winter.

VIRTUES Both white and green portions of leaves and bulbs are used for seasoning and as a potherb. In a garden or in a dried arrangement flower heads conjure up images of silvery skyrockets on the 4th of July.

A. canadense L. ♃ **Δ**
Wild onion

The perennial is found in rich meadows and alluvial woods along waterways of eastern North America. Leaves, 3 or more, are quill-like. Bulbs are very small. Pinkish or greenish-white flowers, often replaced by bulbils, are borne on a stalk to 1 ft.; blooms from May to June.

CULTURE Not known to be cultivated. Grows in moist soil under all light exposures.

VIRTUES Bulbs, bulbils, and leaves have a sweet onion flavor and sustained American Indians, explorers, and pioneers in early spring.

A. cepa L., Aggregatum Group ♃
Shallot, multiplier onion

Shallots were originally named *A. ascalonicum* for a city called Ascalon in Syria to which their origin is traced. The present word, Aggregatum, indicates the bulb is not single, but is a grouping of lateral bulbs or shoots that split—"cloves." Shallot cloves are tinged violet and red. Leaves are slender, cylindrical, and hollow. A flower stalk to 18 in. rarely flowers or sets seed.

CULTURE Propagate from cloves set out late in fall or early spring. Place them root end down, tops just barely visible above ground, and 6 in. apart. Accommodate shallots with a loose, fertile soil in full sun.

VIRTUES A shallot's delicate flavor makes it a seasoning par excellence. Dried shallots keep well. Herb gardens and potagers of frugal cooks are not without shallots!

A.cepa L., Cepa Group ☉
Common onion

Mariska, my close ally in keeping the affairs of a home in order and a political refugee from Hungary, confessed while we prepared chicken paprikash that extreme longing for an onion to season her family's meager and poor food during wanderings in Europe brought her perilously close to stealing one from a neighbor. Since prehistory the onion has been cultivated as a culinary indispensable. Like Mariska, the Israelites longed for them as they wandered in the Wilderness for forty years. Onions are bulbous biennials with flower stalks to 2 ft. Leaves are hollow and cylindrical. Small flowers in round umbels are whitish, bloom the second year, and set seed. A. cepa, Proliferum Group, Egyptian or top onion, produces large bulbils in place of flowers. The weight of the bulbils bends the stalk to the ground, and bulbils take root to form new plants. Nature has her way.

CULTURE Sow seed, plant sets, or bulbils in a fertile, loose soil in the fall where climates are mild or in early spring. After harvesting they should be stored in a cool, dry place.

VIRTUES Bulbs and leaves are seasoning and potherbs. Bulbils of the Egyptian onion are ideal as onions for pickling. Dried bulb skins yield a burnt orange or brass color in dying wool. Eggshells colored with onion skins for Easter turn a dark henna color.

A. sativum L. ♃
Garlic

The globular bulb of garlic enclosed in a membranous sheath is divided into several cloves. Leaves are flat to ½ in. wide. Bulbils and white to pinkish flowers that bloom briefly in July and abort without producing seed are in a round umbel on a scape to 2 ft.

CULTURE Divide a large garlic bulb and set each clove, root end down, 4–6 in. apart in a shallow furrow in late September or October. Cover the furrow with 1–3 in. of soil. Fall planting has a twofold purpose: Cloves have a head start to develop roots, and garlic requires cold treatment to promote bulb development. Planted in full sun, and a light, well-drained, and reasonably fertile soil, leaves will sprout and stay green through the winter in zones 8–10. In early summer to July, when foliage yellows, dig up the bulbs, dry for several days in a well-ventilated area, out of direct sunlight; then braid or cut them 2 in. above the bulb and store.

VIRTUES   The long history in ethno-medicine is equally matched by the flavor fresh garlic has contributed to cuisines around the world, unmatched by inferior convenience powders, salts, and extracts.

A. sativum var. ophioscorodon (Link) Doll. ♃

Rocambole, serpentine garlic

Distinguished from A.sativum by elaborate curves and coils of the scape (flower stalk) at the top to finally form a long, spearlike beak (spathe) pointed neatly downwards. Then it splits open to disclose bulbils which fall to the ground and sprout new plants. Again, nature has her way.

CULTURE   Once established from a bulbil rocambole continues as a perennial and has the same requirements as garlic.

VIRTUES   For a "touch" of garlic flavor pierce a bulbil with a toothpick and swivel it in the oil heated to saute a dish and remove; the garlic flavor is controlled. The curious curved and coiled stalk with its pointed beak around the head is material for a light-hearted cut floral arrangement and known to take a prize.

A. schoenoprasum L. ♃

Chive

Chive, like garlic, and with origins in cold climates needs cold weather to promote ever larger clumps of bulbs. In very early spring slender, hollow, and cylindrical leaves rising to 1 ft. are "first fruits." Rose colored, globular flowerheads with bracts follow to make a show in May and stay if the soil is kept moist. They look well with the neighboring dark green, curled parsley, and there is convenience in snipping with only one bend for a blend.

CULTURE   Sow seed outdoors in fall or separate bulbs of large clumps. Perennial chive self-sows. In warm regions grow chive in partial shade and fertilize in early spring to give it a good start in the cool weather it prefers. Cutting leaves about ½ in. above the soil level encourages new growth; cutting tips discourages it.

VIRTUES   Chive, common and modest, is among the most useful of kitchen herbs. Chopped fresh leaves season spring dishes and many more all through the year. The mild onion flavor is agreeable and harmonizes with many soups and salads as a garnish.

A. scorodoprasum L. ⚃
Spanish garlic, elephant garlic, giant garlic
A mild garlic with cloves 1 in. thick and the outer bulb coat violet colored. Hardier than *A. sativum*.
CULTURE AND VIRTUES   As garlic

A. tricoccum Alt. ⚃△
Wild leek, ramp
Perennial ramp grows in moist places and thin woods from New Brunswick to North Carolina. Unlike most Alliums, leaves are broad, tongue-shaped, coming to a point, 2 in. wide and 5 in. long. Bulbs are single or clustered. On a flower stalk to 12 in. many greenish-white flowers borne on an umbel bloom in June after the leaves die down.
CULTURE   Propagate from seed or bulbs in a natural style garden for native herbs; self-sows. Grows in partial shade or shade.
VIRTUES   Bulbs are pleasant tasting and were used by the American Indians and pioneers for food and medicine.

A. tuberosum Rottl. ex K. Spreng ⚃
Garlic chive, Chinese chive, oriental chive
A bulbous perennial on a stout rhizome with a flower stalk to 20 in. Leaves are slightly keeled. Among the narrow green leaves in late August and September the pretty white, starry flowers in umbels look particularly lovely close to purple-bronze ruffled leaves and flower spikes of perilla. Later the flowers dry to an almond color with shining black seeds in the split capsule.
CULTURE   Propagate by separating bulbous clumps or sow seed in fall; self-sows so prolifically to warrant removing most of the stalks before seed matures. Seed sown indoors or outdoors in spring without stratification regularly fails to germinate.
VIRTUES   Chopped mild garlic-flavored leaves flavor a salad of greens.

Aloe barbadensis Mill. ⚃   Lily family
Aloe
A perennial, stemless succulent with origins in southern Africa from where it spread to the Mediterranean region. Spanish visitors are believed to have introduced it to the West Indies. Clumps form when stolons arising at the base of a plant root and develop an adjoining new plant. The thick leaves are a glaucous-green, narrow, 1–2 ft. long, and armed with teeth. Flowers, on a stalk to 3 ft., are yellow.
CULTURE   Propagate by detaching offshoots from leaves, and root in soil. In areas not reliably frost-free aloe is grown as a pot plant. Pot in a mixture of 2 parts

potting soil and 1–2 parts sharp sand for good drainage. Keep the pot in a warm and bright location through the winter; shade it from the sun in the hot summer. Like all succulents and xerophytic plants, an aloe prefers not being watered too frequently.

VIRTUES   In medicine, a broken aloe leaf applied to a mild skin burn is cooling and soothing. Pain-relieving, healing, and antibacterial claims have been made in the treatment of burns. As the potent elixir of centuries there is at this time little supportive evidence.

Aloysia triphylla (L'Her.) Britt.   Verbena family
Lemon verbena
A deciduous shrub, 5–10 ft. tall; native in warm regions of Argentina and Chile. Spanish conquistadors made it a favorite in Spain from where it moved throughout Europe and into North America, always kept protected from cold temperatures. Crisp, light green, lance-shaped leaves are deliciously lemon-scented. With attention centered on the strong citric-perfumed leaves, little white flowers, scantily arranged in a panicle, are often missed when they bloom in late summer.
CULTURE   Propagate from cuttings taken where new growth begins, and keep chambered until well-rooted to prevent leaf drop. Except in zones 8–11, lemon verbena is generally treated as a pot plant in full sun and moved indoors for the winter. Indoors it is vulnerable to whitefly; to minimize an infestation take the harvest of leaves while the pot is outdoors. Indoors, water the practically leafless plant just enough to keep roots alive until January; then stimulate new leaf growth by watering with a water soluble fertilizer, take cuttings from the new growth to increase your stock, and move the pot outdoors when the weather warms.
VIRTUES   Dried or fresh leaves flavor teas and sweets; use a strong infusion from the leaves as an extract to substitute for the zest of a lemon. Dried leaves are important in potpourri.

Anagallis arvensis L. ☉☠   Primrose family
Poor-man's-weatherglass, shepherd's clock
A low, spreading annual, native to Europe; now widely distributed and weedy. Leaves are shiny, small, ovate. Brick-red flowers borne in leaf axils open to the sun and bloom throughout the summer. The common name refers to the flowers closing their petals in response to a decrease of sun light by cloudiness or its setting; commonly growing around water where sheep were refreshed, shepherds marked the closing of the petals as a sign of rain or day's end. Give expres-

sion to the tradition by keeping poor-man's-weatherglass at the garden's water spigot, from which, of course, it will spread.

CULTURE   Sow seeds in spring in a sunny position; self-sows.

VIRTUES   In ethno-medicine. Though listed in classic French cookbooks as a sauce ingredient, the plant is considered poisonous.

Anchusa officinalis L. ⊙ or ♃   Borage family
Alkanet, viper's bugloss

A coarse, hairy, erect perennial or biennial to 2 ft.; native to Europe and Asia Minor. Leaves are lance-shaped and basal. Bright blue flowers, ¼ in. across, are arranged on one side of a curved stalk and bloom through the summer. Horticultural forms exist.

CULTURE   Seeds sown indoors germinate in 5–10 days. Easily cultivated in a sunny position.

VIRTUES   In ethno-medicine. The root produces a red and blue dye that can be used as litmus.

Anethum graveolens L. ⊙   Parsley family
Dill

An annual to 3 ft.; native in western Asia; naturalized in Europe and North America. Leaves are cut into thread-like divisions, and yellow flowers in large umbels bloom in early summer followed by flattish seeds. Leaves, hollow stalks, and seeds are aromatic. A tetraploid cultivar, 'Green Bouquet' is leafier and produces less seed.

CULTURE   In a sunny position scatter seed over well-prepared light, fertile soil in fall, or two to four weeks before the last frost date; scattering encourages clumping of erect plants to support one another; thin seedlings if necessary. Depend on self-sown volunteers for sturdy and robust plants. Dill's preference for cool temperatures for germination is demonstrated in warm regions where self-sown seed germinates in the winter and harvests are early. Take the leaf harvest before the seeds develop, because as annuals, leaves decline as their stored foods are used to insure progeny.

VIRTUES   Snipped dill leaves, dried seeds, and stalks contribute a common flavoring in pickling, to salads, root vegetables, squash, butters, sour cream sauces, fish, meats, and herb vinegars. Many of the combinations were not invented to satisfy the nose, but as in dill with cucumbers, to aid digestion and diminish "windiness"—medicinal. Lepidopterists grow dill to attract caterpillars of swallowtail butterflies who enjoy feeding on its leaves.

Angelica archangelica L. ⊙   Parsley family
Sweet angelica
A biennial of cool, low, moist habitats; native to northern Europe and Asia. Angelica is imposing in any position and in every part. A hollow stout stem to 6 ft.
supports large compound, deeply cleft, and toothed leaves, and grapefruit-sized
globular umbels of yellow-green flowers in early summer. All parts are aromatic.
CULTURE   Seed germinates as soon as ripe. A self-sown seedling beneath a parent plant must be transplanted to a permanent position in moist soil and light
shade for full growth by the following spring. Growing Angelica in a warm climate is at odds with its genetic make-up. A measure of success is possible by
planting close to the edge of a shaded water garden or in a shaded bog garden
where cooler temperatures prevail.
VIRTUES   Pale green candied pieces of stems and leaf stalks are traditional flavoring and decoration on cake icings in countries of northern Europe; the
unique aroma of a broken stem in a garden is evocative of a long ago birthday
gathering. Angelica is an important flavoring agent in liqueurs, the origin of
which was medicinal—aromatically invigorating and digestive.

Anisostichus capreolata (L.) Bureau **Δ**   Bignonia family
Cross vine, trumpet flower
A semi-evergreen to evergreen woody vine of moist woodlands and along roadsides, native throughout the Southeast. The dark-green, compound leaves with
ovate leaflets and branched tendrils turn purplish in winter. Trumpet-shaped
orange-red flowers appear from April to June. A native herb to cover a fence
or wall.
CULTURE   Propagate from cuttings of new growth taken in June or July. Grows
best in moist soil and full sun to light shade.
VIRTUES   Used medicinally by the Cherokee Indians.

Anthemis tinctoria L. ⊙ or ♃   Composite family
Golden Marguerite, dyer's Marguerite
An erect, branched biennial or short-lived perennial to 3 ft.; native to central and
southern Europe, and Asia; sparingly naturalized in North America. Aromatic
leaves, evergreen in warm regions, are pinnately divided, toothed, and fernlike,
to 3 in. long. Daisy-like golden-yellow flowers, $1\frac{1}{2}$ in. across, bloom in early
spring and late summer.
CULTURE   Sow seed outdoors or start indoors; seed germinates in 4–6 days.
Prefers a sunny location.
VIRTUES   Flower heads yield a yellow, khaki, or gold dye.

Anthriscus cerefolium (L.) Hoffm. ☉   Parsley family
   Chervil
Native in southeast Europe and western Asia; naturalized in North America. An erect annual that grows to 2 ft. with delicate anise-scented, finely cut leaves. Small, white flowered umbels appear in early spring and late summer.
CULTURE   Sown in September, seedlings will overwinter outdoors for an early supply of fresh leaves; seeds germinate in about 14 days; self-sows. Give plants a good soil and partial shade.
VIRTUES   All good cooks appreciate chervil's survival through winter which makes fresh, delicately flavored leaves accessible. It is one of springtime's *fines herbes*, a favorite in French kitchens, and an alternate to parsley. Because it loses its aroma readily after air-drying it is futile to substitute dried chervil for fresh.

Aquilegia canadensis L. ♃△☠   Crowfoot family
   Wild columbine
Familiar in open or rocky woods, on slopes, rarely in bogs, especially common in calcareous soils; native from Canada and west to Minnesota, to Tennessee and Florida. An erect, loosely branched perennial to 2 ft. with numerous leaves divided 2–3 times and redivided. In April and May each red and yellow pendant flower hangs from a nodding stem, causing 5 nectar-bearing spurs to point upward, a never ceasing delight in a natural landscape.
CULTURE   Sow fresh seed outdoors on the soil surface. Moist cold winter temperatures are necessary to break dormancy for germination; or mix the seed with moist sand, place in a sealed container, and store in a refrigerator for 4–6 weeks before sowing indoors; self-sows. Divide crowns in the fall. Grows best in a light, sandy loam with light shade.
VIRTUES   Used by the Cherokee Indians as medicine; parts of the plant are poisonous, similar to monkshood. Nectar in the flower spurs is attractive to hummingbirds.

Aralia racemosa L. ♃△   Ginseng family
   American spikenard
Native in rich woods from Canada to Mississippi and Alabama and in the Southwest. A widely branched perennial to 6 ft. with a single leaf stalk and a spicy, aromatic root. Compound leaves to 2½ ft. long have 3–7 ovate, double toothed leaflets. An elongated, branched flower stalk bears greenish-white flowers in clusters in July and August. Pleasantly aromatic brown to purple berries are not edible.
CULTURE   Doubly dormant seed should be stratified as soon as ripe by storing

at room temperature for 3–5 months, then at 40 degrees F: for 3 months before sowing. Plant in shade or partial shade and rich soil.

VIRTUES   An aromatic extract used to flavor root beer was derived from stout roots and rhizomes. *A.naudicaulis*, wild sarsaparilla, also furnishes the extract. Both were used by American Indian tribes for food and medicine.

A.spinosa L. ▲
Hercules club, devil's walking stick
Native in upland and low woods, rich or thin, throughout the Southeast and northward. A little-branched tree to 30 ft. The trunk has strong spines, and pinnately compound leaves are 3 ft. long. Flowers and fruits are similar to spikenard.
CULTURE   Propagate as spikenard. Adapts to a broader habitat than spikenard.
VIRTUES   Cherokee Indians used pounded roots medicinally. Handling bark and roots causes a dermatitis with blisters for some people. Birds and animals prize ripe fruits.

Arisaema triphyllum (L.) Torr. ♃▲　　　　　　　　　　Arum family
Jack-in-the-pulpit
Common and native in rich, moist woods from Canada to Minnesota and south to Florida and Texas. A perennial to 2 ft. from a corm. Leaves on an 18 in. petiole are trilobed and at maturity in late spring expose a flower on a fleshy green to purple spadex (stalk or "Jack"), enclosed by a hooded striped purple, green, or white spathe (the "pulpit"). In early fall yellowed leaves fall back, and a bright cluster of scarlet berries catch the sun.
Culture   Sow seed outdoors in fall, or detach offshoots from a corm. The plant does best in rich soil of a naturally shaded woodland garden.
VIRTUES   Dried corms were used medicinally by the American Indian and were eaten as palatable food. Corms, as well as other parts of the plant, contain acrid crystals of calcium oxalate known to cause intense irritation and a burning sensation in the mouth.

Armoracia rusticana P. Gaertn., B. Mey. & Sherb. ♃　　　Mustard family
Horseradish
The common English name, "horseradish" means a coarse radish, to distinguish it from the not rough textured leaves of the edible radish; the same prefix is similarly used in the names, horsemint, horse chestnut, horse balm, and horse nettle, all having coarse leaves. The coarse-leaved, deep-rooted perennial herb is native to southeastern Europe and naturalized in the United States. Oblong, rippled, and dissected leaves to 15 in. long and 9 in. wide spring from a crown unrestrained; attacks by snails and chewing insects may leave the plant unsightly,

but deal no mortal blow. Small white flowers, borne on a terminal panicle, are not known to produce viable seed. The long fleshy root contains a strongly volatile, pungent oil quickly released by grating.

CULTURE   In a piece of root with a crown from the produce counter is the beginning of a plant that will never win a prize for good looks. Prepare a soil of sandy loam by removing all stones and other impediments to root growth and add limed compost. Set the root cutting vertically in the soil so the crown is at ground level. Keep moist. Dig roots for harvest in the spring or after the first frost.

VIRTUES   Though gardeners keep horseradish plants out of sight in the garden, the straight, thick, unblemished, not pithy root with a zesty, pungent oil to draw tears while grating has no peer. It is in the limelight of the kitchen prized by cooks. Blend it with grated apples or beets to subdue the fire; soften it with sour cream. Serve it with a piece of boiled beef or smoked tongue. Spread a mixture of sour cream and horseradish on toasted rye bread (minus the ubiquitous caraway with which it is in conflict) to relish and stave off hunger. As an excellent stimulant to the digestive organs it is a medicinal.

Artemisia spp.   Composite family
A large genus of species and cultivars kept in herb gardens by an impressive array of attributes. Deeply divided filigree leaves and near white foliage of *A. ludoviciana* var. *albula*, silver-king Artemisia, *A. arborescens*, or its hybrid with *A. absinthium*, 'Powis Castle', combined with purple-bronze perilla, *Iris pallida*, feverfew, or tricolored sage are superb combinations for decorative effect.

The white, silky foliage is excellent used as a wreath base to emphasize colors of adorning herbs; unlike many herbs in the dried state, leaves and stems do not crumble. One wishes not to be without *A. lactiflora*, white mugwort, a fragrant and white-flowered beauty, and a few more of the more ornamental than herbal members of the genus. Whether or not herbal properties can be ascribed, herb gardeners find it difficult to put aside enhancing plants. Artemisias entered below are included as verifiable herbs.

A. abrotanum L.
Southernwood, old-man
A branched subshrub to 3 ft., evergreen where temperatures do not go below o degrees F:; native to southern Europe and adventive in eastern United States. Finely dissected, fili-form, gray-green leaves have a strong lemony-camphor scent. In warm climates yellowish-white flowers in a loose panicle appear in late summer; rarely are they seen north of zone 7. *A. camphorata* is similar to

southernwood, but smaller with a camphor scent. A form called tree or tangerine southernwood grows to 6 ft. and is fruit-scented.

CULTURE   Take stem cuttings from new growth; divide roots in spring or fall; lax stems of *A. camphorata* will layer. Give southernwood full sun and a loose composted soil. In spring, before new growth starts on established plants, remove all dead material, trim to 6 in., and enjoy newly-formed thick, round clumps. After several years lift, divide, and reset to improve your stock.

VIRTUES   Leaves and stems, dried or fresh, discourage insect infestations in woolens. French closets are known for the aroma; no closet is without a tied bunch or bag of southernwood. Occasionally used as a flavoring in beverages. Medicinal references exist.

A. absinthium L. ♃
Wormwood, bitter wormwood, absinthe

An erect perennial to 4 ft. with hairy stems; native to Europe and naturalized in northeastern United States. All parts are intensely bitter and unforgettable if tasted. Silvery leaves are divided into oblong segments, and small yellow flowers arranged on a loose panicle bloom from July to September.

CULTURE   Propagate from soft or semi-woody cuttings; root divisions; seed requires light and germinates in about 10 days. Prefers full sun and would rather be kept dry than wet. When flowers turn dull, cut the tall stalks back to encourage new growth that takes the shape of an attractive arching clump.

VIRTUES   Used medicinally. A flavoring ingredient in Vermouth, a fortified wine used as an aperitif. Absinthe, a flavored spirit with a high percentage of alcohol and in which wormwood is the dominant ingredient, is prohibited in most countries of the world because it is habit-forming, causes delirium, hallucinations, and permanent mental deterioration. Wormwood's threefold destructive nature has, from ancient times, made it a symbol of hate. It is perhaps the bitterest herb known. An insecticide.

A. annua L. ☉
Sweet wormwood

An erect, symmetrically branched, sweet-scented annual to 10 ft. from Asia and eastern Europe; naturalized in waste places. Light green leaves to 4 in. long are feathery. Greenish flowers from July to September become yellow to golden when dry and nod in loose panicles. When flowers fade and stalks dry, the entire tree-like plant turns reddish-brown. Planted irregularly in a spacious corner, sweet wormwoods bring a spruce forest image into a garden through summer, fall, and winter.

CULTURE   Sow seeds outdoors in fall; seed germinates in 7–10 days indoors; self-sows. Thin seedlings to 3 ft. apart in full sun. An undemanding herb.

VIRTUES   Leaves have been used to flavor wines. Recent studies indicate possible valid use in treating malaria. Graceful in decorative arrangements though dried leaves and flowerheads shatter readily.

A. dracunculus L. var. *sativa* ♃
French tarragon, estragon

A rhizomatous perennial to 3 ft.; native to Siberia. Leaves are narrow, entire, pointed, and anise-flavored. Rarely flowers, and if so, does not produce viable seed. The plant from which French tarragon is derived and with which it is often confused is *A.dracunculus*, Russian tarragon; it is larger, flavorless, and produces viable seed.

CULTURE   Propagate from root divisions or stem cuttings. Genetically adapted to cold climates (can resist below 0° F: temperatures) and not warm ones; brief or absent low winter temperatures reduce a necessary winter dormancy period and cause tarragon to fail in zones 8–10. Starting with good-sized, vigorous plants and keeping them in a cool microclimate or in sphagnum-lined hanging baskets in partial shade is helpful. Frequent fertilizing and cutting back to ground level when 8 in. high until midsummer to stimulate new stem and root growth is worth the effort. Where temperatures are cool and in a sunny position shoots appear in early spring, and entangled roots, for which it was originally called "dragon," need dividing every second or third year to prevent dying out in the center. Give it good drainage.

VIRTUES   One of the most esteemed herbs in cooking; as one of the "fines herbes" it belongs in the spring egg and fish dishes. As the crop increases, it is stashed away in vinegar, dresses the salads, and flavors sauces. Though unimpressive in a garden, it is an aristocrat in the kitchen.

A. pontica L. ♃
Roman wormwood

Native in southeast Europe and naturalized in eastern North America. The often lax perennial, woody at the base, is of all the wormwoods, the most delicate in structure and aroma. Leaves to 2 in. long are gray-green and pinnately dissected. Whitish-yellow flowers are rarely seen.

CULTURE   Propagate from root divisions. Close clipping keeps it attractively erect and useful as a low edging in full sun.

VIRTUES   A flavoring in Vermouth used as an aperitif, and as such, often prescribed as a medicinal in central Europe.

A. vulgaris L. ♃
Mugwort

A naturalized weed in eastern United States from Eurasia. The rhizomatous perennial grows to 4 ft. and is slightly aromatic. Leaves to 4 in. long are dark-green above and grayish-white beneath, variably divided, and each segment pointed at the tip, not blunt. Reddish-brown flowers arranged in dense panicles bloom in late summer.

CULTURE   Divide roots or sow seed; self-sows. Grows in sun or partial shade; spreads to become invasive.

VIRTUES   Dried or fresh leaves are used in pork and goose dishes for flavoring and supposedly to make the fat more digestible. Bitter, aromatic leaves were used to flavor beer before the introduction of hops.

Asarum canadensis L. ♃ △   Birthwort family
Wild ginger

A rhizomatous, stemless perennial, 3–6 in. high; native in rich, moist woods, from New Brunswick south to North Carolina and Missouri. Deciduous leaves are heart-shaped, 2–7 in. across, with long petioles, and mostly in pairs. Curious brownish-purple single flowers are borne near the surface of the ground, quite hidden; blooms from April to June. Rhizomes have an odor and taste suggestive of ginger. An excellent herbal woodland groundcover.

CULTURE   Divide mature plants in fall when dormancy begins by cutting pieces of a rhizome with a pair of leaves attached; place to root 10 in. apart in shade and soil well-prepared with compost or rotted leaves to hold moisture. Sow seed outdoors when fresh.

VIRTUES   American Indian tribes used wild ginger for food, medicine, and flavoring. Early settlers found fresh or dried rhizomes an agreeable substitute for ginger.

Asclepias spp.   Milkweed family
Milkweeds

Where milkweeds take root and grow hosts of Monarch butterflies settle to lay eggs; milkweeds are the larval foodplants for the butterflies. Feeding on poisonous milkweeds the larvae acquire from the latex a toxin and transmit it to the adult butterfly; noxious and distasteful, birds learn to avoid the Monarch and the Viceroy butterfly which it closely resembles. All milkweeds have hoary, pointed, pod-like fruits that split along one side when mature and release a mass of silk-tasseled seeds.

A. incarnata L. ♃ **△**
Swamp milkweed
Native in marshes and moist meadows from Nova Scotia to Florida and Utah, more frequent northward; subsp. *pulchra* is predominant in the Carolinas to Florida. A rhizomatous, stout-stemmed, unbranched perennial to 5 ft. Leaves to 6 in. long are opposite and lance-shaped. Rose-purple flowers arranged in globose clusters bloom from July to September.
CULTURE   Sow seed indoors or outdoors as soon as collected; germinates in 5–10 days; or take root cuttings, positioning 2 in. sections vertically in moist sand. Plant in a sunny position; swamp milkweed can be expected to thrive in drier soil than its name suggests.
VIRTUES   Yields a stem fiber used by American Indian tribes who also used rhizomes medicinally.

A. syrica L. ♃ **△**
Milkweed
The native American milkweed was given the specific epithet *syriaca* by Linnaeus after being misinformed as to its origin. Found in meadows and along roadsides from Canada, south to Georgia and Oklahoma and southward at higher elevations. A rhizomatous, stout-stemmed, unbranched perennial, 3–6 ft. Opposite leaves 3–12 in. long are oblong to oval. Dull purple to white flowers in drooping umbellate clusters bloom from June to August. For a distinctly naturalized effect in its climatic range, follow the usual habit of milkweed by encouraging a colony along a roadside.
CULTURE   Similar to swamp milkweed.
VIRTUES   American Indian tribes used rhizomes medicinally and young shoots for food, both known to be toxic; fibers were used for bowstrings. Plumose silky hairs from seeds made soft pillows and in periods of scarcity replaced imported kapok, a buoyant filling for floats and life preservers. Very early milkweed naturalized in parts of Europe where it was introduced from eastern North America for fiber and as a food plant for bees.

A. tuberosum L. ♃ **△**
Butterfly weed, pleurisy root, milkweed
A perennial to 3 ft. from New England to N. Dakota, and more widely distributed south to Florida, Arizona and northern Mexico. Numerous rough and hairy stems from a woody rhizome may be ascending or decumbent, usually branching at the top. Sap is not milky as in other species of the genus. Alternate leaves to 4½ in. long are linear to oblong-ovate. Flowers in flat clusters vary from yellow to orange to red and bloom from June to August.

CULTURE   Sow seed according to directions for swamp milkweed. In warm climates chiggers besiege plants and discourage digging roots for cuttings. On the other side, the vegetative method insures plants identical in color to the parent. Because butterfly weed grows well in an ordinary well-drained soil with a sunny exposure, but will tolerate light shade, it offers opportunity for inter-planting with numbers of native herbs.
VIRTUES   Rhizomes were used medicinally.

Asplenium rhizophyllum L. ▲   Spleenwort family
Walking fern
A curious fern, native on limestone from Quebec southward to Georgia and Alabama. Evergreen fronds to 9 in. long are lance-shaped, entire, and taper to a taillike long thin tip that usually roots where it touches suitable moist soil to produce a new plantlet.
CULTURE   Propagate from spores or reset a plantlet. Grow in a rock or wild garden with lime conditions on moss-covered calcareous boulders or in lime-stone crevices.
VIRTUES   Used medicinally by the Cherokee Indians.

Atriplex hortensis L. var. *atrosanguinea* ⊙   Goosefoot family
Red orach, French spinach
An erect, branched annual to 6 ft., less in warm climates; of Asian origin. Arrow-shaped, entire leaves are dark red in the variety that offers striking ornamental color in a herb garden. Minute flowers bloom in late spring and turn purplish-red as seeds mature on clustered spikes.
CULTURE   For best results sow seed outdoors in fall to break dormancy and permit self-sowing. Transplant to a desired sunny position.
VIRTUES   Fresh leaves introduce an acetous flavor and color contrast in a salad of greens.

Atropa belladonna L. ♃☠   Nightshade family
Belladonna, deadly nightshade
The rhizomatous, much-branched perennial, 2–3 ft., with red sap is native in Eurasia and North Africa. Leaves to 6 in. long are ovate-pointed. Dull purple-brown, bell-shaped flowers to 1 in. long bloom in July and August. Berries are shiny, round, and black.
CULTURE   Sow seeds indoors in early spring to germinate in 4–6 weeks or divide roots. Germination inhibitors may be responsible for difficulty in germi-

nation which sometimes can be leached out by soaking seeds in water for long periods; soaking for 3–6 hours in vodka or petroleum ether is suggested by the seedsman, J. L. Hudson. Grow Belladonna in partial shade and a rich lime soil kept moist only while the plant is young.

VIRTUES   All parts of the plant are poisonous. Roots and leaves remain one of the main natural sources for the extraction of the alkaloids atropine, hyoscyamine, and scopolamine, all powerful drugs used medicinally. Atropine, because it induces prolonged dilation of the pupils, is an important drug used by the ophthalmologist. In a lighter vein, the specific epithet *belladonna* refers to an Italian or Spanish lady (donna) who used the property by putting distilled atropa water in her eyes; the large and lustrous dilated pupils may have impaired vision, but increased beauty according to Isabella's (bella) sixteenth century concepts.

Baptisia australis (L.) R.Br. ♃ △   Bean family
  Blue false wild-indigo
An American native found in dry thin woods, borders, and prairies of zone 7. Clean lines of the multi-stemmed perennial from 3–6 ft. contribute a refined quality in a garden of native herbs. Blue-green oblong leaves, 1–3 in. long, are ternate and alternate on the stems. Pealike indigo-blue flowers to 1 in. long appear on 8–12 in. spikes in late spring and through summer. Fruits look like over-inflated pea pods and turn charcoal gray. The entire plant blackens upon drying.

CULTURE   Sow seed indoors or outdoors in spring; seed nicked and soaked overnight in hot water germinates in 1–2 weeks. Divide the stout root of a mature plant by cutting pieces from the outer edges. Plant in a well-drained and limed soil with full sun; will tolerate partial shade and is drought resistant.

VIRTUES   Used medicinally by the Cherokee Indians.

B. tinctoria (L.) Venten. ♃ △
  Wild Indigo, horsefly
An erect, much branched perennial to 4 ft.; common in thin woods and dry places from Massachusetts to Florida. Ternate leaves are blue-green, obovate, and less than 1 in. long. Bright yellow flowers, smaller than the blue flowers of *B. australis* and blooming through the same period, are borne on numerous racemes terminating the many branches. Short pods blacken when mature.

CULTURE   As *B. australis*.

VIRTUES   Used medicinally and as a dye plant by the Cherokee Indians. Throughout the colonial period and into the late nineteenth century attempts were made to cultivate wild indigo as a substitute for true indigo, *Indigofera*.

Boehmeria nivea (L.) Gaud.-Beaup. ♃   Nettle family
   Ramie
The coarse, stiff, and hairy-stemmed dioecious perennial to 5 ft., native to China and Formosa, was introduced into the Southeast. Alternate leaves to 6 in. long are broadly ovate with a whitish underside and toothed. Small flowers are borne in axillary clusters, sessile or on a short spike.
CULTURE   Propagation is from seed or division. Prefers full sun, a warm humid climate and a rich, well-drained soil.
VIRTUES   Ramie has been cultivated from ancient time for its fiber harvested from the inner bark layer of stems; spun and woven it becomes a useful strong fabric. Cultivation continues as a minor crop in Florida, Louisiana, Texas, and California.

Borago officinalis L. ☉   Borage family
   Borage
A coarse, thick, and much branched annual to 2½ ft., wholly covered with prickly hairs; native to North Africa and the Mediterranean region, naturalized in most parts of Europe. Alternate, oblong, wrinkled leaves acquire a gray-green color as they become covered with hair. Flower buds arranged along a curved stalk in scorpioid manner are pink. They open into bright blue star-shaped flowers with black anthers conically converged in the center as a fine setting for a precious jewel; blooms from May to October. Fruits are four brownish-black nutlets.
CULTURE   Sow seed outdoors in late fall or early spring in a sunny position and an ordinary alkaline soil; self-sows. Self-sown volunteers are regularly stronger and more vigorous; will tolerate some shade.
VIRTUES   Young fresh leaves with a cucumber-like fragrance that cools were used in summer drinks, wines, and ciders for refreshment and stimulation. To-day herb gardeners are more apt to add a cube of ice with an imbedded borage flower to garnish a beverage and so remember medieval ways with herbs. Flowers continue to be candied.

Brassica hirta Moench ☉   Mustard family
   White mustard
An erect, branched annual to 4 ft. from the Mediterranean region and naturalized in North America to become widespread in fields and waste places. Leaves are deeply cleft. Four petaled and pedicelled yellow flowers on an unbranched stalk bloom from late spring through summer. The fruit, a silique, to 1½ in. long, spreads horizontally from the flower stalk, and contains pale yellow seeds in the swollen bristly base that ends in a flattened beak.

CULTURE   Plants come readily from seed sown and can become aggressive in full sun by self-sowing.

VIRTUES   The vast culinary use of ground mustard seed for a pungent condiment, whole seeds to season meats and vegetables, greens for salads, and extracted oil is as broad as mustard's medicinal use. Both are dated to place mustard as the most ancient herb used by peoples throughout the Eastern Hemisphere. Mustard's wide distribution has made it economically accessible to all people.

B. nigra (L.) W. D. J. Koch ⊙
Black mustard

A Eurasian and widespread naturalized weed. Distinguished from B. hirta by shorter and not bristly fruits, ½–¾ in. long, lying closely pressed to the stalk rather than spreading with black seeds about one half the size of white mustard seeds; plants are taller and flowers smaller.

CULTURE   As B. hirta.

VIRTUES   As B. hirta.

Brugmansia x candida Pers. [Datura x candida (Pers.) Saff.]; According to Hortus III, most material cultivated as Datura arborea is B. x candida. ☠

Nightshade family

Angel's-trumpet

A small tree, 10–20 ft.; native in Ecuador and widely grown in the tropics; winter hardy to zone 9. Oblong-elliptic leaves and calyx are pubescent and coarsely toothed. The impressive pendulous trumpet-shaped white flowers, 10–12 in. long, are very fragrant in the evening hours.

CULTURE   Sow seed in early spring indoors at 55°–65° F: or outdoors in zone 9–10; germination is slow, 2–6 weeks. If given full sun, ample space, and a deep rich soil, plants will bloom in their first summer. As tub plants in the more temperate zones they can be overwintered indoors.

VIRTUES   Angel's-trumpets are very poisonous; the violent narcotic alkaloids in the leaves and seeds were from ancient times used in cultural practices of Andean Indians and continue. The alkaloids are also used in medical treatments.

Buxus sempervirens L.   Box family
Common box, common boxwood

The compact, aromatic, evergreen shrub or tree, 6–15 ft., is native to southern Europe, North Africa, and western Asia. Except around the very warm Gulf area, common box does very well in the Southeast. The successful seventeenth century introduction and common use of box in southern gardens gives it unmatched priority among traditionally-minded southern gardeners. Dark green leaves to ½–⅔ in. long, lustrous and leathery, are ovate and opposite on the twig. Small yellow-green flowers in auxiliary clusters bloom in spring.

CULTURE Propagate from 3–5 in. cuttings; use softwood in spring and early summer; semi-hardwood in late summer and fall; place cuttings in the ground where there is protection from cold winds and the soil remains moist. Division, separation of sucker growth, and layering are also successful propagation methods. The very slow growth of seedlings discourages using seeds. Transplant young plants with a ball of soil around their roots. Box does well in sun or partial shade, requires a well-drained soil, and benefits from a fertilizer treatment (1 teaspoon of 5-10-10 for each square foot of canopy) in early spring. Keeping all dead leaves and branches (organic matter) out of box and treating the soil with lime tends to deter fungus infections and improves green leaf color. Spraying with very cold water pressure about once a week during hot, dry weather periods diminishes spider mite infestations. As shallow-rooted shrubs, avoid deep cultivation around their base, and use a non-decaying mulch during winter to prevent dehydration. Box responds well to shearing and shaping; severe pruning is best done in very early spring and light clipping at any time.

VIRTUES Allegedly in herb gardens as a medicinal plant, the assertions are dimmed by non-use and disregard since the seventeenth century. The hard and close-grained wood is used for wood engraving and musical instruments. Leaves yield a hazel dye.

B. sempervirens 'Suffruticosa'
Edging box, edging boxwood
The slow-growing dwarf box is used successfully as an edging plant when there is compatibility with the soil, climate, herbs enclosed by it, and gardener who keeps it properly clipped. At maturity it may reach 4 ft. and that may be after twenty or more years.

CULTURE As common box.
VIRTUES As common box.

For the collector many other valued cultivars of B. *sempervirens* are available. In the warm and humid Gulf area B. *microphylla* from Japan and B. *balearica* from the Balearic Islands, Sardinia, and Spain do better than B. *sempervirens*. For lack of herbal documentation purists may wish to exclude these two species.

Calamintha cretica (L.) Lam. ♃   Mint family
There is a comely quality in the densely gray-pubescent and intensely aromatic perennial that enjoys calcareous crevices of Crete and is hardy in our zone 7 Mediterranean herb collection. The spreading decumbent stems to 12 in. have

broadly-ovate ¼ in. long petioled leaves. Small white flowers in axillary clusters bloom through the summer.

CULTURE   A good many years ago a barely rooted cutting from Dorothy Bonitz flourished in the sun and prepared calcareous soil; in the mortar between red paving bricks the alkaline requirement of now self-sown progeny is satisfied and the effect is blessed, friendly informality.

VIRTUES   A minty-scented tea in Cretan ethno-medicine.

C. nepeta (L.) Savi. ♃
Common calamint

An aromatic, hairy and bushy perennial to 2 ft.; native to southern Europe and the Mediterranean region. Gray-pubescent, petioled leaves to ¾ in. long are broadly ovate. White or lilac catnip-like flowers in axillary clusters bloom through the summer.

CULTURE   Propagate from seed, division, or cuttings. Provide a limy soil, good drainage, and full sun.

VIRTUES   A tea in ethno-medicine.

Calendula officinalis L. ☉   Composite family
Pot-marigold, calendula

An erect, branched annual to 2 ft.; native to southern Europe and Mediterranean region. Clasping leaves are oblong. Flower heads from 1½–4 in. across are pale yellow to deep orange; blooms from May to August. Seeds are curved and rough.

CULTURE   Sow seed in fall or very early spring where it can grow in full sun in most any soil; where self-sown and grown uncontrolled, their scattered and cheerful faces induce relaxation. Deadhead promptly to extend the blooms.

VIRTUES   In times past a yellow dye from the petals flavored and colored custard dishes, baked goods, butter, and cheeses—"a poor man's saffron." Medicinal uses have been promulgated.

Callicarpa americana L. ▲   Verbena family
French mulberry, beautyberry

A native deciduous shrub, 4–6 ft., ranging from Virginia to Texas and the West Indies. It grows in moist, sandy, rocky woodlands. Opposite leaves, 4–6 in. long, are elliptic-ovate, sharply pointed, and toothed. Bluish flowers in June and July are small and clustered in the angles of leaves and stems. Striking and conspicuous violet fruits in crowded clusters on the stems ripen in September and persist after the leaves drop.

CULTURE   Propagate by division of the clump, by layering lower branches, and by softwood (root in 7 days) or hardwood cuttings; sow seed as soon as ripe.

Provide sun or partial shade and sufficient moisture. Pruning back encourages new growth on which flowers are borne.

VIRTUES According to Raymond L. Taylor in "Plants of Colonial Days," Alabama Indians used beautyberry for malaria and the Choctaws for dysentery.

Calycanthus floridus L. △ — Calycanthus family
Sweet shrub, Carolina allspice

A deciduous native shrub, 4–10 ft. high, distributed from Virginia to Florida. Leaves, 3–5 in. long, are opposite, ovate-lanceolate, entire, and aromatic when crushed. Terminal and solitary maroon flowers blooming in April and May are highly fragrant. Large brown seeds are borne in a closed, dry receptacle.

CULTURE Sow seed in fall, divide, or layer lower branches. Prefers an acid soil, partial shade of fertile woodlands, and sandy soil of stream banks.

VIRTUES Used medicinally by the Cherokee Indians. The perfume never ceases to be appreciated.

Capparis spinosa L. — Caper family
Caper bush

A spiny, sprawling shrub to 5 ft. growing in rocky, dry soil of the Mediterranean region. The slightly fleshy, alternate leaves are roundish; 4-petaled white to yellow flowers 2 in. across on long pedicels are solitary and nodding with stamens protruding beyond the corolla.

CULTURE Propagate from cuttings with 65°–75° F: bottom heat. Seed also requires warmth for germination; about 10% of fresh seed germinates in about 10 days and another 5–10% over the next month or two. Guard against seed drying out. Total germination percentages supply sufficient plants for a non-commercial herb gardener. Grow in full sun and along a south-facing wall for winter protection; replicate a Mediterranean alkaline, dry, rocky soil.

VIRTUES Pickled unopened flower buds contribute a piquant flavor to vinegars and sauces used to complement specific foods or counteract blandness.

Capsicum spp. ☉♃ — Nightshade family
Peppers

Although all species in the genus are perennials they are grown as annuals. All are native to tropical America, moved into the Old World only after Columbus reached the New World (where he hoped to find black pepper), and since then have thoroughly naturalized all over the world. Leaves of the much branched shrubby herbs that can grow to 30 in. are alternate, simple, ovate, entire. Whitish, sometimes tinged violet, axillary and pedicelled flowers are solitary or in small clusters. The many-seeded fleshy fruits ripen to red, orange, or yellow, and vary in size, shape, and pungency.

C. annum L.

Var. *annum* includes the Grossum Group represented by the bell pepper, green pepper, sweet pepper, and pimento whose mature fruits are red or yellow; large and fleshy; and mild in flavor. The Longum Group is represented by hot and pungent capsicum pepper, cayenne, chili pepper, long pepper, and red pepper with elongated, tapered red, yellow, or green fruits. Other groups in the variety enter the garden as ornamentals.

CULTURE   Sow seed barely covered indoors or outdoors when the ground is thoroughly warm; germinates in about 14 days. Fertilize to develop a good root system; pinch the growing tips to encourage branching. Because peppers are wind-pollinated and cross-fertilize easily, collected seed may not breed true.

VIRTUES   Fruits of the Grossum Group are used for seasoning and nutrition; fruits of the Longum Group are the source of the culinary chili powders; paprika's importance as a culinary seasoning is matched by the role it played in the vitamin C discovery by the Hungarian, Albert Szent-Gyorgi, Nobel prize winner for the work in 1937; other medicinal uses are also ascribed to Capsicum.

C. frutescens L.

Tabasco pepper

Similar to *C. annum*, but flowers, paired at the nodes, are greenish or yellowish-white. Fruits are smaller, pungent, incendiary. Seeds are $\frac{1}{16}$th–$\frac{1}{8}$th in. in diameter.

CULTURE   Similar to *C. annum*.

VIRTUES   Used in the production of hot sauces; in the United States plants are commercially grown in the Gulf States for the purpose.

Carthamus tinctorius L. ⊙   Composite family

Safflower, false saffron

An erect annual to 3 ft., branching at the top; so ancient as a cultigen in central Asia, the Mediterranean region, and central Europe that its native habitat can only be supposed to be Eurasia. Ovate to lanceolate leaves are spiny like a thistle and sessile. At maturity yellow florets of thistle-like flower heads, 1 in. across, turn red, and seeds on the conical heads become shiny white.

CULTURE   As a herb from arid regions scatter seed outdoors in a warm, lean, and dry soil with full sun as its permanent position; allow 5–10 days for germination; safflower resents being transplanted. Thin seedlings to 6 in. apart. High humidity can be ruinous. A cluster of colorful yellow to red safflowers makes a dazzling display in July and August.

VIRTUES   In ancient times the dried florets were an important source of dye for silk and linen, yielding yellow, orange, red, and shades of pink in accord with acids and alkalies used in the process. Origin of the common expression "red tape" is founded in the application of safflower dye to color tapes used to tie together legal documents. Equally ancient, particularly in India, is the use of the seed as a source of cooking oil. In our time the herb is cultivated on a large scale as a "polyunsaturated" oil-seed crop. The dried petals have long been used to color sauces and rice as a substitute for costly saffron. Young shoots are edible.

Carum carvi L. ☉   Parsley family
  Caraway
An erect biennial to 2 ft. with a thick overwintering tap root, like parsnip and Hamburg parsley of the same family; native to Europe and naturalized to weed status in North America. Leaves are carrot-like. On ends of flower stems that rise during the second growing season white to pinkish flowers are borne on flat umbels. Slender aromatic seeds are slightly curved and rough.
CULTURE In good garden soil sow seed in the fall where plants will mature and have full sun through the winter, light shade in the summer; self-sows. Thin seedlings to 10 in. apart. See Chapter 7 for harvesting seeds.
VIRTUES Dried seed or distilled essential oil from seed is an important flavoring for dark breads, English sweet cake, meats, cheeses, sauerkraut, and the basis of the liqueur, "kümmel." When sauerkraut is served at formal dinners in German communities a liqueur glass of "kümmel" is placed above the dinner plate; sips of the liqueur are considered an aid to digestion and dispel flatulence; in this guise the medicinal value of caraway is supported.

Catharanthus roseus (L.) G.Don. ☉ or ♃   Dogbane family
  [*Vinca rosea* L.]
  Madagascar periwinkle
An attractive erect perennial to 2 ft., treated as a garden annual; native from Madagascar to India. Oblong, glossy leaves are 1–2 in. long. Rose-pink to white tubular flowers are borne in leaf axils; many are marked at the center with a red or pinkish "eye." Cultivars give gardeners a broad choice of flower colors and plant sizes.
CULTURE Seed sown indoors germinates in 5–10 days; self-sows. Give periwinkle full sun and ordinary garden soil. Pinch tips to encourage branching.
VIRTUES During the last five decades medical researchers have taken a special interest in *Vinca rosea*, today *Catharanthus roseus*. Slowly, yet dramatically, a story unfolded that covered botanical, pharmacological, and old folk-medicine of all *Catharanthus* species to bring into medicine a lifesaving drug. Cognizant of alkaloids in the dogbane family from which a number of useful drugs have been

derived and to which the periwinkles belong, pharmacognosists studied old folk-medicine uses of all the species. The trail moved to the laboratory where a crystalline alkaloid called vincaleukoblastine, abbreviated to VLB, was isolated from leaves, stems, and roots of C. *roseus*, and it was found to have antitumor action. Individual cases differ, and cancer therapy focuses on many accepted methods of treatment; today VLB is among them. The chronicle is much abbreviated here.

Ceanothus americanus L. ▲   Buckthorn family
New Jersey tea
The native low shrub to 3½ ft. is found throughout the Southeast and north to Maine in mixed deciduous forests and along roadsides of forest margins. Leaves are alternate, ovate to lanceolate, toothed. Small whitish flowers in terminal clusters on long stalks bloom from May to July.
CULTURE   Propagate from terminal softwood cuttings of vigorously growing bushes; or layer. Grow in light to partial shade in ordinary soil. Difficult to transplant from the wild.
VIRTUES   Roots are used medicinally by a number of American Indian tribes; leaves were steeped for a tea by the Indians and white settlers during the American Revolution.

Centranthus ruber (L.) DC. ♃   Valerian family
Red valerian, Jupiter's beard
An erect Mediterranean perennial to 3 ft. with a sweet-scented vigorous root system; branching is from its base. Lanceolate leaves to 4 in. long are opposite. Small rose to red flowers, rarely white, are in dense clusters at ends of branches; each sweet-scented flower is marked by a spur at the base of the tubed corolla and has one protruding stamen. Blooms from late spring and into fall.
CULTURE   Seed sown indoors germinates in 5–10 days. Plant in an alkaline, dry soil about 10 in. apart. A good plant for the Mediterranean rock garden or in front of a stone wall from which it will spread.
VIRTUES   In Europe leaves are enjoyed in salad or cooked; in France roots are cooked for a soup. Seeds were used in ancient embalming.

Chamaemelum nobile (L.) All. ♃   Composite family
[*Anthemis nobilis*]
Roman chamomile
A branched, pleasantly fruit-scented perennial to 1 ft. with prostrate sterile shoots of tufted foliage; native to western Europe, the Azores, and North Africa.

Leaves of upright stalks are finely cut. Terminal, solitary flower heads have yellow flowers on a conical disc and white ray flowers; blooms throughout the summer. The frequent absence of ray flowers and presence of tufted foliage in basal rosettes growing from prostrate running stems distinguish Roman chamomile from the annual German chamomile; see *Matricaria recutita*.

CULTURE   When the weather is warm sow seed outdoors, tamp, and cover with a thin sprinkling of sharp sand; germinates in 12–14 days. Give chamomile a well-drained soil and full sun or light shade where summer temperatures are high. From zone 6 northward give winter protection.

VIRTUES   A tisane of dried flower heads has long been used as a restorative, calming tonic.

C. 'Treneague'

A non-flowering, creeping form of Roman chamomile with tufted foliage used for lawns and the "chamomile bench."

CULTURE   Propagate by dividing and resetting prostrate stems, each with a basal rosette. In late fall move one rosette of tufted foliage to a 14 in. clay saucer with soil and keep it indoors; by the time the weather warms again tufts will hang over the saucer's edge and move into nearby saucers. If the outdoor plants survived you have starters for friends. Carpets and paths of chamomile require careful hand weeding.

VIRTUES   To revive one's self after hours of physical work in the garden, walk barefooted on a path of chamomile, or sit on a chamomile bench with feet resting in a patch below. As wafts of the fruit-scented aroma move through the air you may recollect the soft, smooth sounding Spanish word "manzinella," little apple, for chamomile; let it roll off your tongue, sigh, and relax.

Chelone glabra L. ♃△   Figwort family
Turtlehead, snakehead, balmony

A perennial 3–4 feet of moist habitats in eastern North America, south to Georgia. Lanceolate leaves to 6 in. long are opposite. White, tinged with rose, 1 in. turtle-shaped flowers in a compact spike bloom from September to October.

CULTURE   Divide roots in spring or fall; sow seed in moist ground where the germinated plants can grow undisturbed to maturity. Prefers sun, but will tolerate partial shade.

VIRTUES   Cherokee Indians and Shaker communities have documented medicinal uses; the U.S. Pharmacopoeia finds no place for the Shaker's balmony.

Chenopodium ambrosioides L. ☉   Goosefoot family
Wormseed, Mexican tea, "epizote"
An erect, branched, aromatic annual to 3½ ft. from tropical America, naturalized
in North America, Europe, and Asia. Coarsely toothed leaves are 5 in. long; small,
yellow-green flowers clustered in thick spikes bloom in late summer.
CULTURE   Sow seed in fall to stratify in a sunny position with fertile soil;
self-sows.
VIRTUES   Cultivated for the essential oil of chenopodium in leaves and seeds
used as a fermifuge and insect repellent. Leaves used in a tea give off a strong
odor of the oil. In Mexican and Guatemalan cooking leaves are a seasoning.

C. botrys L. ☉
Jerusalem oak, ambrosia
An erect, gray-green annual to 2 ft., less in warm climates; native to Eurasia,
North Africa, and naturalized in North America. Hairy, glandular, viscid, pleas-
antly and intensely aromatic leaves are shaped like small oak leaves; in early
summer tiny light green blossoms wreath about the leaves in heavy clusters.
CULTURE   As *C. ambrosioides*.
VIRTUES   Bag dried material and hang in closets for the sweet scent and insect
repellent property. Graceful arches developing from the weight of flower clusters are useful in flower arranging on a wreath or in a vase, fresh or dry.

Chimaphila maculata (L.) Pursh. ♃ **Δ**   Heath family
Pipsissewa, spotted wintergreen
An evergreen perennial to 12 in., spreading by rhizomes; common in shaded
alluvial woods of eastern North America, south to Georgia into the c.p. and Alabama. Lanceolate, sharply toothed leaves, appearing whorled, are variegated
white (maculate) along the veins. 1-3 creamy-white fragrant flowers are borne
on each flower stalk from May to August.
CULTURE   Propagate by dividing rhizomes, and plant in a woodland situation.
VIRTUES   American Indian tribes used leaves and fruits medicinally; pharmaceutical investigations made the plant an official drug and formulated doses for
relieving urinary system disturbances.

Chrysanthemum balsamita ♃   Composite family
    var. *tanacetoides* (Boiss.) Boiss.ex W.Mill.
Costmary, alecost, Bible leaf
An aromatic, erect, almost evergreen perennial to 3 ft.; native to Europe and
western Asia. Grey-green leaves with glandular hairs release a spearmint scent

when touched, a good reason for keeping the 6–12 in., oblong, toothed leaves in Bibles not only for markers, but for retrieving and stroking during a tedious sermon. Basal, upward pointing leaves are petioled; smaller leaves along the 3 ft. high flowering stalks are sessile. In var. *tanacetoides* flowers are buttonlike yellow discs, white ray flowers are absent.

CULTURE   To propagate, divide a crown in fall or early spring; plant vigor is increased by resetting the divisions in fresh soil. Full sun is necessary for blooming, but partial shade is favored for taller growth in warm climates. Flower stalks may need staking.

VIRTUES   Dried leaves contribute a refreshing scent to potpourri. A herb class participant from northern Italy near the Swiss border regularly stirred a bruised costmary leaf through the heating butter when preparing an omelette to be filled with a preserved fruit. Alecost refers to its use as a flavoring in ale. As book markers Bible leaf ought never to be abandoned.

C. cineriifolium (Trevir.) Vis. ♃
Dalmatian pyrethrum

A glaucous perennial to 15 in. high; native to Yugoslavia. In July and August, from a crown with an attractive tuft of long, grey, finely divided leaves, long stems arise with 1½ in. across, bright white, daisylike heads; a showy plant.

CULTURE   Sow seed indoors; germinates in 7–10 days; blooms the second year. Give Pyrethrum full sun and an ordinary garden soil; avoid a moist and rich soil.

VIRTUES   Dried flower heads are the primary source of insecticidal pyrethrum; prolonged human contact with pyrethrum can cause skin irritation and other allergic symptoms. C. *coccineum* Willd., painted daisy, also contains pyrethrum. Plants are appreciated for pink, red, and white flowers, 3 in. across.

C. parthenium (L.) Bernh. ♃
Feverfew

An aromatic, erect, bushy, short-lived perennial to 2 ft. from southeastern Europe. Ovately divided leaves are crisp, yellow-tinged green. They are covered with clusters of daisylike flowers having flat, pale yellow discs and notched, white rays; blooms from June to September. Evergreen in mild winters. C. 'Selaginoides' has fernlike leaves; C. 'Aureum' are golden-yellow.

CULTURE   Sow seed outdoors in fall; self-sows. Divide clumps in spring or fall and reset. Grow feverfew in sun or partial shade in ordinary soil; a tolerant plant. Deadhead to keep flowers coming.

VIRTUES   The profusion of feverfew's medicinal uses penetrate ancient ethnomedicine; recent research has given the old-time herb a positive value that side effects in treatment negate.

Cimicifuga racemosa (L.) Nutt. ♃ Δ   Crowfoot family
Black cohosh, black snakeroot
An eastern American native, south to Georgia; common at the edge of rich
woods. The erect, rhizomatous perennial, 3–8 ft., has large leaves of 3 compound divisions, each further dissected. On leafless long, slender stems white
flowers in elongated wandlike racemes bloom from May to July. (See plate 18.)
CULTURE   Propagate from rhizome divisions made in fall. Plant in light shade
and a soil of moist humus.
VIRTUES   A favorite remedy among American Indian tribes; known to be toxic.

Cistus spp.   Rock rose family
Rock rose
If you keep unpruned, gnarled rosemarys, lavenders, and Santolinas in the herb
garden and can grasp with your mind's eye the sight of them growing under a
hot sun in an infertile soil on an open, arid, rocky site, then rock roses—low,
untidy and sprawling shrubs—add and brighten an evergreen or evergray Mediterranean picture. Aromatic, viscid, hairy leaves range from gray or pale green to
dark green, are opposite on the stem, frequently wrinkled and undulating. Tre-
mendous blossoms, bursting open in white, pink, rose, crimson, or purple, with
yellow centers, give you relieving sparks of color and gladness until early afternoon; by that time, like single roses, petals fall to the ground.
CULTURE   Sow seed indoors; germinates in 7–12 days. Stem cuttings under
glass to hold humidity may take 3–5 months to root. Layering is successful and
occurs in the garden when sprawling branches lie on the ground; plant a removed rooted branch or a rooted stem cutting to a garden position in spring,
not in autumn. Full sun exposure, a well-drained, slightly alkaline soil, and protection from winter winds are necessary. Rock roses may succumb after periods
of frost combined with frosty winds, but replacements grow quickly. Given the
proper soil, species benefit from warm Southeast temperatures.
VIRTUES   Several species exude a gum resin "ladanum" or "labdanum," a dark
brown, fragrant, bitter substance used in perfumery and medicine. It is collected
by dragging a rake with leather prongs through the shrubs in the heat of the day;
shepherds remove it from beards of goats where it adheres as they browse
through the bushes. Leaves are used in a tea.
    Two familiar species are:

C. incanus L. subsp. *creticus* (L.) Heyw.
Native to Greece and the Aegean region, the shrub grows to 3 ft. and is distinguished by oblong, gray-green, viscid leaves with ruffled margins. Rose-pink
crinkled flowers are 2½ in. across and bloom from May to June.

C. ladaniferus L.

A shrub to 5 ft. with very fragrant, sticky branches; native in the western Mediterranean region. Dark green leaves, sessile and lanceolate, are white-tomentose beneath and very viscid above. Solitary flowers to 3½ in. across are white with a purple blotch at the base of each petal. (See plate 19.)

Coccoloba uvifera (L.) L. △   Buckwheat family
Sea-grape, platterleaf

A tree to 20 ft. of subtropical and tropical beach margins in Florida, the Caribbean and into South America. Rounded leaves to 8 in. across are leathery and glossy. White flowers are borne in dense clusters to 10 in. long. Purple fruit.

CULTURE   Propagated from seed, cuttings of ripe wood, or layering. Prefers a rich, sandy soil on a sunny beach.

VIRTUES   Fruits make a tasty jelly. Fruits, roots, and bark have been used medicinally.

Colchicum autumnale L. ♃☠   Lily family
Autumn crocus, meadow saffron

A cormous perennial; native to Europe and North Africa. In early spring large, rich green leaves rise from an underground stem. In late August or September, when the leaves have disappeared, there is an unannounced appearance of single, slender stalks holding purple to white crocuslike flowers, with six yellow anthers on six stamens, not 3 as in the true crocuses. Cultivars of various flower colors and sizes are available.

CULTURE   Plant corms 2–3 in. deep; make divisions after the leaves have withered, and reset clumps under and around shrubs in a loamy soil for the moisture and partial shade.

VIRTUES   Dried corms and seeds contain the highly poisonous alkaloid colchicine which was used in ancient Egypt and into the 20th century in Europe and North America as a valid treatment for gout. The ability of colchicine to effect chromosome changes in nuclear and cell division has applications in the development of horticultural plant varieties as well as in medical research.

Conium maculatum L. ☉☠   Parsley family
Poison hemlock

A large branching biennial to 10 ft. with hollow, red-spotted stems and an unsavory aroma; native in Europe and naturalized in North America; rare in the c.p. Dark green leaves are pinnately compound with further finely cut segments. Small, white flowers in compound umbels bloom from June to August. Fruit (seed) is ovate, flat, and ribbed with oil glands. Very poisonous in all parts, fatal if eaten.

CULTURE   Sow seed outdoors in autumn in partial shade as background herbs; germination rate is high; self-sows to become weedy.

VIRTUES   Although Dioscorides' description of the plant in the first century is too general there are reasons to believe he gave the first written use of poison hemlock in medicine; Pliny the Elder with others followed. On the other side is its use by the Grecian State at Athens as a mode of execution for those condemned to death. The best description of the potion composed of fresh juice from the leaves and green seeds and its poisonous effect is found in Plato's "Phaedo," a story of the death of the Athenian philosopher Socrates in 399 B.C., available in most every library.

Conradina canescens (Torr. & A. Gray) A.Gray ▲   Mint family
Wild rosemary

An upright, evergreen, branched shrub to 2½ ft. with limited native distribution in barren, sandy soil and open pine woods of southern Alabama and northwest Florida. Gray-pubescent linear leaves to ¾ in. long make a dense foliage. Two-lipped, ¾ in. long pale violet flowers borne in upper leaf axils bloom from April to May. Winter-hardy to zone 7.

CULTURE   Propagate from stem cuttings; newly rooted cuttings resent a moist potting soil; water sparingly. A full sun and well-drained soil satisfies.

VIRTUES   The slight resemblance in appearance and aroma to rosemary led early settlers in Alabama to use it as such.

C. verticillata ▲
Cumberland rosemary

A prostrate, branched shrub growing along gravelly river banks of the Cumberland plateau in Kentucky and Tennessee. Dark green leaves like rosemary are slightly less than 1 in. long. Showy lavender-pink to white flowers more conspicuous than *C. canescens* bloom through the early summer. An endangered species.

CULTURE   Propagate from stem cuttings. Cumberland rosemary is not as resentful of water as wild rosemary and makes a fine evergreen groundcover in gravelly soil along the edge of a stream.

VIRTUES   It is said the early Cumberland settlers recognized the spreading mounds and foliage scent as rosemary and used it as a seasoning.

Coreopsis tinctoria Nutt. ⊙▲   Composite family
  Calliopsis
A native from central United States south to Louisiana, and introduced in the
Southeast to Georgia and Alabama. The erect, branched annual to 4 ft. with leaves
dissected into linear to lanceolate segments bears flower heads in solitary or
loose clusters; disc flowers are crimson-brown; ray flowers deep yellow with a
crimson-brown band at the base, blooms from late May to October.
CULTURE   In late summer sow seed outdoors in full sun or light shade where
plants are to grow; self-sows. Large basal rosettes develop during the autumn
and winter months. Though moisture is necessary for germination and during
the seedling stage, mature plants not only survive dry periods in ordinary garden
soil, but continue to give a blaze of bright flowers. Stems carrying abundant
blooms are inclined to slump; in a mixed planting with rigid-stemmed species
as cone flowers, the flaw is minimized, or follow the English gardeners and use
brushes for support.
VIRTUES   Dried flower heads yield a bright yellow, burnt orange, and brick
red dye.

Coriandrum sativum L. ⊙   Parsley family
  Coriander, Chinese parsley, "cilantro"
A strong-smelling erect annual, 1–3 ft.; native to southeastern Europe. Lower
leaves are broad; upper leaves threadlike. Small, pinkish-white flowers in
composite umbels are followed by round, white to yellowish brown seeds;
blooms in May and June.
CULTURE   By sowing at intervals from January to April in full sun and a well-
drained, slightly alkaline soil seeds can germinate in their preferred time, and a
good harvest of broad leaves, "cilantro," can be anticipated; as temperatures rise
coriander will concentrate on the production of flowers and seed. To encourage
"cilantro" water to keep the soil moist and cool. Harvest seeds when ripe and
before they drop; self-sows.
VIRTUES   Seeds have a pleasing aroma, suggestive of a combination of lemon
or orange peel and sage scents, and are used as seasoning in European and Mediterranean cuisines. "Cilantro" is associated with Chinese, Spanish, and Mexican
kitchens. Sprouted coriander seeds have the same flavor as "cilantro" and can
be substituted when leaves are unavailable; sprout seeds between pads of moist
paper toweling. Powdered seeds and essential oil extracts were formerly added
as flavors to disguise unpleasant potions in medicines.

Crocus sativus L. ♃   Iris family
  Saffron crocus
The floral parts (perianth) of perennial and cormous Mediterranean wild saffron
is 6-segmented and 1½–2 in. long, has 3 stamens with yellow anthers, and
a deep red stigma on a style. The cultivated form is a rich purple. Both bloom in
autumn. (Avoid confusing saffron crocus with poisonous Colchicum autumnale
which also blooms in autumn.) When the flowering period ends tufts of grasslike, dark green leaves rise from the corm.
CULTURE In July plant corms 3–4 in. deep and 4–6 in. apart in a well-drained
soil. Each year new corms form above the old ones causing new plants to be
pushed out of the soil. Remedy the problem by digging out corms after the
leaves die down, dry, store, and replant at the proper depth in July.
VIRTUES Red stigmas are harvested and yield the saffron aroma after drying to
flavor and color a large number of traditional dishes and baked goods; many
originated in the countries bordering the Mediterranean Sea where saffron is
native; after its successful introduction in Great Britain English golden saffron
bread and Cornish saffron buns came to the tea table. A dye yields a rich golden
color for cloth. Saffron's familiar odor formerly attached to the doctor's bag
made known its application in medicine. Not all climates and soils are favorable
for producing a product of distinct potency. Threads (stigmas) of unadulterated
saffron from Spain are best, costly, and used prudently.

Cuminum cyminum L. ☉   Parsley family
  Cumin
A tender, erect annual to 6 in. from the Mediterranean region. Leaves are thread-
like; compound thin umbels hold white to rose flowers followed by thin, aro-
matic seeds.
CULTURE Sow seed when the soil is warm in full sun. Harvest mature seeds
before they drop.
VIRTUES Seeds, many times blended with other herbs and spices, have con-
tributed an important seasoning from ancient time in North African, Middle East,
East Indian, and Mexican dishes. Similar to dill and caraway as a digestive aid.

Cymbopogon citratus (DC.ex Nees) Stapf. ♃   Grass family
  Lemon grass, fever grass
An aromatic, dense, clump-forming perennial grass; native in southern India and
Ceylon. Vertical form and graceful arching leaves to 3 ft. long and ½ in wide
tapering at both ends give it worth in a herb garden. The cultigen available in the
United States seldom flowers.

CULTURE   Propagate by division of the clump. Not winter hardy from zone 7 northward. In such case cut back leaves to 3 in. from the ground in the fall as your harvest, make divisions of the clump, and pot to keep indoors in good light through the winter; water sparingly to avoid root rot.
VIRTUES   Chopped fresh leaves season many southeast Asian dishes; used for a tea. The essential oil is distilled from the leaves for use in perfumery, cooking, and medicine. Cultivated in Florida for the commercial production of the essential oil.

Cyperus papyrus L. ♃   Sedge family
Papyrus, bullrush, paper plant
The papyrus of the ancients is native along banks and shores of quietly flowing water to 3 ft. deep in northern and tropical Africa. The perennial has a short rhizome from which thick, woody, triangular stems to 15 ft. rise. Leaves are reduced sheaths. Inconspicuous flower clusters in an umbel are surrounded by a plumage of threadlike rays, each 12–18 in. long.
CULTURE   Propagate from rhizome divisions. Keep the dramatic aquatic plant in a large container with openings at the side and bottom to hold the soggy soil, and submerge it in a pool of water exposed to full sun. Occasionally add a soluble fertilizer. Keep a papyrus indoors above zone 9 through the winter. Divide the rhizome as it outgrows its container.
VIRTUES   In ancient times stems, split into strips and pressed while wet, became papyrus paper rolls; the pith was eaten, men built boats of stems, and wood of the rhizomes was made into utensils.

Datura spp. ☠   Nightshade family
Common names for the "magical drugs," violently narcotic, hallucinatory, and poisonous, are thornapple, Jamestown weed (jimson weed), angel's-trumpet, Indian apple, devil's apple. Bizarre magic-medicinal rituals and cultural customs bind the plants, poisonous in all parts, to men, women, and children. Out of the past came confusing records about the origin of D. *stramonium*, thornapple. Found growing in waste places (often characteristic of introduced species) in the vicinity of Jamestown, Virginia suggested American origin; as one might expect, Jamestown or jimson weed became common names. Observed growing near homes of white settlers, American Indians called it "the white man's plant." Today Old World origin is accepted, and evidence points to world-wide distribution as the result of seed carried in earth put on ships for ballast from one country to another. Shrubs and trees called angel's-trumpet are native to South America; though formerly classed with *Datura* spp., they now belong to the genus

Brugmansia; see Brugmansia x candida. Annuals and short-lived perennials kept in herb gardens from Mexico and southwestern United States are Datura inoxia, sacred Datura or Indian apple, and its subsp. quinquescuspida; D. metel, horn-of-plenty, entered the garden from southwest China. All Daturas have alternate, ill-smelling leaves. Large funnel-form night flowers are solitary, borne in axils of branches, bloom from July to September. In the still of a hot summer night their haunting, evasive fragrance pervades the air and is unsettling. In the morning the flowers, lasting only one day, are wilted and scentless. The almost globoid fruits are prickly with spines.

CULTURE Seed sown indoors in cool climates in January or February, barely covered, and kept at 55°-60° F: germinates in 6–8 weeks; expect irregular germination; sow outdoors in spring when the soil is warm; self-sows from zone 7 southward. In a pot or in garden soil Daturas respond to full sun with rapid growth, blooming in one season. From zone 7 northward perennial species are moved indoors when winter comes. Daturas cannot escape attention in a herb garden where eyes more often than not focus on small flowers and the nose is pleased. Added descriptive statements for the species:

D. inoxia Mill. ⏀☠
Grows to 3 ft. Leaves are gray-green, ovate; flowers white or pink. Subsp. quinquescuspida (Torr.) A.S.Barcl., is more spreading, always perennial, widely used as an ornamental and incorrectly referred to as D. meteloides.

D. metel L. ☉☠
An annual to 5 ft. with ovate leaves. Flowers are white, yellow, and purple. Cultivars in various hues of color are available.

D. stramonium L. ☉☠
A much-branched annual to 5 ft. Leaves to 8 in. long are irregularly toothed and angled. Flowers to 5 in. long are white or violet-purple.

VIRTUES Since ancient times leaves and seeds have been used in religious rites, cultural customs, and in medicine for the poisonous alkaloidal drug, hyoscamine or scopolamine. An extract prepared from the seeds of Stramonium is used to reduce choking attacks of asthma. Pharmacognosists continue research among the Daturas.

Dianthus spp. ⏀   Pink family
Pinks, clove pinks, cottage pinks
In today's herb gardens perennial pinks are mostly hybrids and cultivars of Dianthus spp. They are derived from species native to dry, rocky, and calcareous

soils of the Mediterranean region, central Europe, and western Asia. Foremost as the ancestor of all modern pinks is D. x *allwoodii*, a hybrid between the matt-forming cottage pink, D. *plumarius* and the carnation, D. *caryophyllus*. Out of it, and from D. *deltoides*, D. *gratianopolitanus*, D. *plumarius*, and others, countless cultivars have come from which gardeners can select favorites. Stems of everbluish-gray plants vary in height from 2–15 in. and form compact clumps or lie prostrate. Paired leaves rising at more or less swollen nodes are slender. Solitary flowers have 5 fringed petals; an additional number of sepals below the petals are joined into a tube; petals are pink to white, and a number have darker pink or red circles near the eyes. The sweet clove fragrance is one of the invigorating, welcome notes of spring, blossoms appear in April and may continue into September.

CULTURE   Seed sown indoors germinates in 5 days. Because hybrids and cultivars may not produce viable seed nor breed true, reliance on vegetative propagation methods are preferred to preserve characteristics of a favorite pink. Root stem cuttings or divide clumps. Stems can be rooted outdoors by layering; spread sieved compost mixed with sharp sand over prostrate stems in the fall; in early spring cut away rooted stem portions, reset, and water. Pinks thrive in full sun, a slightly alkaline, well-drained soil, and warm temperatures. Humid situations are disliked. Plant pinks in a sloping rock garden, along a pathway, in a raised simulated stone trough to cascade over the side, or in a paved garden as situations tending to be more dry than wet.

VIRTUES   Whole flowers or petals were added to wine cups in place of costlier spice cloves. Dried petals are aromatic spice clove substitutes in potpourri or sachet and add color. D. *caryophyllus* is the carnation of the florist trade and is used in perfumery.

Dictamnus albus L. ♃   Rue family
Gas plant, fraxinella
A long-lived perennial to 3 ft. high, growing from a crown; native on sparse slopes from southern Europe to northern China. Aromatic leaves are shiny, dark green with 9–11 leaflets, each to 3 in. long. White to pink flowers are arranged along an unbranched, terminal stalk; blooms in zone 7 and northward from May to July.

CULTURE   Sow seed outdoors from ripe pods turned brown in the fall, and do not expect to move seedlings until the following year. Successful cultivation depends on giving gas plant a position well apart from other herbs in full sun or partial shade and garden soil. Once established, though difficult in warm climates, plants are known to live and thrive in an open lawn for more than two generations of the property's occupants, despite lawnmowers regularly striking plant stalks. We have dubbed gas plant "Greta Garbo" for its excellent performance distanced from other plants in a paved garden. After experiencing severe dermatitis upon contact, many individuals avoid the plant.

VIRTUES   Crushed leaves were used in a tea for a lemony fragrance. A fragrant essential oil emitted from leaves on warm, humid evenings releases an inflammable vapor that can be ignited. Applications are found in folk-medicine.

Digitalis spp. 💀   Pigwort family

By scientific interpretation of folklore and examination of early writings Digitalis, from leaves of foxglove, became a care-giver to the heart. The herbal connection began in remote time when people of central Europe lived in close association with the plant world, gathered plants for healing, and took note where they grew. Among them was Hieronymous Bock, a German herbalist. He is said to have assigned the genus name Digitalis from the Latin "digitus" for finger, drawn from the German common name "fingerhut," thimble. In his 1538 German herbal is a description of Digitalis. In England the blossom was seen as a gloved finger, hence foxglove; "fox" remains in question. The physician Leonhard Fuchs mentions Digitalis in his 1542 Latin herbal. Beginning in the thirteenth century, writings of physicians in Wales and England referred to the use of foxglove leaves, roots, and seeds in herbal mixtures. Versed in folklore and folk-medicine, a "wise" woman made a curious and serious Dr. William Withering (1741–1788) aware of a herbal mixture containing Digitalis leaves used to treat dropsy and other circulatory ailments. After careful investigations Dr. Withering could state in 1785: " . . . digitalis has the power over the motion of the heart, to a degree yet unobserved in any other medicine, . . ." After more than another century modern chemistry and pharmacology determined the cardiac principles (glycosides) and chemical molecular structures of Digitalis leaf extracts. As yet the synthesis of the cardiac drugs has eluded pharmaceutical chemists. The extraction and purification of the drugs from Digitalis leaves provide important standard, suitable, pharmaceutical dose forms. Three *Digitalis* spp. of a number from which extractions are prepared are given here as plants for the herb garden.

D. *lanata* F. Ehrh. ☉♃💀

Grecian foxglove

An erect biennial or perennial to 4 ft.; native in the Danube region and Greece. Dark green lanceolate leaves are in basal rosettes. Tall, narrow stalks bear grayish-white, violet-streaked flowers in dense racemes.

D. lutea L. ♃☠
Small yellow foxglove

An erect perennial to 3 ft.; native in southwestern and central Europe and north-western Africa. Leaves in rosettes are dark green, lanceolate. Pale yellow flowers, ⅜–1 in. long are arranged on a stalk in a one-sided raceme, an identifying characteristic that distinguishes it from the subsp. *australis* (Ten. Arcang.) from central and southern Italy, and which has ⅜–⅝ in. long pale flowers not one-sided on the raceme.

D. purpurea L. ⊙ or ♃☠
Common foxglove, purple foxglove

An erect, biennial or perennial to 4 ft., centered in southwestern Europe and naturalized through much of the European continent and the British Isles. Light green, ovate, and wrinkled leaves form a rosette. Stalks with pink to purple or white drooping, thimblelike flowers, spotted inside, to 3 in. long are on a one-sided raceme to 2 ft. long.

CULTURE   Seed sown indoors, uncovered and exposed to light, germinates in 10–20 days; self-sows. Transplant self-sown seedlings where you want them to grow in the fall; they will bloom the following year. All foxgloves prefer a fertile, well-drained soil and light shade; a not moist soil in thin woods with a slightly moist woodland atmosphere is ideal. As biennials or perennials flowering begins in the second year and usually extends from May to July. The smaller yellow foxgloves grouped in "sweeps" in front of taller purple foxgloves displays them as striking ornamentals in color and form. Progeny of purple foxgloves as a species of variable colors and forms can be expected to reproduce a miscellany of soft flower colors, variations in flower markings, and lengths of racemes. The narrow spires of modestly drooping soft-colored, singular racemes of flowers in a scattered or group planting through thin woods present an uncontrived woodland garden scene from a distance or close-up.

VIRTUES   All parts of *Digitalis* spp. are poisonous. Dried leaves of D. *lanata* are the source of the prescription drug, digoxin, more potent than Digitalis. D. *lutea* yields cardiac glycosides that are used, but not as widely as those of D. *lanata* or D. *purpurea*. Dried leaves of D. *purpurea* are the principal source of the drug, Digitalis.

Dryopteris cristata (L.) A. Gray ▲   Polypody family
Crested shield fern

A fern native in swamps, bogs, and marshes of the Northern Hemisphere, south to Virginia in eastern North America. Fronds (leaves) arise from a crown of the

rhizome. Sterile fronds are evergreen, spreading, and smaller than deciduous, upright, fertile fronds with round and kidney-shaped sori (reproductive bodies) covering the underside of the frond midway between the midrib and margin. CULTURE A divided rhizome with a crown can be planted anytime; keeping the crowns where new growth initiates at soil level is important as well as keeping the soil moist with plenty of water. A desirable fern for a moist and shady garden or woods.
VIRTUES The rhizomes, crowns, and basal portions of fronds are used medicinally in a tea or extract for the expulsion of tapeworms; irritant poisons causing coma, muscular weakness, and blindness come with the tea and extract and should only be used under strict medical supervision. A number of other *Dryopteris* spp. and fern genera in southeastern Asia, South Africa, South America, and Europe are similarly applied.

Echinacea purpurea (L.) Moench ♃ △   Composite family
Purple coneflower
The erect, coarse, long-lived perennial to 3 ft. is a native of the American prairie and occasionally appears east of the Mississippi River in thin woods and along roadsides from Kentucky to Georgia and Alabama. Alternate leaves are ovate-lanceolate and toothed. Coloring a sunny garden or natural landscape from June to September are flower heads to 4 in. across with rose-purple ray flowers slightly drooping and deep purple conical disc flowers.
CULTURE Sow seed indoors in early spring; germinates in 7–10 days; self-sows. Divide mature clumps in fall or spring. Coneflowers prefer full sun and a well-drained garden soil with added lime if very acidic (lower than pH 6); partial shade and untreated soil are tolerated; resistance to drought is in their genes.
VIRTUES Roots were used medicinally by Plains Indians. The entire plant is under close scrutiny as a medicinal in United States research laboratories and foreign countries.

Elettaria cardamomum (L.) Maton ♃   Ginger family
Cardamon
The perennial spice grows wild and is cultivated in the rain forests of southern India and Sri Lanka. From a seedling a crop of fruits are produced in 4 years. A large, fleshy rhizome gives rise to 7 ft. high stems sheathed by fragrant leaves to 2 ft. long and terminating in a point. Horizontal flowering stems to 2 ft. long bear small, yellowish with a violet lip flowers in small racemes. Smooth, ovoid, pale yellowish-gray fruits are about ⅜ in. long when dried and contain small, dark-brown, aromatic seeds in tight rows of the 3-celled fruit.

CULTURE   Propagated by rhizome divisions. As a tropical plant, cardamom is not winter-hardy from zone 8 northward and is kept as a pot plant, cut back, and taken indoors through the winter. Its sculptured effect is used to advantage in a tropical Florida herb and spice garden. Coming from the rain forest, cardamom wants a rich humus soil and partial shade.

VIRTUES   Pleasantly aromatic seeds are used in breads, cakes, confectionery, curries; flavors coffee in Arab countries and hot wine cups in Scandinavia. Because oil of seeds removed from fruits dissipates in a short time, cooks remove seeds and pound or grind them when required for use. Medicinally seeds are helpful in flatulence.

Ephedra distachya L.   Ephedra family
Joint fir ephedra
A scraggly, much-branched, almost prostrate shrub with jointed, slender green stems, and tiny scale leaves; native in southern Europe and northern Asia; hardy through zone 6. Dioecious; flowers not considered an attraction.

CULTURE   Propagate by division or layering. Prefers a dry, well-drained alkaline position in full sun.

VIRTUES   "Ma Huang," a species of Ephedra used medicinally in China for over 5000 years is among the earliest recorded medicinal plants. In 1923 Dr. K.K. Chen of Eli Lilly introduced the drug to Western medicine. *E. distachya*, as one of the sources of the drug ephedrine, is regularly kept in pharmacy school gardens and medicinal plant collections.

Equisetum hyemale L. ⌃Δ   Horsetail family
Horsetail, scouring rush
Perennial horsetails belong to a class of plants allied to the ferns and are found in wet places—stream banks and ditches along roadsides. *E. hyemale* is widely distributed in the Northern Hemisphere. Var. *affine* is native in eastern North America, south to Georgia and Alabama. From deeply buried rhizomes erect, evergreen, hollow-jointed stems rise, harsh textured by prominent siliceous ridges. Deciduous scalelike leaves are fused into a sheath at nodes. Terminal conelike reproductive bodies on stems appear from May to September.

CULTURE   Easily propagated by dividing rhizomes. Plant a division in ordinary moist soil at the margin of water in the wild or at the side of a garden pool under a full sun or in light shade from which it will spread unless held in a container.

VIRTUES   Wherever scouring rush was readily available a handful of the abrasive sandpapery stems were used to scour pans. The abrasive quality continues to be used to polish tools and reeds of wind instruments. Their special affinity to concentrate gold in solution makes them valuable indicators for miners as a test for the presence of gold in solution in soil water.

Eruca vesicaria subsp. *sativa* (Mill.) Thell. ☉   Mustard family
Rocket, roquette, rugala
A branching, erect annual to 2 ft. from the Mediterranean region. Leaves are irregularly lobed. Flowers to ¾ in. across have 4 cream colored petals with deep violet colored veins; blooms from May to July.
CULTURE   In early spring sow seed in fertile garden soil and repeat sowings at intervals through the growing season for a continuous supply of young, tasty leaves; self-sows. Or, cut back the fast-growing annual repeatedly to encourage new growth; leaves on old stems become unpleasantly strong-tasting. Grows in full sun or light shade.
VIRTUES   Cultivated for young leaves enjoyed in a salad of mixed spring greens dressed with oil and vinegar. Formerly grown in the Mideast and Europe for the oil-bearing seeds used medicinally and as a substitute for pepper.

Eryngium yuccifolium Michx. ♃ ▲   Parsley family
Rattlesnake-master, button snakeroot
A perennial to 3 ft. with a single, erect flowering stem; native along sandy road-sides and open woods throughout eastern United States. Rigid, basal leaves to 2 ft. long are linear, sufficiently yuccalike to assign the specific epithet, *yuccifolium*. Small, whitish-green flowers are borne terminally on the stem in tight globose umbels; the plant's inclusion in the parsley family is well-camouflaged by the compacted umbels; blooms in July and August.
CULTURE   To stratify sow seed outdoors as soon as ripe where soil can be kept moist, but not wet. Expect germination towards spring to be slow and irregular. When roots are well-formed transplant young plants with basal rosettes to a permanent sunny position in well-drained soil; additions of sharp sand improve drainage. The structurally bold form of rattlesnake-master introduces excellent contrast in a collection of sun-loving native herbs with broader and less rigid leaves.
VIRTUES   Roots were considered effective in treating snakebites and as an emetic by the Cherokees and other American Indian tribes living where the plant grows. *Eryngium* is from the Greek, to belch, from carminative properties assigned to European species used medicinally.

Euonymous americanus L. ▲☠   Spindle family
Strawberry bush, bursting heart
The deciduous shrub to 6 ft. has a rounded crown or is sparsely branched and
upright; native in mixed deciduous forests and low woodlands throughout
the Southeast. Thin leaves to 3 in. long on smooth green stems are opposite.
1–3 greenish-cream flowers about ½ in. across are borne on a terminal or axillary
stalk from May to June. Ripe fruits are warty, pinkish-red when ripe, and split to
expose scarlet seeds; in autumn a bright sun spotlights the superb colors from a
distance or nearby.
CULTURE   Seeds that drop to the ground scarify with winter temperature fluc-
tuations, germinate, and healthy seedlings can be positioned as group plantings
in partial shade of woodland or along its stream in late summer, fall, or the
following early spring. Nature's way is difficult to replicate. Growth is rapid in
fertile, moist, well-drained soil.
VIRTUES   Cherokee Indians prepared a root tea for medicinal use. Do not in-
gest fruit, seeds, or bark; they may be poisonous. Stems and root barks of
E. atropurpureus, wahoo, another native species, though documented as medicinal,
is considered dangerous and poisonous; similar documentation is applied to the
European spindle tree, *E. europaeus*; the winged spindle tree, *E. alatus*, native in
temperate eastern Asia, is applied in Chinese medicine.

Eupatorium spp. ♃▲   Composite family
Erect, clump-forming perennial species entered in the Descriptive Catalog are all
native to eastern North America, common in the mts. and pied., less frequent in
the c.p. Masses of flowers in large trusses at the tips of flowering stems color
roadsides, meadows, and stream borders from late summer to early fall. Walking
through thin woods gentler formed white flowered species brush legs. Common
names—Joe-pye-weed, boneset, and white snakeroot belong to the American
Indians and white settlers who borrowed them. In all respects they belong in a
native herb collection.
CULTURE   Seed sown outdoors in a seedbed from a fall collection for germination in the spring is more successful than sowing indoors. Move young plants
to sunny or lightly shaded positions. Ordinary moist to wet soil is favored and
watering is necessary to prevent young plants from drying out during dry periods. Plants reach maturity in the second year. Divide large clumps in fall. We
keep tall species on sunny banks and in a roadside ditch where they have moisture and wave in the wind for passers-by'. White flowered species prefer a moist,
shaded woods.

VIRTUES For a host of ailments American Indians of eastern North America boiled roots of *Eupatorium* spp. and drank the liquid as a medicinal tea. A tea of boneset, as the name implies, was thought beneficial for the healing of broken bones. Whistles were made for calling deer from boneset root fibers combined with roots of *Asclepias syricus*, milkweed.

E. *maculatum* L. ◭

Joe-pye-weed, queen-of-the-prairie

Inhabits moist meadows, marshes, and woodlands of the southeastern mts. Rigidly erect, solid stems to 8 ft. are purple-spotted. Lanceolate leaves are in whorls of 3–6. Purple flowers in 9–20 flowered heads are arranged in a flat-topped, dense and large inflorescence.

E. *purpureum* L. ◭

Joe-pye-weed, queen-of-the-meadow, gravel root

Inhabits the southeastern mts. and pied. Similar to E. *maculatum*, but has greenish, not purple-spotted stems, and a vanilla scent when bruised. Pale pink to light purple flowers in 5–7 flowered heads are arranged in an open, rounded inflorescence.

E. *perfoliatum* L. ◭

Boneset

Inhabits wet ground throughout the Southeast. An erect, solid stem to 5 ft. has opposite, lanceolate leaves, joined at the stem. White flowers in 10–40 flowered heads are arranged in a flat-topped inflorescence.

E. *rugosum* Houtt. ◭ ☠

White snakeroot

Inhabits rich, moderately moist woods; not common to the c.p. A solid stem to 5 ft. has opposite leaves, broadly ovate, and pointed at the tips. White flowers in 15–30 flowered heads are arranged in an irregularly-shaped inflorescence. A poison in the plant not only kills a grazing animal, but can be transmitted to people using milk or butter from the animal.

Foeniculum vulgare Mill. ☉ or ♃   Parsley family
  Fennel

An aromatic, erect perennial to 6 ft.; native to southern Europe and known to escape from gardens and naturalize along roadsides in warm climates. Branches from the base of shiny stalks bear large yellowish-green leaves that are pinnately divided into very fine linear, threadlike segments. Morning dew or a soft sum-

mer rain covers the leafy masses with a misty veil that beams of sunlight transform into a sparkling one. Upon evaporation the dry, airy plumage majestically
ascends into place. From July to September small golden flowers bloom in
wide, flat-topped umbels. Ribbed, slightly curved, $\frac{5}{16}$ in. long seeds have a
strong anise or licorice flavor. A bronze to purple-leaved fennel decoratively
shows off colors of the yellowish-green leaves and white flowers of feverfew
or the glossy leaves and rose-pink flowers of Madagascar periwinkle planted in
the foreground.

CULTURE   In spring sow seed in full sun where plants are to grow and will not
hide smaller herbs; seed germinates in about 10 days; thin out seedlings to 8 in.
apart; self-sows. Fennel grows rapidly in well-drained garden soil. From zone 6
northward treat fennel as an annual. Harvest seeds in October before they drop.
Bronze fennel is similarly cultivated; somewhat smaller, its position in the garden
is more flexible. If large, green larvae of sphinx moths called hornworms feeding
on fennel leaves disturb you, consider that attached to hornworms are numerous parasitic wasps and flies, their natural predators. Glove hands and remove
them to foliage away from the garden where predators will cause their demise
or squash them underfoot. Swallowtail butterflies flit and light on fennel leaves
to lay eggs; hatched caterpillars feed on leaves, but damage is not serious. The
large green, black, and yellow caterpillars may be offensive when you come
upon them unawares, but I have yet to meet the gardener who does not pause
to take delight in the fluttering performances of a swallowtail.

VIRTUES   Seeds and leaves contribute an anise to licorice flavor useful as a seasoning; leaf branches and stems flavor a grilled or baked fish; seeds are a requisite
for Italian sausages; crushed seeds are added to sauces, sweet cakes, breads, salad
dressings. A tea steeped with seeds is used medicinally as is the oil extracted
from the seeds of var. *dulce*. The oil is added to liqueurs for flavor.

Fragaria sp. ♃   Rose family
**Strawberry cultivars as 'Baron von Solemacher', 'Alexandria', 'Fraises
du Bois', 'Improved Rugen' are included here.**

The neat, mound-like perennial cultivars to 10 in. high without runners and ev-
erbearing are forms of F. *vesca*, a strawberry native in the Northern Hemisphere.
Glossy leaves are compound with 3 coarsely toothed leaflets. Dainty white flowers in loose clusters bloom from May to December. Fruits are slender, conical,
and of delicate flavor.

CULTURE   Seed sown outdoors in early spring on the soil surface germinates
in about 10 days; self-sows. Rhizomes with roots can easily be teased apart in the

spring, reset 8 in. apart, and watered. The cultivars thrive in all but heavy, wet clay soil. An enriched soil and considerable sunshine improves flavor and fruit production. In partial shade little attention is required for cultivation; watering is necessary in a hot, dry, and full sun situation. Winter-hardy and almost evergreen to zone 5, strawberry cultivars are suitable for attractive edgings.

VIRTUES   The fragrance of the strawberry cultivars closely resembles American wild strawberries enjoyed with a dollop of sweetened sour cream. Leaves are steeped for a pleasant, comforting tea.

Galium odoratum (L.) Scop. ♃   Madder family
Sweet woodruff, "Waldmeister"

A perennial of the woods; native in central Europe. From a creeping, slender rhizome erect stems rise to 10 in. In succession along the stems are whorls of 6–8 linear, dark-green leaves. In May stems are capped with clusters of small, starry, white flowers, and the surrounding air becomes deliciously fragrant.

CULTURE   Because seed germinates only when fresh and can be difficult, divisions of rhizomes is the preferred method of propagation. Grow sweet woodruff as a ground cover in soil of cool, moist, and shaded mixed woodland containing leaf mold. From zone 6 northward a winter mulch of hay is necessary. Without the litter of a woodland floor to keep a soil properly moist watering may be necessary. In a year's time a single plant can increase to become a large patch.

VIRTUES   The fragrance of coumarin present in the leaves is suggestive of new-mown hay and vanilla; the aroma is more intense in dried leaves and is retained for many years. Dried leaves steeped in Rhine wine contribute a distinctive coumarin fragrance to May wine or "Mai Bowle" traditionally enjoyed when celebrating the rites of spring in May; fresh strawberries are the traditional accompaniment. Coumarin's presence in plants is not uncommon. Its property as a blood thinner was discovered when cows grazing on sweet clover, *Melilotus offi-cinalis*, died of lethal hemorrhaging. After careful investigations and laboratory research coumarin came to the fore as an anticoagulant in medicine; on the other side, Warfarin was developed to give fatal doses of coumarin to rats and so reduce their populations. Dried sweet woodruff leaves are used in potpourri and for a pleasant tea.

G. verum L. ♃
Lady's bedstraw, yellow bedstraw

An erect or decumbent slender perennial to 3 ft. with creeping roots; native on dry slopes in Europe and Asia; slightly naturalized in North America. Small, linear leaves are in close whorls along the stems. Small, bright yellow flowers are densely massed in panicles from June to August.

CULTURE   Propagate by dividing creeping roots, reset in a prepared soil adjoining a rock or on a slope; water. Masses of wiry stems with crowded leaves and abundant bright yellow flowers are well-fitted spilling over a large rock's contours in full sun and ordinary garden soil.

VIRTUES   Having the property of curdling milk as rennet and yielding a yellow dye, leaves and stems were used in making cheese. "Lady's bedstraw" is derived from its use as a stuffing for her more comfortable bed. Roots yield a red dye.

Gaultheria procumbens L. **Δ**   Heath family
   Wintergreen, checkerberry, teaberry
A diminutive, prostrate, aromatic shrub of dry to moderately moist, acid, often sandy soils of eastern North America, south to Georgia and Alabama; rare in the pied. Look for wintergreen in a pine woods of sand and humus, beneath wild rhododendrons and kalmias. Stems are creeping. Ovate, evergreen, shiny leaves are 1–2 in. long. Solitary, nodding, pinkish or white flowers are urn-shaped and bloom from June to August. Fruit is a red berry.

CULTURE   Propagate in early spring or autumn by carefully cutting away from a colony a portion, reset in a prepared very acid soil mixed with leaf mold and sharp sand (as prepared for wild rhododendrons), and water thoroughly. Successful transplanting is dependent on the similarity of the soils and quality of filtered light of the two sites and keeping the transplant well-watered until it is established.

VIRTUES   American Indians were the first to use leaves of wintergreen, the original source of aromatic wintergreen oil, to treat pain and valid for the salicylic acid in its leaves. Dried leaves are used for a tea, marvelously fragrant blended with dried basswood or linden blossoms. Oil of wintergreen flavors tooth powders and pastes.

Geranium maculatum L. ♃**Δ**   Geranium family
   Wild Geranium, wild cranesbill
A rhizomatous perennial to 2 ft.; common in rich, moist woodland and wet meadows of eastern United States west to the Plain states; rarely in the c.p. Broad leaves are cut into 5–7 toothed segments. Lavender-rose, 5-petaled flowers, 1–1½ in. across, are borne on 5 in. long stalks rising from a rhizome; blooms from April to July. Mature fruit retains the style of the pistil which develops into a beaklike structure that gives the plant its common name, cranesbill.

CULTURE   Sow seed outdoors in a shaded seedbed. Expect slow and irregular germination as seeds require two seasons of alternating cold and warm temperatures to break dormancy; self-sows. Division of rhizomes in the fall is a good way to multiply plants. Grow wild geraniums in moist, rich soil of partially shaded woodland where fertilizer and moisture from the litter of the woodland floor encourages naturalization.

VIRTUES   American Indians and early settlers used powdered roots and extracts medicinally for astringent properties.

Gillenia trifoliata (L.) Moench. ♃▲   Rose family
Indian physic, bowman's root

A much-branched, slender-stemmed perennial to 3 ft.; common to woods of eastern United States, south to Georgia and Alabama in the mts. and upper pied. Alternate leaves are divided into 3 almost unstalked, lanceolate, unequal toothed leaflets. 5 linear, twisted flower petals are white with a reddish tinge; blooms from April to July.

CULTURE   Propagated by dividing roots in spring. Thrives and multiplies in rich woodland soil and partial shade.

VIRTUES   Powdered dry roots and root bark were used as an emetic by American Indians living where the plant grew. *G. stipulata*, American ipecuc, of soils in the lower pied. in Georgia, Alabama, Mississippi, and Louisiana was similarly used and is considered potentially toxic.

Hamamelis virginiana L. ▲   Witch hazel family
Common witch hazel

A deciduous shrub or small tree to 15 ft. of dry to moist woods and woodland margins throughout eastern United States and north into Canada. Leaves are alternate, obovate, and wavy-toothed. When golden-yellow leaves drop in October small yellow flowers bloom in tight clusters above the leaf scars; the leafless tree remains golden into December; flowers have 4 linear and twisted petals about ½ in. long. Fruits with 2 lustrous black seeds mature the following year.

CULTURE   Double dormancy of seeds that require repeated stratification and germinate after 2 years discourages most gardeners. Sucker growth at the base of shrubs or trees can be layered; soft wood cuttings root. Witch hazel does well in shaded woods and is tolerant of a great range of soils; though drought resistant, a moist soil is its first choice. In rich soil and full sun where forked branching is not impeded a lovely urn-shaped tree develops.

VIRTUES   Twigs, leaves, and bark yield an extract used by American Indians for astringent properties; settlers made further remedies. Pharmacists' alcoholic solution of the extract is still available as a refreshing astringent applied to skin surfaces. Settlers noted its likeness to European hazel used in England as divining rods and applied their supposition; the shrub became "witch hazel."

Hedeoma pulegioides (L.) Pers. ⊙▲   Mint family
   American pennyroyal

An aromatic, erect, branching, and hairy annual to 12 in. of woodlands and meadows in north central and eastern United States south to Georgia, Alabama, and Mississippi; rare in the c.p. Small leaves are elliptic. Small, bluish-lavender flowers are in few-flowered axillary clusters; blooms from July to September.

CULTURE   The best way to get American pennyroyal started in a garden of native herbs is to collect a rooted plant from a friend which might well have been tossed in the compost; self-sown plants are always in excess. Starting from seed at a new site may take at least two seasons before your nose leads you to a seedling; indoor and outdoor germination is irregular, and the procedure is best left to nature's way that does not fail. Once a growing plant matures, self-sown seedlings are found in sun or partial shade and ask for no special attention; you in turn will supply friends with starters for it is a charmer.

VIRTUES   American Indians and early settlers used infusions of American pennyroyal medicinally as Europeans applied English pennyroyal, *Mentha pulegium*. Inland fishermen, woodsmen, and gardeners of meadows and woodland place sprigs in their caps to repel gnats, mosquitoes, ticks, and fleas. Contact with the pure essential oil can cause dermititis.

Helichrysum angustifolium (Lam.) DC. ♃   Composite family
   Curry plant

An evergray, xerophytic, woody-based perennial to 2 ft. high with a curry aroma; native in the Mediterranean region. A dense covering of matted, short, wooly hairs gives a grayish-white appearance to stems and slender leaves to 1 in. long. Golden yellow flowers in heads are in flat-topped clusters to 2 in. across.

CULTURE   Propagate from stem cuttings in late summer or in early spring from plants wintered indoors for lack of reliable winter-hardiness from zone 8 northward. Run your fingers along the length of the stem to be inserted in the medium to rub off excess matted hairs that hold disease organisms; use a mixture of sharp sand and vermiculite or perlite to reduce water-holding capacity. Pot rooted cuttings in a well-drained potting soil with bonemeal and top with a thin covering of chopped oyster shells. Avoid over-watering. Keep contained in a raised sunny position.

VIRTUES   The fragrance of curry, a blend of herbs and spices, exists in leaves, but can hardly be considered a substitute; a questionable plant for a herb garden by the purist.

Heliotropium arborescens L. ♃   Borage family
  Heliotrope
A branching, hairy perennial to 4 ft.; native to Peru. Alternate leaves are elliptic.
Sweet, vanilla-scented flowers, purplish to white, are ¼ in. long and arranged in
2–4 in. dense clusters.
CULTURE   Seed germination is slow and irregular. As not winter-hardy from
zone 9 northward, plants are taken indoors through the winter; in such case
rooting stem cuttings from indoor plants is easy; rooting outdoors in warm climates is even simpler. Potted heliotropes trained as standards add ornament to
a garden; bringing fragrant flowers closer to the nose without bending pleases
visitors. A rooted cutting taken in the fall and grown through the winter is suitable material for a standard. Keep watch for whiteflies on indoor plants. Heliotrope takes full sun or light shade and needs a rich soil that holds moisture; in
tropical Florida a number of potted standards on a terrace garden or sunk into
the ground decorate and perfume the air throughout the year. Fertilize a potted
plant with a soluble fertilizer at half strength at three-week intervals.
VIRTUES   The sweet fragrance is used in perfumery.

Helleborus niger L. ♃☠   Crowfoot family
  Christmas rose
An evergreen, rhizomatous, low-growing perennial of moist, limestone soils and
shaded woods; native in Europe and well-adapted to cold temperatures. Dark
green, shining leaves are divided into wedge-shaped segments. White, saucer-
shaped flowers sometimes with a pinkish cast bloom in December.
CULTURE   Seed requires fluctuating winter temperatures for germination; since
most self-sow permit nature to take its course and position seedlings as you
discover them. To propagate by division, lift clumps and divide creeping rhizomes into pieces with 2–3 buds, reset with buds below the soil surface in partial
shade, and water thoroughly. Hellebores want a moist, well-drained garden soil
further enriched with compost and manure. From zone 6 northward give the
Christmas rose a sheltered location against a warm wall where a winter sun encourages winter or early spring bloom; provide a winter mulch.
VIRTUES   All parts of the plant are poisonous. Cardiac and narcotic glycosides
in rhizomes have been used medicinally. Similar properties exist in *H. foetidus*,
H. orientalis, and *H. viridis*, appreciated for different flower color, forms and leaf
patterns.

Hepatica americana (DC.) Ker-Gawl. ♃   Crowfoot family
   Round-lobed hepatica, liverleaf
A spring-flowering, low-growing perennial of rich woods in eastern United
States; chiefly on the pied. south to Georgia, Alabama, and Mississippi. Rounded,
three-lobed leaves, purplish beneath, are persistent through the winter. Single,
pinkish-blue flowers on hairy stalks bloom from early February to April before
new leaves appear. H. *acutiloba*, more frequent in the southeastern mts., has
pointed leaf lobes and whitish-pink flowers.
CULTURE   Best propagated by root divisions of mature plants after flowering.
Patches of hepatica tend to spread among rocks in rich, shaded woodland soil,
often dry, with the woodland litter all around.
VIRTUES   American Indians used a tea made of chopped leaves as a medicinal.
The popular demand of the leaves to treat liver ailments by European immi-
grants to the United States in the nineteenth century brings into question
whether the fanciful resemblance of the leaves to the liver reflected the influence
of the Doctrine of Signatures promulgated in Europe.

Hesperis matronalis L. ☉ or ♃   Mustard family
   Rocket, dame's rocket
An erect, branching biennial or perennial to 3 ft.; native in central and southern
Europe and naturalized in the United States. Leaves are lanceolate to 4 in. long.
Light purple flowers, ½ in. across, are borne on the top of tall stalks in dense
panicles; they emit a lovely sweet-violet fragrance in the evening; white and
double flower forms are available; blooms from early April to July.
CULTURE   Sow seed outdoors in late summer to bloom the following year; self-
sows. Seed sown indoors on the soil surface and exposed to light germinates in
6 days. An easy plant that flourishes in ordinary garden soil with full sun.
VIRTUES   Gather edible leaves before flowering for the sharp, piquant flavor.
Formerly used for the prevention of scurvy, as Vitamin C is used today.

Heucheria americana L. ♃ △   Saxifrage family
   Alumroot, rock geranium
A rhizomatous, evergreen, clump-forming perennial of dry, rocky woodlands in
eastern and north central United States, south to Georgia, Alabama, and Mississippi. Long-petioled, shallowly multi-lobed leaves, 2–5 in. across, are mottled
gray and green. After midsummer and through winter leaves develop an appreciated reddish-bronze cast. In May slender stalks to 2 ft. high bear tiny bell-
shaped greenish-white to pink flowers. Clumps massed among rocky outcroppings create a handsome evergreen woodland groundcover.

CULTURE   Sow seed indoors; mixing tiny seeds with sand gives better distribution and when wet holds seeds in place; water from beneath; germinates in 10–20 days; self-sows. Divide large clumps in early spring or fall. Alumroot belongs to the shaded, not moist rock garden environment; as a drought resistant plant, full sun and a rich, moist soil is tolerated, but vigorous appearing plants decline earlier than plants of the dry woods.

VIRTUES   Astringent property of alum in roots and leaves was applied medicinally by American Indians and early settlers.

Humulus lupulus L. ♃   Hemp family
Common hop, European hop
An aromatic, rhizomatous, rough, twining perennial vine reaching to 20 ft.; native to Eurasia, widely distributed in temperate climates, and naturalized in eastern United States south to Georgia. Stems and heart-shaped, 3–5 lobed, toothed leaves are bristly. As dioecious male and female flowers are on separate plants and bloom in July. Female flowers in spikes surrounded by rounded papery bracts that fit together like scales of a pine cone are 1¼ in. long. After drying aromatic resins contained in the cone can be shaken out.

CULTURE   Propagated from divisions of rhizomes; each piece should have at least two pairs of buds. In early spring plant 2 or 3 pieces together in a hill where plants are to grow, about 1 in. deep in a rich garden soil. Supply an arbor, trellis, or pole in full sun on which the rapidly growing vines can twine. Hop is a long-lived plant that thrives under extreme seasonal rises and drops in temperatures. During dry spells watering is required.

VIRTUES   An extract from resins in the flower cone is added in the fermentation process of brewing beer to help clarify and preserve, as well as adding a bitter flavor and aroma. Hops was valued medicinally as a tonic and soporific; pillows stuffed with dried flower cones were respected in the treatment of insomnia. In the spring tender, blanched shoots are prepared as asparagus, delicious in a soup or salad. Hop vines spread across an arbor block out a hot sun or screen a view.

Hydrangea arborescens L. ▲   Saxifrage family
Wild hydrangea, sevenbark
A much-branched shrub to 9 ft. among ledges and along stream banks of shaded moist woods in eastern United States, south to Georgia, Alabama, and Mississippi. Opposite leaves are ovate to 6 in., long, pointed, and toothed. At the tops of the current season's shoots creamy-white flowers bloom from May to July;

small fertile flowers are surrounded by showy sterile flowers to form a rounded cluster 2–6 in. across. "Sevenbark" is derived from the tendency of the smooth bark to peel, with each layer a different color.

CULTURE   Tiny fresh seed sown indoors germinates in about 4 weeks; likewise seed sown outdoors in moist soil. Separate sucker growth with roots from the shrub and reset in moist, well-drained soil. Divide shrub roots early in spring before growth starts. In full sun or partial shade blooms are heavier than in full shade. Pruning almost to the ground in the fall or early spring combined with a fertilizer feeding when soil is lean encourages production of strong new shoots and an abundance of flowers.

VIRTUES   Dried roots were used medicinally by Cherokee Indians; potential toxicity is now known to exist.

Hydrastis canadensis L. ♃ **△**   Crowfoot family
   Goldenseal
A rhizomatous, erect perennial to 12 in. of rich woods in eastern and north central United States, south to Georgia and Alabama. Two unequal sized leaves on a forked branch are rounded, heart-shaped at the base, 5–7 lobed, double-toothed. Solitary flowers lacking petals have numerous greenish-white stamens; blooms from April to May. Fruit resembles a large red raspberry.

CULTURE   Propagate by dividing a rhizome when goldenseal is flourishing in shaded, rich, moist soil of woodland litter. Over collection caused by an unrealistic aura assigned to goldenseal has made it rare; protection in woodland set aside for native herbs is appropriate in the interest of preservation. When a small specimen plant is surviving, give it protection; do not remove it.

VIRTUES   Thick yellow rhizomes were applied in treating a number of ailments by the American Indians and pioneers. A yellow dye from the rhizome was used for clothing and implements of Indian warfare.

Hyssopus officinalis L.   Mint family
   Hyssop, European hyssop
An almost evergreen branching subshrub to 2 ft. of southern Europe. Opposite dark-green leaves are small and lanceolate. Small two-lipped blue flowers with long perky blue stamens to match bloom on one side of a spike from June to September; pink and white flowering forms are available.

CULTURE   Seed sown indoors in early spring germinates in 4–7 days; self-sows. Non-woody stem cuttings root; clumps can be divided. In well-drained, alkaline garden soil hyssop grows and keeps a compact habit in sun or partial shade;

better suited to partial shade in warm climates. Prune mature plants back to the ground in spring. For an edging place plants 12 in. apart.

VIRTUES   A musky civet odor of the essential oil is employed in perfumery and in flavoring blended liqueurs. A bee plant. These and past acclaimed medicinal applications plus winter-hardiness in cold climates keep handsome hyssop in the herb garden where its successful use in clipped borders is unlikely to be relinquished.

Ilex spp.   Holly family
  Holly
Of four herbal species described, three are native in the Southeast, proudly and well-used as landscape plants. All are evergreen shrubs or trees with gray bark and alternate leaves. Usually dioecious, it is essential that both male and female plants are nearby to ensure the development of globose red, orange or yellow fruits.

I. *opaca* Ait. ∆
  American holly
Native in deciduous woods from eastern Massachusetts to the Southeast, and to about 5000 ft. elevation in the southern Appalachian mts. A medium to large tree; in gardens to 20 ft. Leaves are oval to elliptic, leathery, and spiny. Small flowers bloom from April to June. Red or orange fruits, rarely yellow, ripen in September and October. Winter-hardy to zone 6; many of the cultivars are less winter-hardy.

I. *vomitoria* Ait. ∆
  Yaupon, cassine
Native in maritime woods, pond margins, and swamps of the southeast c.p. into Louisiana and Texas. A small tree or large shrub. Shiny, leathery leaves are ovate and wavy-toothed. Flowers bloom from March to May. Red fruits, rarely yellow, ripen in October and November. Not all cultivars are winter-hardy to zone 6. Dwarf yaupon makes a fine native hedging or screening shrub for a herb garden; a herbal replacement for boxwood, difficult along the Gulf coast.

I. *cassine* L. ∆
  Dahoon
Native in wet woodland soils, bogs, and cypress ponds of the southeast c.p. A small tree or large shrub. Shiny, leathery leaves are elliptic to obovate. Flowers bloom in May and June. Red, occasionally yellow or orange, fruits ripen in October and November. Var. *myrtifolia* is distinguished by narrower leaves.

I. *paraguariensis* St. Hil.
Yerbe-mate, Paraguay tea
A tree to 20 ft.; native in Paraguay and adjacent Argentina and Brazil. Leathery leaves are elliptic to obovate, 1–5 in. long, coarsely toothed in the upper ⅔. Ripe fruit is deep red, less than ¼ in. in diameter. Grows in zone 10.

CULTURE   Seeds of *Ilex* spp. have double dormancy and individual species vary in required treatments. A simple method for sprouting slow germinating seeds can be applied. Place seeds in a polyethylene bag with moist sand or peat moss in fall, and place it in a safe container outdoors to undergo seasonal changes and be ready for sowing in the second spring. Softwood cuttings taken through mid-summer root in an outdoor cutting bed or cold frame by spring. Rooted cuttings should not be transplanted for 2 years. Plant in early spring or fall; water thoroughly and frequently during dry periods; as a whole hollies want an acid soil, rich in humus. American holly prefers partial shade, but tolerates full sun. Yaupon holly accepts a wide variety of conditions; sun to partial shade, wet to dry sites, indifference to pH, sandy or clay soil; and best of all, lends itself to shearing. Fertilize the slow-growing yaupon frequently with small amounts. Cassine is satisfied in an ordinary garden soil kept moist. Yerbe-mate requires a subtropical to tropical climate. In early spring and late fall scatter on the soil to the outer branches a fertilizer prepared for acid-loving broad-leaved evergreens, about a pound for each inch of trunk diameter. Mulches of leaf mold are effective. Prune at Christmas time to shape, and remove dead, injured or crowded branches. Damage from fungus diseases or insect attacks can be reduced by not planting species or varieties not adapted to the area and giving trees ample growing space. Infections on leaves may degrade appearance, but are usually not serious. Trees normally lose half their leaves in late April or May, just as new growth appears; old leaves turn yellow and spotted before dropping.

VIRTUES   Fresh bark and fruits of *I. opaca* were used by southeastern American Indians to treat intermittent fevers associated with common maladies. A decoction of boiled dried leaves used by Swedish settlers in New Jersey was reported by Peter Kalm. An infusion of green yaupon or Cassine leaves became the "black tea" that entered into American Indian ceremonies which only males were allowed to use as purifiers of the body; it induced vomiting; yaupon is a caffeine-containing plant, unique as a North American native. *I. paraguariensis* is cultivated in Paraguay as the source of dried leaves containing caffeine, widely used in a tea.

Illicium floridanum Ellis **∆**   Illicium family
Purple star-anise, Florida anisetree
An aromatic, broad-leaved evergreen shrub to about 10 ft.; native in the coastal Gulf area from Florida to Louisiana. An enormous interest in the plant began in

July, 1765 when a W. Clifton, Esq. (Justice of West Florida) sent a servant into the woods to collect specimens of remarkable trees and shrubs about Pensacola. Two specimens were sent to John Ellis, F.R.S. in London. The discovery was confirmed when John Bartram found Florida anisetree on banks of the St. John's River in eastern Florida. Henceforth seeds and plants were requested for ornamental quality by recognized English plantsmen, botanists, gardeners, and royal personages of the period. Herbists and spice collectors have adopted the species as a counterpart of I. *verum*, star-anise of southern China and northeastern Vietnam. Elliptic-lanceolate leaves when crushed emit an odor of spice and turpentine mixture. Nodding burgundy-colored flowers to 2 in. across have numerous narrow petals; blossoms in May. Wheel-shaped dried brown fruits hold a brown shiny seed in each boat-shaped ray around the central disc.

CULTURE   Propagated from semi-ripened soft wood cuttings in an outdoor bed. Position the shrub in full sun or partial shade and a rich, moist soil; growth rate is moderate; winter-hardy to zone 7.

VIRTUES   Oil of star-anise is used for carminative and stimulant properties in medicine and as a flavoring similar to anise seeds, but richer and sweeter. Crushed seeds or oil flavor sweet baked goods at Christmas, Asian cooking, and in tea. Manufacturers of liqueurs as anisette use the oil of star-anise as a more productive source than anise seed.

Inula helenium L. ♃   Composite family
  Elecampane, horseheal
A stately perennial to 6 ft. rising from a mucilaginous rhizome; native to Asia and naturalized in moist, shaded places of Europe, Japan, and North America, south to North Carolina. Enormous basal leaves to 18 in. long with 12 in. long petioles are elliptic, wooly beneath. Bright yellow daisy flowers, 3–4 in. across, bloom from June to August.

CULTURE   Sow seed outdoors in fall for seedlings in spring; self-sows. Divide rhizomes in spring or fall. Plant 2–3 feet apart in a moist garden soil, partially shaded; lovely near a patch of red bee balm.

VIRTUES   Antiseptic and tonic properties of the rhizome have been applied to respiratory ailments. Used for cutaneous diseases in veterinary medicine. Agreeable, aromatic and pungent rhizomes were used for flavoring the liqueur absinthe; or candied and eaten as a prophylactic.

Ipomoea tricolor Cav. ☉ or ♃   Morning-glory family
  Morning-glory
A stout twining perennial vine of tropical America treated as an annual in eastern United States, except in tropical Florida. Large rounded leaves are heart-shaped

at the base. Angled funnelform flowers are purplish-blue; various colors exist in cultivation; blooms from July to September.

CULTURE   Seed requires scarification; before sowing outdoors in spring when soil is warm, soak seed in tepid water overnight and nick lightly any that do not swell. In moist soil seeds usually germinate in 2 weeks. In full sun and garden soil vines have a rapid growth rate; overfertilizing produces heavy foliage and few flowers. Provide a support for the twiners; twining up a tall pole adds height in a garden of medium-sized herbs and utilizes less space than a trellis.

VIRTUES   Seeds were used as an hallucinogen in Aztec religious ceremonies and in medicine.

Iris cristata Ait. 24 Δ   Iris family
Crested dwarf iris

A spreading perennial from densely scaly rhizomes on the soil surface; native from Maryland south to Georgia, Alabama, and Mississippi on wooded slopes of the mts. and on the pied. Sword-shaped leaves to 8 in. long are slightly arched toward the tips. Flower sepals and petals are pale lilac with a white and yellow crest to 1¼ in. long on the sepals; dwarf Iris, I. *verna* has no crest, but a yellow to orange smooth band on the sepals; both bloom in April and May.

CULTURE   Divide rhizomes in late summer or fall by cutting runners connecting rhizomes; reset separated rhizomes even with a soil surface on a low mound of loosened soil; spread attached roots downwards at an outward slant; firm the soil and water thoroughly. Filtered light is preferred over full sun. Forced growth by over-fertilizing and over-watering creates a favorable environment for rot. Naturalized crested Iris in a gently sloping dryish rock garden or light woodland between large boulders remains in good health and is an effective, heavily blooming spring beauty.

VIRTUES   Cherokee Indians used rhizomes in a medicinal tea; blended with animal fats, an ointment was prepared for surface ailments.

Iris x germanica var. florentina (L.) Dykes 24
Orris, Florentine iris

A robust hybrid with a thick perennial rhizome, broadly sword-shaped leaves, and a branched flowering stem to 3 ft. bearing numerous flowers in April and May. Cultivation in southern Europe for centuries influenced naturalization in the Mediterranean region and made dim its original habitat. Large violet-scented flowers are nearly white, better described as "dead white," flushed with pale blue.

CULTURE   Florentine irises, even when growing well, need to be moved at the end of the fourth growing season; after the heat of midsummer has past divide rhizomes of old clumps. Cut away all soft spots and borer damage; leave rhizomes exposed a day to allow cuts to callus; trim leaf blades to 6 in.; set the top of a rhizome in the same manner as crested iris in sun or light shade. By spacing rhizomes among herbs in well-drained soil, and not indulged in heavy fertilizings nor large amounts of water, diseases common to irises are slow to spread. Forced growth in combination with mechanical injury to rhizomes, winter injury due to sudden changes of temperatures, or damage from iris borer are the usual causes of soft rot. Cut back spent flower stalks to prevent seed formation which weakens rhizomes. Except for Florida and the Gulf coast area, Florentine iris does well in eastern United States.

VIRTUES   Orris, from violet-scented rhizomes, is used dried and powdered as a fixative, the quality of holding fast fragrant volatile oils of other ingredients in a perfume, sachet, or potpourri. Medicinal use has much declined except in cosmetics.

I. pallida Lam., native to southern Tyrol, is another iris grown for orris. Fragrant lavender-blue flowers veined with brown-purple and a white beard tipped yellow distinguish it from Florentine iris. Lovely in front of an old Damask Rose by the good fortune that blooming usually coincides.

I. pseudacorus L. ♃
Yellow iris, yellow flag

A rhizomatous perennial with sword-shaped leaves and flower stalks from 3–5 feet tall. Large flowers are yellow. Of wet areas in western Europe and North Africa; naturalized in wet places in eastern United States south to North Carolina.

CULTURE   Remove seeds from ripe capsules collected in the wild or garden, and sow outdoors in a soil likely to remain moist; look for seedlings in the spring; self-sows. Like I. cristata the short brownish rhizomes are connected by slender runners; lift out a clump and separate runners in early fall; reset and water well. Keep yellow iris in sun at the edge of a stream, in a bog or pond, or near a downspout close to the house; in not over-fertilized soil healthy plants bear a quantity of flowers in May.

VIRTUES   Rhizomes were formerly used in medicine. A sweet-smelling powder made of dried rhizomes perfumed linens. Flowers yield a yellow dye, rhizomes a black one so powerful that it was used in place of galls in the making of ink.

Isates tinctoria L. ☉   Mustard family
Dyer's woad

An erect, branching biennial to 3 ft. with a basal rosette of oval leaves in the first year of growth; native to Europe. Smooth, clasping stem leaves are oblong to lanceolate. The bluish bloom of the leaves contributes a pleasing contrast when clusters of small yellow, 4-petaled flowers cover the top in April and May. Capturing attention are pendulous flat black seeds that remain on stems a long time and move with the slightest wind.

CULTURE Sow seed outdoors in late summer; self-sows. Transplant seedlings in spring while the soil is moist to a rich, well-drained soil with full sun in a cool climate; in a warm climate position plants to receive early morning sun and partial shade when temperatures rise.

VIRTUES From ancient time, long before East Indian indigo was introduced into Europe in the 16th century, woad was the European source of indigo to give a blue color. Julius Caesar's accounts of the Romans' entrance to Great Britain in about 51 B.C. tell of their meeting Picts, ancient people of Great Britain, whose bodies were stained with woad. Indigo is produced from a fermentation process of the leaves.

Juniperus virginiana L. **Δ**   Cypress family
  Red cedar

A medium-sized cone-bearing evergreen tree of well-drained soils and open areas. Widely distributed through middle and eastern United States; not at high elevations. Leaves are scalelike and overlapping. Mature seed cones are berrylike. Bark flakes off in narrow strips. *J. silicola*, southern red cedar, occurs in the c.p. of Florida, west into Mississippi, and north into North Carolina; it tends to have a rounded crown in contrast to the tapering top of *J. virginiana* and has smaller scale leaves.

CULTURE Self-sown seedlings from natural species are variable; they are common wherever red cedar or southern red cedar are growing and can be transplanted to a sunny position in well-drained soil. Cuttings of select cultivars taken with a heal in early winter after the last season's growth root outdoors in a prepared bed by early summer.

VIRTUES Pungent aromatic oil in the wood is a traditional fumigant used in insecticidal preparations, medicinal linaments, and perfumed soap. Boxes made of red cedar wood deter insects from infesting the contents. Red cedar wood is used in the manufacture of lead pencils and is valued for structural durability. Volatile oil of blue juniper berries from *J. communis*, distributed in the Northern Hemisphere, provides the important flavoring in alcoholic gin. Dried whole berries are used in stews and sauerkraut for a distinctive, subtle flavor and to reduce flatulence.

Laurus nobilis L.   Laurel family
   Laurel, bay
The aromatic evergreen tree with smooth olive-green bark is native to the Mediterranean region where it grows to 40 ft. and suckers freely at the base. In American gardens a height of 12 ft. is attained or kept by shearing. Alternate dark, glossy green leaves to 4 in. long ar elliptic to lanceolate. Small yellow flowers in clusters blooming in spring are only seen in subtropical gardens and are followed by one-seeded dark purple or black berries.
CULTURE   Propagate from cuttings of ripened wood; see Index. Rooting is slow, 6 weeks to 6 months. In zones 8–10, bays grow outdoors throughout the year in well-drained soil with plenty of sun; in spring keep the soil moist, give it light fertilizing; minimize watering and fertilizing through the summer. Sensitive to extreme cold winds a garden's outdoor bay may take a bruising to the above ground portion or be desiccated by high, but not cold winds. Cut away old wood; young shoots will come in late spring or early summer; root exposure to frost in the soil is seriously damaging. From zone 7 northward the traditional practice of removing sucker growth early and training a potted bay as a shaped standard facilitates moving and keeping it indoors through the winter. Size of a standard can be controlled by root pruning matched with tip pruning when roots crowd the pot's drainage opening. In addition to nutrients in potting soil, supplement with a feeding of ground bonemeal in spring, 1–2 tablespoons to a 14 in. pot, and a soluble fertilizer at six week intervals only after the bay is well-established; growth proceeds at a slow but steady rate. A potted standard bay tree makes a striking focal point in a herb garden. Red spider mites are known to attack growing tips under hot and dry situations; thin webs in growing tips usually indicate an infestation. Regular flushes of cold water during hot, dry periods before infestations arise is a simple control procedure.
VIRTUES   The symbol of accomplishment is conveyed by antiquity's wreath of laurel leaves used to crown the victor. Today a cook is more likely to receive a wreath from which the indispensable pungent leaf is drawn as a single seasoning for the stew pot, a soup, or fish in preparation; as one herb of a blend in the *bouquet garni*, fibrous leaves broken into pieces, difficult and unpleasant to swallow, are kept from being lost in the pot. Contrary to most seasoning herbs, remember that hand-picked fresh leaves from a bay tree impart more flavor than dried ones.

Lavandula spp.   Mint family
   Lavender
On arid Mediterranean calcareous slopes with lots of sunshine and high temperatures seas of gray clumps of feltish foliage with spikes of lavender flowers

are seen and smelled; lavenders are native in the well-drained, lean soil. Declared clean, comforting, and of the country, the mix of fragrances is in leaves, stalks, and flowers. Flower colors, leaf shapes, fragrances, and winter-hardiness among species, varieties, and cultivars vary in part or degree.

L. *angustifolia* subsp. *angustifolia* Jord. ex Billot
Lavender, English lavender

A subshrub to 3 ft. in the native habitat. The entire plant is covered with densely matted, short wooly hairs. Linear, gray-white leaves from ⅜–2 in. long are downy when young and become light green with maturity. Dense spikes to 2¼ in. long bear lavender to purple flowers, each ¼–½ in. long. The species is winter-hardy through zone 5. Common cultivars are 'Hidcote' with deep purple flowers; 'Munstead', an early bloomer with lavender flowers; 'Jean Davis' with pink flowers. A lavender devotee will accumulate many more; all have a sweet lavender scent. Blooms come to a peak in June and are sporadic until September. Natural hybridization of species with L. *angustifolia* is not uncommon. A natural hybrid noted for high quality perfume and the result of a cross with L. *latifolia* is L. x *intermedia*, lavandin, first described in 1828. Lavandin blooms from early mid-July, is available at herb nurseries, and from it many cultivars with excellent lavender perfume fragrance have been derived.

L. *dentata* L.
Toothed lavender

A subshrub from 1–3 ft. tall with a pleasant lavender-balsam fragrance. Narrow green leaves to 2 in. long have margins deeply cut into small rounded teeth. Flowers in spikes to 1½ in. long are lavender to light purple; pale pink conspicuous bracts, ovate to ⅝ in. long extend from the spike tip; blooms from July to September. Toothed lavender is not winter-hardy from zone 7 northward; a pleasure-giving winter houseplant. Var. *candicans* has larger leaves with a grayish cast when dense matts of wooly hairs cover young leaves.

L. *stoechas* L.
Spanish lavender, French lavender

A subshrub to 3 ft. tall with narrow, soft gray-green leaves covered on both surfaces with dense white, velvety hairs. Dark purple flowers are arranged in dense quadrangular spikes, ¾–1½ in. long; 2 large purple bracts to 2 in. long extending above the four-sided spike of dark flowers and a resinous-lavender scent make L. *stoechas* unusual and unmistakable. Blooms in early spring and repeatedly when spent spikes are removed from early May to September.

CULTURE   By prechilling fresh lavender seed 4 weeks in moist vermiculite germination percentages are much improved; seed germinates in 14–24 days, sometimes less. Hybrids and cultivars that are unlikely to breed true are propagated from two year old stem cuttings, division of clumps in spring, or by layering in the fall. L. *dentata*, without feltish stems, is propagated from stem cuttings by the regular method. Lavenders need a brilliant sun and its heat, a well-drained, calcareous soil, and a dry atmosphere to grow and bloom well. Where soil acidity decreases availability of calcium and micronutrients lime in some form is added to raise the pH. Treat feltish lavenders as xerophytes. Plant them on a dry rocky slope, not crowded, in raised beds, in a paved garden where water dries up quickly, and on mounds. Avoid organic mulches. A feeding of 1 teaspoon to 1 tablespoon of bonemeal around small to large plants in spring stimulates root growth; spoons of chopped egg shells keep soil sweet. Not all lavenders respond well to drastic cutting back; clipping back a previous year's grow is safe.

VIRTUES   The role of sweet-smelling and long-lasting flowers, leaves, and stems in lavender bundles, potpourri, sachets, and commercial production of essential oil in perfumery has never approached disuse. A hand of fresh or dried lavender stalks brought to a sickbed or tucked between linens helps to restore a low spirit; fingering bowls of dried flowers is pleasant. Folk-medicine used lavender salts as a stimulant; L. *stoechas*, a medicinal plant of antiquity, is still used in Islamic medicine. In a dried culinary herb blend of Provence lavender blossoms are an ingredient that lift a salad of greens dressed with olive oil, tarragon vinegar, and the blended herbs to a high pedestal of aromatic delight. Lavender blossoms supply nectar for a fine honey.

Levisticum officinale W.D.J. Koch ♃   Parsley family
   Lovage
A stout perennial to 6 ft. in temperate climates; native in southern Europe, occasionally escaped from gardens in north central and northeastern United States south to Virginia. All parts, from the thick, fleshy root, 5–6 in. long, to hollow stems, leaves, and seeds, are strongly aromatic of celery with a hint of angelica. Leaves to 2½ ft. on erect stalks rising from a crown are arranged in 3 segmented leaflets, coarsely toothed, suggestive of celery. In June and July flower stalks rise high, topped with large umbels of yellow flowers. Ripened seeds are elliptic and ribbed with oil glands.

CULTURE   Sow fresh seed outdoors where plants are to grow or transplant self-sown seedlings to a permanent position. Roots of mature plants that include a portion of the crown can be divided. A sunny position and a rich, well-drained soil applies to lovage culture in cool climates, from zone 7 northward. Look for a cool microclimate with partial shade in a warm climate. High temperatures in midsummer may not support flower stalks with seeds, but a harvest of leaves is worth the effort, and a second growth of leaves can start up in cooler autumn weather if the soil is moist and fertile. Flowers are attractive to aphids; dip supple flower stalks in soapy water to float them off. Not a herb to grow in Florida or the Gulf coast area.

VIRTUES Leaves, fresh or dried, are a superb seasoning, better than celery for soups and stews. A cook with credentials depends on lovage for the chicken stock. The rich flavor and potency of lovage compared to celery require restraint in amounts added to the pot and is best learned with experience. Roots, stems, and leaves were formerly used in folk-medicine.

Liatris spicata (L.) Willd. ♃ **△**   Composite family
  Blazing-star, button snakeroot, gay-feather
A stiffly erect perennial to 5 ft. of moist areas; native in eastern United States, south to Florida; var. *resinosa* is represented in the c.p. Narrow basal leaves to 12 in. long form a grasslike clump; stem leaves decrease in size upward. Many lavender to purple disc flowers are borne in a dense spike to 2½ ft. long; uniquely, flowers open from the top to the bottom of the spike; blooms from July to September.

CULTURE When seed is ripe in September or October, lay down spikes in an outdoor seedbed, cover with ½ in. of sieved compost, and look for seedlings in spring. Transplant seedlings to a permanent position in full sun where fertile soil is moist; in a less fertile and drier soil plants will be shorter, but equally attractive. Blazing-star is regularly cultivated as an ornamental. In a naturalized garden for native herbs it fits well with yellow flowers of sweet goldenrod, black-eyed Susan, and calliopsis.

VIRTUES Cherokee Indians and Shakers gave the root wide use as a medicinal.

Lindera benzoin (L.) Blume **△**   Laurel family
  Spicebush, Benjamin bush, allspice bush
A deciduous shrub, 6–15 ft. high, of moist woods in eastern North America; in the Southeast chiefly in the mts. and pied. The spicy aroma of a broken twig, a crushed leaf, or berry captivates. The winter aspect of naked, slender twigs is dressed and brightened as a dependable event in March with round clusters of small yellow flowers. Obovate leaves tapering at the base follow. In autumn leaves turn a clear golden yellow, and when they fall in September and October small, elliptic red berries shine.

CULTURE   To propagate from seed do not let it dry out; break dormancy by stratifying seed as soon as ripe at 40°F: in the refrigerator for 4 months; sow outdoors in a moist seedbed and watch for seedlings. Softwood cuttings can be rooted. In rich, moist soil and partial shade spicebush grows rapidly.

VIRTUES   A decoction of the fragrant bark, twigs, or fruit was used medicinally by American Indians. Powdered, dried berries were used as an allspice seasoning substitute during the Revolutionary period. Leaves were used as a tea substitute during the War between the States.

Magnolia virginiana L. **Δ**   Magnolia family
  Sweet bay, swamp magnolia

A tree of low ground and swamps where water may stand during a rainy season. Sweet bay can reach a height of 60 ft. in the South, but grows as a multi-stemmed shrub or medium-sized tree elsewhere; native from Massachusetts to Florida, gradually extending inland in the southeast pied. Fully evergreen south to semi-evergreen and deciduous further north; var. *australis* is more nearly evergreen northward. Lustrous leaves to 5 in. long are elliptic with a silvery lower surface that creates an impressive flashing light among wind-moved blades. From May to July fragrant creamy-white, cup-shaped flowers to 3 in. across make a display. Seeds are in a small red conelike fruit.

CULTURE   Ripe seed, fresh and cleaned, sown in the fall in a moist bed can be expected to germinate in spring; protect seedlings and do not transplant for 2 years; then give them a permanent position; repeated transplanting retards growth. Layer 1–2 year old basal shoots in spring; allow two seasons for well-rooted branches. Sweet bay responds favorably to a wet, fertile, acid soil with a great deal of humus and full sun or partial shade.

VIRTUES   A decoction of the aromatic bark and fruits and a leaf tea were used medicinally by American Indians. Though recognized as the finest scented flower of American magnolias, the cool, fruity, and sweet perfume causes a physical oppression in the chest and dizziness, a not uncommon phenomenon among persons sensitive to strongly odorous flowers.

Marrubium vulgare L. **♃**   Mint family
  Common horehound

Horehound is a bitter herb. The erect perennial, 18–30 in. high, is a native of dry slopes and waste ground in central Asia and the Mediterranean region; occasionally escaped from United States rural gardens southward into the pied. and mts. to Alabama. White-wooly hairs cover stems and opposite, round-ovate, toothed, wrinkled leaves to give the entire plant a gray-green color. Small white flowers arranged in whorls bloom from May to September. M. incanum with downy gray-white to silvery leaves enters the garden for ornamental effect; difficult to maintain in a humid climate.

CULTURE   Seed sown indoors germinates in 7–10 days; after 1 year germination percentages drop rapidly. Propagate 2-year old plants from root divisions. Give horehound a well-drained garden soil and full sun; avoid over-fertilizing and over-watering the borderline xerophyte. Contrast gray-green stalks and rounded leaves of horehound with bronze-red stalks and arrow-shaped leaves of red orach.

VIRTUES   A cough syrup has been made of an infusion of dried bitter horehound leaves and sugar. The familiar bitter-sweet lozenge of folk-medicine is prepared by boiling fresh leaves in water until the bitter principle is extracted and reboiling the strained infusion with sugar until the syrup hardens when poured into a pan.

Matricaria recutita L. ☉   Composite family
   Chamomile, German chamomile
A fruity, sweet-scented, branched annual to 2 ft. high from Europe and western Asia. Leaves are finely dissected into linear segments. White ray flowers are drooping; yellow disc flowers are on a conical head; blooms from May to July. Not to be confused with M. matricarioides, pineapple weed.

CULTURE   Sow seed outdoors in early spring; thereafter, if not all flowers are harvested, abundant self-sown seedlings are identified each spring. A sunny position, garden soil, and spring rains bring chamomile to maturity. Snip off and dry enough blooms for post-theater evening cups of tea with a friend.

VIRTUES   Traditional and occasional cups of fragrant chamomile tea are acknowledged more beneficial than harmful. Has been used in a rinse for blond hair.

Melilotus officinalis (L.) Pall. ☉ or ☉   Bean family
   Yellow sweet clover
A sweet-scented, erect, much branched annual or biennial to 4 ft.; widely naturalized from Eurasia along roadsides in North America with working bees taking copious nectar from the flowers. Alternate leaves are divided into 3 small, ovate leaflets. Small yellow peaflowers are arranged in spikelike racemes to 4½ in. long; blooms from June to September. Seeds are in pods. M. alba, a white flowering sweet clover, has similar characteristics.

CULTURE   Seed sown indoors germinates in 3–5 days; self-sows. Under temperate climatic conditions in a garden or along roadsides with full sun and ordinary soil sweet clover grows and thrives.

VIRTUES   The fragrance of coumarin in the leaves, more distinct when leaves are dried, is preserved in a paste made from curd and dried leaves pressed into molds by the Swiss to become a hard cheese, sapsago; grated and blended with butter the pronounced flavor is welcome on a piece of crusty bread or as a base for a white sauce used to dress a cooked vegetable. Dried leaves supply scent to snuff and tobacco. Nectar in the flowers supplies a delicately scented honey.

Melissa officinalis L. ♃   Mint family
   Lemon balm
A bushy perennial to 2 ft. high of southern Europe and Asia; occasionally found escaped from gardens in eastern United States. The most common of lemon-scented herbs has hairy, ovate, round-toothed leaves to 3 in. long. Small, nearly white to pink flowers arranged in whorls in the axils of opposite leaves bloom from May to September.

CULTURE   Sow seed outdoors in fall on the soil surface and let winter moisture and temperatures prepare the seed for optimum germination conditions in spring; self-sows. Transplant 2 in. seedlings to a permanent position. In spring cut runners that connect young rosettes of a clump, reset rosettes with roots 15 in. apart, water. In well-drained garden soil growth is rapid; cut back tall, leggy growth to encourage fresh, new growth. In an infertile, dry, alkaline soil the lemon oil scent is more intense. Lemon balm thrives in sun or partial shade, the latter preferred in warm climates. Lemon balm is difficult in warm climates of zones 9–10; but the superb lemon aroma of a lemon-scented verbena is an enviable replacement, coveted by northern herb gardeners who must take the large shrub indoors in winter. A golden variegated form of lemon balm has a visually distinguished aspect when leaves are forthcoming in spring. Seedlings of the form do not carry the trait, and in most environments it is rarely carried through the entire season.

VIRTUES   A tea prepared from lemon-scented fresh or dried leaves has been used in folk-medicine. Dried leaves were applied to wounds as surgical dressings to ward of infections. Lemon-balm oil is a flavoring in liqueurs. A handful of fresh leaves rubbed over scratched furniture corrects the blemishes, polishes, and benefits the wood. Honey bees are attracted to lemon balm blossoms for nectar. As potpourri material, the scent of dried leaves is not lasting.

Mentha spp. ♃   Mint family

The perennial, uninhibited and interbreeding aromatic mints of herb gardens are for the most part of European, Asian, and North African origin. Given a rich moist soil, or a poor one, a brash hybrid mint succeeds. Marvelously adapted to spreading by underground and surface stolons or runners, a hybrid mint can reach into a patch of another hybrid species; successful interbreeding produces a good percentage of fertile seeds and resulting progeny with an essential oil usually inferior to parent plants. Some hybrids are quite sterile and never set seed. Most hybrids are variable in their characteristics. Adaptability for survival is in their genes. Despite an imperious habit specific hybrids as peppermint or bergamot mint created in nature are cherished for distinct and high quality essential oils.

CULTURE   To maintain identity hybrids, varieties, and cultivars are propagated from stem cuttings, by dividing roots and runners, or by layering stems. M. *Pulegium*, English pennyroyal, and M. *Requienii*, Corsican mint are uniform species and come true from seed; sow seed indoors or out doors in spring; or propagate vegetatively. Both prefer a lightly shaded position while the hybrids do well in sun or partial shade. Mints thrive in summer climates that are fairly warm and moist and in a rich, moist soil; soil and climate have an important influence upon the quality of a mint oil. M. *suaveolens*, apple mint, likes a dry spot. Mints exhaust a soil in 3–4 years and rotating is advised. M. *Pulegium* requires winter protection from zone 6 northward; M. *Requienii* is not reliably winter-hardy from zone 7 northward; a scoop from a narrow trowel transferred to a saucer with potting soil becomes 10 in. in diameter indoors through the winter. Keep invasive mints restricted in above ground containers; plant in ground where natural obstructions or arranged impediments hinder unwelcome spreading. Eight Mentha spp. are entered in the Descriptive Catalog as well-fitted to herb gardens. A collector will want more.

M. *arvensis* var. *piperescens* Malinv.

Japanese mint

A freely branching, hairy plant to 3 ft., variable in odor, vigor, leaf shape, and resistance to mildew. Not winter-hardy from zone 5 northward. Lilac to white flowers are in globular whorls of leaf axils; blooms from June to September.

VIRTUES   An important source of menthol, the distinctive oil in peppermint oil used in medicine. Has been grown commercially in North Carolina and Michigan.

M. x gentilis L.
Red mint, Scotch mint
A small sweet-scented, spearmintlike mint with erect red-tinged stems to 1½ ft. high; naturalized in North America from Canada to Georgia; the result of a cross between M. arvensis and M. spicata. Leaves are variable in form. The cultivar 'Goldenapple mint' is a variegated mutant with a fruity aroma and leaves marked yellow or ivory.

VIRTUES   Commercially cultivated for the production of spearmint oil.

M. x piperita L.
Peppermint
The erect, branching, not hairy mint to 3 ft., often purple-tinged, is a natural hybrid of M. aquatica and a M. spicata variety. Its strong peppermint odor that can clear nostrils is identifying. Dark green leaves are lanceolate to 2-1/2 in. long, petioled, and sharp-toothed. Lilac to pink flowers are in close spike-forming whorls.

VIRTUES   Oil of peppermint distilled from fresh leaves is used in confectionery, chewing gum, perfumery, dental preparations, soaps, pastes, liqueurs, and medicine as a digestive aid. Contains menthol used medicinally. Dried or fresh leaves are used in tea and as seasoning; high amounts of tannic acid are contained in the leaves. Many variable forms are recognized as cultivars.

M. x piperita var. citrata (J.F.Ehr.) Briq.
Bergamot mint, lemon mint, eau de Cologne mint
Though erect to 1 ft., branches to 2 ft. tend to recline. Dark green ovate leaves, ½–2 in. long, are petioled and finely toothed. Pinkish flowers are in terminal and unequally spaced whorls of opposite leaf axils. A mutant of M. x piperita. A common plant of home gardens in tropical Florida and the Bahamas.

VIRTUES   The citrus-bergamot scent of fresh leaves gives a special tang to iced tea; dried leaves contribute a clean, citrus smell to potpourri. Extracted oil is an ingredient in the liqueur Chartreuse and in perfumery.

M. spicata L.
Spearmint
An erect, branching, non-hairy mint to 2½ ft., strongly sweet-scented; though of unknown origin, hybrid origin is probable since progeny is very variable. Leaves are lanceolate to 2 in. long, sharply toothed, not petioled to very short petioled. Arrangement of lilac or white flowers is variable, usually in a loose spike. The cv. 'Crispii' is distinguished by crisper leaves; spearmint odor is intact.

VIRTUES   In a versatile cook's garden spearmint is grown without question. A

British lamb joint requires mint sauce with spearmint. It is indispensable in cuisines of the Near and Middle East. Oil of spearmint is employed in pastes, chewing gum, confections. A jelly is prepared by adding an infusion of spearmint leaves to the base liquid with sugar.

M. *suaveolens* J.F. Ehrh.
Apple mint
An erect, branching, hairy mint to 3 ft.; fruit-scented. Leaves are oblong to ovate, with or without a short point, not petioled, and sharply toothed. White to pink flowers are in long, branched, dense spikes. Cv. 'Variegata', a smaller attractive form with creamy, pale green leaves, pineapple-scented, fails to hold its scent when dried.

M. *pulegium* L.
English pennyroyal
A decumbent, creeping mint with stems to 1 ft. long and a strong peppermint scent. Ovate leaves to 1 in. long are entire or toothed. Lilac colored flowers are in dense upright interrupted whorls. A herb to plant between flagstones in a pathway or as a carpetlike groundcover.
VIRTUES   A mosquito repellent; oil of English pennyroyal is used to repel fleas on cats.

M. *requienii* Benth.
Corsican mint
An extremely flat, creeping plant with threadlike short stems and a habit of forming a dense mat. The strong peppermint-scented species is native in Corsica and Sardinia. Tiny, petioled round leaves are ⅜ in. across. Minute lavender flowers in few-flowered whorls bloom sporadically in summer.
VIRTUES   The earliest sweet mint liqueur was flavored with the essential oil of Corsican mint.

Mirabilis jalapa L. ☉ or ♃   Four o'clock family
Four o'clock, marvel-of-Peru
A branched perennial to 3 ft. tall with tuberous roots; native in tropical America. Grows as a perennial in the southeast c.p. and is treated as an annual northward. Leaves to 5 in. long are opposite and heart-shaped. Narrow-tubed funnelform flowers 1–2 in. long and borne in axillary clusters are red, pink, yellow, or white; flowers open at about four o'clock in the afternoon and bloom throughout the summer.
CULTURE   Seed sown in spring where plants are to grow germinates in about

8 days; self-sows. Tuberous roots can be lifted in fall, dried and stored over winter, and replanted in April or May. Prefers a light, well-drained soil and full sun.
VIRTUES   Tuberous roots are the source of a purgative drug known as jalap.

Mitchella repens L. ♃ ▲   Madder family
Partridgeberry, squawberry
A prostrate, aromatic, evergreen perennial with trailing, rooting stems of deciduous woodland; native in eastern North America from Canada south to Florida and eastern Mexico. Opposite, rounded and glossy leaves to ¾ in. long are often with white lines. Small white to tinged pink flowers in pairs are funnel-shaped, 4-parted; blooms from May to June.
CULTURE   Sow seed outdoors in fall to stratify and expect germination in spring, or root stem cuttings outdoors in early summer where soil is kept moist. Give partridgeberry a moist to wet woodland soil with partial to full shade.
VIRTUES   Eastern American Indians made a medicinal tea of dried or fresh leaves and berries.

Monarda didyma L. ♃ ▲   Mint family
Bee balm, Oswego tea, wild bergamot
A stout, upright, aromatic perennial to 4 ft.; native in moist, open woods from New England south to the mts. of Georgia and Virginia. Opposite leaves on square stems are ovate-lanceolate to 4 in. long, petioled, and sharply toothed. From June to August intensely red, lipped flowers to 1¼ in. long crown each stem in layered, dense whorls. Over a patch of bee balm hummingbirds, bees, and butterflies hover and buzz. In midsummer leaves are coated with a harmless powdery mildew. For gardeners sensitive to special hues an impressive array of flower colors is accessible. The native is appreciated as an ornamental in Europe. As early as 1637 the younger John Tradescant of England, gardener to Lord Salisbury and later to Charles I, returned from a collecting trip in Virginia and introduced England to *M. didyma*.
CULTURE   Because seedlings are slow-growing sow seed indoors in January for germination in 2–3 weeks; self-sows. Division of mature clumps in early spring is easy; remove woody dead portions before resetting divisions. Select flower colors are maintained by divisions. Plant single clumps in open woods from which they will spread. In the garden masses are effective and appropriate; place hyssop in the foreground to screen lower leafless stalks. Bee balm thrives in a moist soil and partial shade; plants in full sun require frequent watering. Cutting spent flowers encourages a second bloom.

VIRTUES   Oswego Indians made an infusion of dried leaves for a palatable tea. In pre-Revolution days after the revolt against England's tea tax, manifested at the Boston Tea Party, American colonists followed the Indian usage. The bergamot-scented dried leaves find a place in potpourri and dried bright red flowers add color. Oil of wild bergamot, less costly than true bergamot, is blended with oils and perfumes to mask the odor of unpleasant-smelling chemicals.

M. fistulosa L. ♃△
Lavender wild bergamot
In contrast to M. *didyma*, lavender wild bergamot is native in dry sandy meadows and along roadsides in eastern North America, south to Georgia, Alabama, and Mississippi, more frequently in the mts. than on the pied., rare in the c.p. The less-scented bright lavender flowers appear in July and August.
CULTURE   Propagate by cutting runners attached to clumps, reset, and water well. Prefers full sun and a dry situation.
VIRTUES   A tea made of leaves has been used medicinally by American Indians.

M. punctata L. ♃△
Dotted horsemint
An erect, aromatic perennial to 2 ft. of sandy soils in the c.p. from Long Island to Florida and Louisiana. Pungent leaves are lanceolate to 3 in. long. The striking color combination of purple-spotted yellow petals with leaflike pink to lavender bracts in tight, tiered clusters on the end of each flowering stem draws attention from July to September.
CULTURE   Seed sown indoors germinates in 6 days, an easy method to supply a mass planting. Grow in full sun and sandy soil; a winter mulch saves roots from freezing temperatures.
VIRTUES   A source of thymol, an antibacterial essential oil. During World War I when thymol was unavailable from thyme fields in Europe field growing of T. *punctata* was government subsidized in the United States as a source of necessary thymol. American Indians prepared a medicinal leaf tea.

Myrica cerifera L. △   Bayberry family
Wax myrtle, candleberry
An oval to round-shaped evergreen shrub to 25 ft. tall of sandy pinelands from New Jersey to Florida, chiefly in the c.p. Olive-green leaves to 3 in. long are toothed above the middle; yellow resin dots on both leaf surfaces release a spicy fragrance when crushed. Grayish-white fruits about ⅛ in. in diameter are borne in dense clusters close to the stem and are covered with a resin or wax. Related

herbal species are: M. *pensylvanica*, bayberry, with deciduous leaves, sometimes evergreen, to 5 ft. in sun and dry soil; winter-hardy to zone 5. M. *heterophylla*, similar in height, is evergreen, extends into the upper pied., grows in moist to average soil, and is winter-hardy to zone 6.

CULTURE   Propagate by layering lower branches in fall; cut away sucker growth with attached roots in spring or fall; or divide roots in early spring; softwood cuttings taken in May, July, and August root successfully. Supply an acid soil with adequate moisture and position in full sun or light shade. For protection against cold temperatures plant a shrub against a wall where it can be pruned and espaliered. Fertilize in early spring.

VIRTUES   Wax myrtle is so named because the fruits are favorite food of myrtle warblers, and it yields an abundance of wax from which candles are made. Wax is removed from the fruit by melting in hot water; then separated from the water for perfumed candlemaking when it cools. Bark of stems, root, leaves, and wax have been used medicinally by American Indians and early American settlers; warnings of toxicity are to be heeded.

Myrrhis odorata (L). Scop. ♃   Parsley family
Sweet cicely

An elongated and gracefully formed perennial to 3 ft. high; native to temperate Europe. Stalks of fernlike leaves are strongly anise-scented. Small, creamy-white flowers in large umbels bloom from May to June. Stunning ripe seeds to 1 in. long are shiny black, strongly ribbed and upright.

CULTURE   Sow fresh seed as soon as ripe for germination in early spring; self-sown seedlings are the most vigorous. In spring position young plants in partial shade where soil remains moist and is well-drained. In warm climates look for a cool microclimate in shaded woods. *Osmorhiza longistylis*, aniseroot cicely, is native in deciduous woodlands from Quebec south to Georgia, Alabama, and Mississippi, chiefly on the pied. Like the European sweet cicely, fernlike leaf stalks have a strong anise flavor. Seeds are smaller, not shiny black.

VIRTUES   American settlers introduced sweet cicely and used the stalks as a flavoring for springtime potherbs. The sweet licorice-anise flavor has been suggested as a sweetener and flavor enhancer in conserves and tart dishes for individuals on low sugar diets. American Indians used aniseroot cicely in a medicinal tea.

Myrtus communis L.   Myrtle family
  Classic myrtle, myrtle
An aromatic, evergreen shrub to 9 ft.; native to the Mediterranean region. Glossy
green ovate leaves are strongly scented when crushed. Stalked, starry white flowers to ¾ in. across are borne in leaf axils; flowering is sporadic from May to
August. Ripened fruit is a blue-black berry. Not winter-hardy from zone 7 northward; a gift of outdoor, year-round fragrance southward.
CULTURE   Stem cuttings taken from new growth on indoor plants in February
root in 3–4 weeks. Keep year-round outdoor plants exposed to full sun in a
sheltered position, shielded from desiccating winds; a spot against a wall is protective. When and if tops are caught in a freeze, cut back and wait for new
growth. Myrtles moved indoors through winter and kept in containers can be
trained without much difficulty as standards and shaped topiaries; see Index. In
this guise myrtles properly announce their herbal and classical connections in a
garden or at its entrance.
VIRTUES   A perfume oil, "eau d 'ange" is extracted from bark, leaves, and flowers. Myrtle wood is durable and recommended for its fine grain. Bark and roots,
used for tanning fine Turkish and Russian leather, impart a distinctive scent. As a
symbol of divine generosity and emblematic of peace and joy, central European
brides wear myrtle wreaths; they were worn by magistrates and winners of
Olympic games. Medicinal uses have been applied.

Nepeta cataria L. ♃   Mint family
  Catnip, catmint
An aromatic, branched perennial, 2–3 ft. high with origins in Eurasia; widely
naturalized and often a weed in North America. A soft gray-hairy down on stems
and both leaf surfaces gives catnip a hoary aspect. Opposite gray-green leaves are
heart-shaped to 2 in. long, petioled, round-toothed. Small purple-dotted white
flowers in dense whorls form spikes to 5 in. long; blooms from June to September. *N. mussinii*, a decumbent catnip to 1 ft. high, bears a heavier foliage of smaller
leaves covered with sprays of blue flower clusters in May. It makes an easy, fit to
be seen edging that tumbles out of a raised bed and reduces stiffness. 'Citriodora'
is a lemon-scented cultivar.
CULTURE   Seed sown outdoors in fall germinates in spring; seed sown indoors
in March germinates in 10–20 days; self-sows. Divide mature plants in spring;
root stem cuttings. Though catnip grows in waste places, give garden plants a
moist, rich, well-drained soil. Under a warm sun plants are shorter and sturdier
than in partial shade. Keep in good foliage by cutting back before flower buds

form; after the first flowering of N. nussinii cut it back hard to encourage new growth and a second flowering.

VIRTUES Catnip odor is attractive, stimulating, and addictive to all felines and suggests a combination of mint, pennyroyal, and lemon; Charles Millspaugh treats catnip as a feline aphrodisiac. In years past women drank cups of catnip tea for stimulation and a number of ailments based on folk-medicine.

Nicotiana rustica L. ☉   Nightshade family
   Wild tobacco

The original tobacco and first to be introduced to the Old World is a course annual to 3 ft. with hairy and viscid stems; native in the Andes and naturalized in eastern United States. Leaves are ovate to 8 in. long. Small, tubular greenish-yellow flowers bloom along a terminal stalk from June to September, varying with locality. N. *tabacum*, tobacco, originating in tropical America, is larger than N. *rustica*. It is the principal commercial source of agrinomic tobacco forms for the production of leaves used after drying as smoking tobacco.

CULTURE Seed sown indoors, uncovered and exposed to light, germinates in 6–8 days. Commercial cultivation aside, give the herb in disgrace full sun and a well-drained sandy or sandy-clay soil in the herb garden. Sensitive to frost, plant outdoors only after all danger of frost is past.

VIRTUES Nicotine, an important garden insecticide, is extracted from wild tobacco. Used by South American natives as an addictive narcotic from prehistoric time in rituals and as medicine. Risks upon health imposed by tobacco are well-known.

Nigella sativa L. ☉   Crowfoot family
   Black cumin, fennel flower, nutmeg flower,
   Roman coriander

A stiffly erect, branched annual to 1½ ft. from the eastern Mediterranean region. Grayish-green leaves are deeply cut into linear segments. Solitary gray-blue flowers to 1½ in. across are 5-petaled and bloom in early summer. Fruit is a 5-lobed inflated sac filled with three-cornered black, spicy-pungent seeds.

CULTURE Sow seed outdoors when the soil is warm in full sun and a well-drained, slightly alkaline garden soil. Thin seedlings 4–6 in. apart; resents transplanting. Harvest seed when ripe before it falls to the ground.

VIRTUES N. *sativa* plants are the "fitches" of the Bible (Isaiah 28:25 & 27). It has been suggested that seeds were scattered in the spring sowing with wheat and barley in ancient Biblical time to inhibit insects, and for the same purpose seeds were added to milled grain used in baking breads. Over the millennia, if such was the case, by adding spicy seeds to breads, sweet or otherwise, an acquired taste may have developed since the custom of using seeds continues among eastern Mediterranean ethnic groups. Very old writings relating to gardening and textiles mention insecticidal properties of N. *sativa*.

Ocimum spp.   Mint family
   Basils
Fragrant basils are annuals or short-lived perennials of subtropical and tropical regions in the Old World. Clearly marked mint family features are 4-sided stems, leaves opposite on the stem, and small flowers arranged in whorls usually in a terminal spike. Each flower produces 4 nutlets or seeds. Some species show considerable variation in form, size, color and shape of leaves, and aroma; other species remain noticeably uniform. An assortment of essential oil mixtures produced in epidermal gland cells on the leaves are responsible for variation in fragrances. Scents include anise, camphor, cinnamon, cloves, lemon, rose, floral, and thyme—all variously blended.

Listed in the Descriptive Catalog are species, hybrids, varieties, strains, and cultivars likely grown in American herb gardens.

CULTURE Basils are easy to grow from seed; stem cuttings root without difficulty. As truly subtropical to tropical, seeds or plants cannot bear being put outdoors too soon in temperate climates, and plants blacken at the first hint of a frost. They want full sun, revel in the hot sunshine of moist Florida, and carry on as perennials if kept de-budded. Seed sown indoors germinates in 3–6 days; seed sown outdoors when daytime temperatures are about 70°F: and nightime temperatures are above 45°F: germinates in 10–14 days. High germination percentages require thinning; seedlings transplants well. In warm and humid climates basils thrive in good garden soil; when repeatedly grown in the same area a complete fertilizer is added yearly according to soil test suggestions. Native to regions with wet monsoon periods, growth and vigor is outstanding after heavy rains. Pinch out tips of 4-leaved seedlings to encourage a dense and compact habit; pinch flower buds away to sustain foliage growth; retain flowers on at least one plant to harvest plump, brown or black ripe seeds that fall from crushed, dried calyces. As insect pollinated, cross-pollination is normal and uniformity in progeny cannot be expected when varieties, strains, or cultivars of O. *basilicum* are grown in close proximity. Attention-receiving unfamiliar combinations of characteristics appear to be received as possible gracious winners. Basils are naturally resistant to fungus diseases. Japanese beetles are known to cause damage, and whiteflies are a bother on indoor plants.

O. basilicum L. ⊙
Sweet basil
Annual sweet basil, native in subtropical India, is generally 1–3 ft. tall with variable branching. Leaves of variable size are ovate, smooth, and glossy with margins entire or slightly toothed. Lipped flowers in whorls form long spikes, are white or purple, stamens and style always white; blooms appear from early summer onward. Within the species are definable categories. Two tall, slender, open types have sharply-pointed and toothed leaves. One from Persia has a distinct cinnamon odor, the other a soft anise aroma; the usual clove scent is masked. Robust types include the cultivars 'Italian', 'Crispum', 'Ruffles'; all have a strong, sweet basil aroma and large leaves, not pointed. Within dwarf types is 'Minimum', rounded and bushy, 8–10 in. wide; leaves from ⅜–1 in long. Small white flowers in whorls are scattered on stems among leaves or in short terminal spikes. A unique globular dwarf type has purple leaves on the upper part of the sphere and green leaves below. *O. basilicum* var. *purpurescens* is applied loosely to eye-catching sweet basils with mixed or mottled green and purple colored foliage. Flowers are lavender and white; calyces, bracts, and stalks purple. 'Dark Opal', a cultivar with total purplish-bronze foliage, is a horticultural form, developed at the University of Connecticut for ornamental quality but maintains a pungent sweet basil fragrance. It is known to carry a virus disease.
VIRTUES   Spicy oils in leaves and flower stalks are stimulating seasonings; 'Opal basil' foliage makes a lovely claret-colored vinegar of superior flavor blended with robust sweet Italian basil; 'Cinnamon' is attached to Southeast Asian and East Indian cookery; sweet Italian basil will always represent the Italian kitchen and Genovese pesto demands it. Basil is said to deter flies; a bee plant. The essential oils are used in perfumery. Stored frozen leaves are more potent than dried. Dried basil leaves are used in a preparation of salt and spice-free dietetic meat products.

O. canum x *O. basilicum* var. ⊙
Spice basil
A uniform, self-sowing and annual hybrid basil commonly grown in herb gardens as *O. sanctum*, sacred basil or tulsi. Tulsi is native to India and revered in Hindu religious practices; though available from basil specialists, it is not common in American gardens. Other than the name of spice basil's parents, no reliable botanical name is available. Hairiness of the entire bushy plant to 2½ ft. high with ovate, toothed leaves, and spikes of pink flowers in groups of 3 or 5 terminal branches are identifying features. Its strong, penetrating and peculiar odor is unlike all other basils. The scent has been described by Hindus as characteristic

of tulsi. Having kept *O. sanctum* for several years, I could not detect any similarity; however, soils and climate influence essential oil production in volume and mixtures. Gather and transplant self-sown seedlings into a drift for an abundance of soft pink spikes rising above the grayish foliage. More frost-resistant than all other basils, and the only basil known to self-sow north into zone 5.

O. gratissimum L.

A shrubby basil to 6 ft. high of tropical Africa; cultivated and commercially grown for its fragrant clovelike essential oil where it is native, in the West Indies, South America, and to a small extent in tropical United States. Treated as an annual in temperate climates. Ovate leaves, 5–6 in. long with toothed margins, are densely hairy and petioled. The densely hairy leaves give a gray-green aspect to the entire plant. Pale yellow flowers to ½ in. long with long, protruding bright yellow stamens are arranged in whorls on branching stalks. Roundish seeds are reddish-brown. *O. gratissimum* merits a prominent place with all other basils in herb gardens of tropical and subtropical zones.

VIRTUES   Clove oil from *O. gratissimum* is used in perfumery, industry, and medicine; the essential oil has antibacterial properties with low human toxicity and irritability. Seed has been used in African folk-medicine. Cut fresh plants act as mosquito repellents. Steeped leaves, fresh or dried, make a pleasant tea with a clove flavor.

O. kilimandscharicum Guerke
Camphor basil

A branched, strongly camphor-scented shrub, 5–10 ft. high in its tropical eastern Africa (Kenya) native habitat. Gray-green leaves are hairy, ovate to elliptic, petioled, and toothed. Small white to pink flowers are in close whorls forming slender spikes to 12 in. long; blooms from June to September. Not winter-hardy from zone 8 northward. Plants or stem cuttings taken indoors to root are subject to whitefly.

VIRTUES   A commercial source of camphor for medicinal use.

O. americanum L. [O. basilicum 'Citriodorum'] ⊙
Lemon basil

A uniform natural hybrid of *O. canum* and *O. basilicum* var. *purpurescens*, native to northwestern India. The annual, 1½–2 ft. high, is semi-compact, lemon-scented with sweet basal undertones. Light green leaves are narrowly ovate, long-petioled, entire, 1–2 in. long. White flowers are in whorls which form a lax spike, 5–7 in. long; blooms from June to September. Black seeds have a lemon fragrance; self-sows through zone 7. As the least leafy basil, lemon basil can better survive dry conditions. Its stratagem of folding leaves upward when soil and air is dry further preserves moisture in the leaves.

VIRTUES Lemon basil entered our garden through an Austrian friend and exacting cook who believed it contributed a proper subtle basil and lemon flavor to Austrian dishes. Less robust than sweet Italian basil, unlike spicy strains East Indians prefer, but like the story of Goldilocks and the three bears, just right for a delicate Austrian veal stew. Nuances of herbs in the cooking pot are subtle and recognized by discriminating noses.

Oenothera biennis L. ☉▲   Evening primrose family
Evening primrose
A weedy biennial to 6 ft. tall of roadsides, fields, and waste places in eastern North America, south to Georgia, Alabama, and Mississippi. An erect flowering stem, sometimes reddish, rises from a basal rosette in the second year. Alternate leaves along the stalk are lanceolate to 6 in. long and diminish in size upward. Yellow, 4-petaled flowers, 1–2 in. across cap stalks in crowded, branched clusters from June to October. From dusk to late evening tightly rolled flower buds swell, and with a suddenness sepals separate and luminous pale yellow petals spring apart to reveal 8 stamens and a cross-shaped stigma. A rich lemon scent is exuded which attracts nocturnal moths to take nectar; honey bees visit flowers in the morning until they close, and new buds follow the act when the sun goes down.

CULTURE Seed sown indoors germinates in 4–8 days; self-sows. Small rosettes attached to mature clumps can be separated, reset, and watered to produce flowering stalks the following year. Flowers abundantly in full sun, is drought tolerant, and satisfied with any soil that is not constantly wet.

VIRTUES American Indians used roots for nutrition and medicine. An extract made from fresh plant material was used by settlers through the nineteenth century. Recent investigations for medicinal properties center on essential fatty acids contained in oil extracted from the seed. In Germany and France where *O. biennis* has naturalized edible roots, shoots, and leaves are eaten pickled, or raw.

Opuntia humifusa (Raf.) Raf. ♃▲   Cactus family
[*O. compressa* (Salisb.) Macbr.]
Prickly pear cactus
A perennial, prostrate, spreading cactus with flat obovate stem segments, "pads", to 1 ft. high of dry, sandy or rocky open habitats from Massachusetts south to Florida and west to eastern Texas. Short-lived, small, fleshy, pointed leaves are

attached below tufts of tiny bristles and a solitary spine to ¾ in. long. Bright yellow waxy flowers, 3–4 in. across, bloom from May to June and sporadically thereafter. Fruit is an edible fleshy berry with seeds, 1–2 in. long, reddish-brown when ripe. (See plate 20.)

CULTURE   In late summer break off one or more segments from a mature, spreading clump, reset in a soil to which several shovels of sand have been added for fast-drainage; a cactus would rather be dry than wet. Roots form in 3–4 weeks to establish a new planting in full sun. For a pleasing display of evergreen segments and shining flowers let them spread at the base of a large tree trunk or in front of a large rock.

VIRTUES   American Indians used poultices of "pads" on wounds. Indian usages were adopted by pioneer settlers who added applications for numbers of ailments.

Origanum spp. ♃   Mint family
Oregano

The common name oregano, often with slight differences in spelling, is derived from the Latin genus name *Origanum* which has its origin from two Greek words, "oros" mountain and "gano" joy, for the joyous appearance plants give to their native arid hillsides of the Mediterranean region. Since the lusty, bitterish to sweet aroma with broad nuances also exists in essential oils of other genera (*Thymus, Thymbria, Satureja, Coleus, Salvia, Lantana, Monarda, Lippia*) "oregano" is defined as an identifiable aroma. Associating aroma with plant form, color, shape, or habitat invariably increases confusion between herbal common and botanical names. Botanical names can for the most part be disregarded when an oregano is smelled for culinary use; but a herb gardener needs complete identification accompanied by a specific botanical name to grow a particular herb.

Origanum spp. are perennial with slightly wooden stems (subshrubs). Winter-hardiness varies among species and varieties. Opposite leaves are ovate to elliptic, petioled and not petioled, often purplish on the lower surface. Flowers with bracts are in round or flat-topped clusters. Exact identification of herb garden species is partially based on whether a calyx has 5 teeth or 1 slit and length of bracts; a good magnifying glass is necessary.

CULTURE   Propagate from seed when proper identification is assured. The trade on occasion inadvertently or heedlessly packages not exactly identified species or describes aromas inaccurately. Seed sown indoors germinates in 6–8 days. For better distribution mix dust particle size seed with sand before strewing. Stem cuttings are easy to root, and when taken from properly identified plants you get what you want; carrying over rooted cuttings of questionable winter-hardy species indoors through the winter is practical. Grow oreganos in full sun and a well-drained, slightly alkaline soil; avoid over-fertilizing and over-watering. Excessive moisture, especially in winter, can be devastating. Pinch tips repeatedly for bushy growth. A rock garden environment on a slope or mound for spreading or bushy oreganos and upright thymes is functional and goodlooking; excess water runs off and rocks absorb heat to keep roots in rock crevices alive through the winter. Foliage tumbling over rocks keeps dry; chopped oyster shells or pea gravel mixed with soil benefits a species from an arid climate. Intensity of fragrance is dependent on individual growing conditions.

VIRTUES   Greek ethno-medicine includes many Mediterranean oreganos; special emphasis is placed on dittany-of-Crete, *O. dictamnus*. Varying pungent, balsamic, bitterish to sweet fragrances are significant seasonings in ethno-Mediterranean dishes. Americans have adopted oregano seasoned pizzas with gusto and increased variety in their cooking with oregano. Until the Middle Ages *O. vulgare* was used to flavor beer; flower clusters yield a dye to color woolens purple and linen a reddish-brown; neither are brilliant nor durable. Goats and sheep graze on wild oregano. Greeks and Romans crowned young couples with sweet marjoram, *O. marjorana*, called "Amaracus" by ancient Greek writers.

O. dictamnus L.
Dittany-of-Crete
A dwarf, gray-woolly, aromatic shrub to 12 in., native in the mts. of the Greek mainland and on Crete. Dittany-of-Crete is not reliably winter-hardy from zone 7 northward; Rounded leaves appear gray by the presence of soft-wooly hair. Flowers to ½ in. long are pink-lavender; calyces are 2-lipped; chartreuse overlapping bracts turn rose-purple as seeds develop; blooms from May to June. Attractive in the winter as a profusely blooming indoor window plant.

O. heracleoticum L.
Oregano, winter marjoram
An erect or decumbent, branched, and slightly hairy oregano to 12 in. closely related to *O. vulgare*. Flowers are white; calyces have 5 equal teeth; inconspicuous bracts are no more than ⅛ in. long, shorter than in *O. vulgare*; blooms from June to September. A pungent oregano aroma for the Italian kitchen.

O. majorana L. ⊙
Sweet marjoram
Erect and branching to 12 in., sweet marjoram from North Africa and southwestern Asia is naturalized in southwestern Europe. For lack of winter-hardiness it is usually treated as an annual. Flowers are white; calyces 1-lipped, deeply slit;

rounded bracts are closely overlapping; blooms through the summer. A sweet fragrance, with little assertion of oregano's lustiness, is appreciated by the Portuguese and central Europeans, often blended with thyme. More fragrant than leaves, developing flower heads are collected just before the flowers open.

O. x marjoricum

A natural hybrid between *O. marjorana* and *O. virens* that rarely if ever produces seed; native of southwestern Europe. Hardier than sweet marjoram. Whitish-pink flowers have 2-lipped bell-shaped calyces with the upper lip deeply 3-toothed and the lower 2-toothed; bracts closely over lapping. The aroma of fresh leaves and flower heads is similar to sweet marjoram; dried material has a delicate oregano scent and is not substituted for sweet marjoram.

O. onites L.
Greek oregano, "rigani"

"Rigani," growing abundantly on mainland Greece and its islands east to Turkey and Syria, is a favorite in the region's cuisines. The bright, sharp aroma is less pungent than a pizza oregano and is combined with a suggestion of lemon to fill a gap for just a tang of oregano. Not reliably winter-hardy from zone 7 northward. Flowers are white; calyces 1-lipped, deeply slit; overlapping bracts pointed. Collect developing flower heads before the flowers open.

O. vulgare L.
Common oregano

A decumbent oregano, native to Eurasia and naturalized in eastern United States; self-sows. Winter-hardy through zone 5. Leaves are often purplish. Pink flowers are in flat-topped clusters; calyces have 5 equal teeth; purplish bracts. Plants grown in the soils and climate of its native habitat have a strong oregano aroma; fragrance is much reduced elsewhere. Useful as a groundcover. Var. *prismaticum*, more erect than the species, has white flowers; calyces are 5-toothed. Its pungent aroma is fit for a tomato sauce. 'Aureum' is a spreading cultivar of negligible aromatic quality, but useful when its golden-green leaves on decumbent stems lie close and flat to carpet a pathway; hardy through zone 5.

Oregano scented plants grown and used in zones 9–11 where *Origanum* spp. are less successful are: *Coleus amboinicus*, Cuban oregano or Spanish thyme, from Cuba; *Poliomintha longifolia* from Mexico; and *Lippia graveolens* from Mexico.

Panax quinquefolius L. ♃ ▲ Ginseng family
Ginseng, American ginseng

A perennial with a solitary stem to 2 ft.; native in rich, moist woods from Quebec south to Georgia and Oklahoma. A mature spindle-shaped, fleshy root, 2–4 in.

long, often forked, is sometimes interpreted as taking a human form. Petioled, palmately compound leaves with 3–5 elliptic leaflets about 5 in. long and sharply-toothed are borne in a whorl. Greenish-yellow flowers in round umbels are inconspicuous, but bright red fruits borne in the axils of the compound leaves in September are identifying.

CULTURE   Seed sown ½–1 in. deep as soon as ripe in the same rich soil of the parent plant germinates a year from the following spring. Left to itself a plant grows at a slow rate but is long-lived. For large scale cultivation methods that benefit commercial growers the United States dept. of Agriculture supplies Bulletin No.2201, "Growing Ginseng." North Carolina and Wisconsin with climates and soils favorable for commercial production also provide useful information for commercial growers. Collection of roots from the wild is discouraged as wild stands decrease and need protection.

VIRTUES   American Indians used the American species as a medicinal in the same manner as Chinese and Koreans use species native to Korea. The value placed on the medicinal stimulating properties by some Chinese and Koreans has influenced exportation of dried roots by commercial growers and the zeal of collectors in the United States.

Papaver somniferum L. ⊙   Poppy family
  Opium poppy
An erect annual, 2–3 feet high, from southeastern Europe and western Asia. Gray-green glaucous leaves are clasping, wavy, coarsely toothed. Terminal, solitary, nodding flowers are delicately colored white, pale pink, or mauve with a dark blotch in each petal; blooms from May to July. Fruit is a capsule containing a large number of small steel-gray or white seeds.

CULTURE   Fall sowings in a sunny position succeed in garden soil; self-sows. We are permissive and let opium poppy seedlings grow where they will after experiencing the mellowing effect of glaucous leaves and pastel flowers distributed freely in a charming Spanish garden.

VIRTUES   A hardened milky sap taken from unripe capsules is the source of the addictive, narcotic drug opium and its derivatives as morphine. Seeds lacking the narcotic property have been used since ancient time to flavor bread and cakes. An extracted oil is used in cooking.

Pedicularis canadensis L. ♃△   Figwort family
  Lousewort, wood betony
A hairy perennial to 1½ ft.; native in dry to well-drained moist, open woods from Quebec to Florida. Grayish-green leaves to 5 in. long are tansylike. Flowers to

¾ in. long are 2-lipped, yellow tinged with brown, and arranged in a compact spike; blooms from April to May.

CULTURE   Best propagated from division of a clump. Though given a position in an open, dry woods with partial shade and woodland litter all about, louse-wort has a habit of dying down when transplanted; as partly parasitic on roots of certain grasses it may take two seasons to reestablish. Despite the odds, the rare combination of heavy haired tansylike leaves and curiously colored 2-lipped flowers on short stout spikes provokes an effort to include the herb in a wood-land rock garden.

VIRTUES   Cherokee Indians placed roots and leaves on the dog bed to delouse pups and to rid sheep of lice. American Indians of several tribes used the root medicinally.

Pelargonium spp. ♃   Geranium family
   Scented geraniums

Scented-leaved geraniums, classed as perennials, become shrubs where they grow and are native among the scrub on hot, sunny mountainsides in South Africa. From the beginning of the seventeenth century they were brought to England by English and Dutch navigators. Few herbs of a single genus have, over such a long time, contributed the diversity of fragrances, leaf textures, and form. In our country, even before the American Revolution, colonists enjoyed the rose, lemon, fruity, mint, and spicy scented foliage of plants brought from En-gland. Whether potted for a windowsill through winter or moved to an outdoor garden in summer, scented-leaved geraniums have never ceased to charm. Touching a leaf for a single aroma or deriving a potpourri effect by fingering an assortment of fragrant varieties taps the endocrine system and generates sensual delight. From time to time all display attractive flowers with detailed purple col-ored veins or blood red strokes, spots, and blotches on their petals; but scent brings them into a herb garden. Ease of culturing scented-leaved geraniums, hybridization among species, and a strong tendency towards variation have introduced confusion in the grouping of hybrids and variable forms. Growing the plants over three centuries in varying climates and soils can be given some responsibility for changes in form. Claims for a scent are not only subject to a soil, temperatures, and sunshine when sampling, but are also influenced by per-sonal olfactory perceptions.

CULTURE   To preserve identity of hybridized and variable forms propagation from stem cuttings is best and easy. Geranium propagators advise leaving cuttings exposed a day to encourage callus tissue formation which decreases infection. Keep an indoor pot in the sunniest of windows or under fluorescent light. Water only when the soil is dry to the touch; then water until water drains from the pot. An occasional watering with a complete soluble fertilizer, 1 teaspoon to a gallon of water, encourages foliage growth, over-fertilizing diminishes fragrance. Pinching and cutting back produces a desirable bushy plant. In summer (throughout the year in zones 9–11) scented-leaved geraniums thrive in full sun in garden beds, tubs, boxes, or pots on a terrace except P. *tomentosum*, peppermint-scented geranium, which prefers partial shade. Indoors some varieties are susceptible to whitefly and precautions are suggested.

VIRTUES   Geranium oils have been distilled at Grasse in France since 1800 as a substitute for the costlier attar of roses. Sprigs or tiny leaves of lemon-scented geranium are floated in finger bowls. A rose-scented leaf placed at the base or top of each glass holding hot apple jelly imparts a delicate rose flavor. Add chopped leaves of 'Cinnamon' rose to a rich biscuit batter or line a tin with rose-scented leaves to flavor a pound cake. A variety of dried scented leaves enter potpourri or sachet bags placed among bed linens or in a handkerchief drawer.

The following scented geraniums are representative; the list is not all-inclusive.

P. *capitatum* (L.) L'Her.
Rose-scented geranium
Sprawling to 1 ft.; rose-scented. Heart-shaped leaves are lobed above the middle, ruffled, toothed, hairy, and long-petioled. Derived cultivars from hybrids and otherwise are 'Shrubland Rose', 'Attar of Roses', 'Shotesham Pet'; from hybridization with P. *quercifolium*: 'Elkhorn', 'Fringed Oak', 'Logee's Snowflake', 'Round-leaved Rose', 'Skelton's Unique'; with P. *radens*: 'Carlton Corsage'.

P. *crispum* (L.) L'Her. ex Hait.
Lemon-scented geranium
Erect, pyramidal, woody, medium-sized; lemon-scented. Small leaves with crisped margins have long petioles. Suitable for bonsai and small standards. Cultivars derived by hybridization or otherwise are: 'French Lace' with white leaf margins; 'Minor' with leaves not petioled and tiniest of all; 'Prince Rupert' with small and crisp leaves and largest of the *crispum* group.

P. x *fragrans* Willd.
Nutmeg-scented geranium
Sprawling, woody, to 1½ ft.; good in a hanging basket. Grayish leaves are slightly lobed, rounded, and crinkled. Cultivars are: 'Cody's Fragrance', also referred to as 'Old Spice' with compact, larger, and velvety-textured leaves; 'Variegatum', also listed as 'Snowy Nutmeg', is variegated green and white.

P. *graveolens* L'Her. ex Ait.
Attar of roses geranium

Erect, branched, and woody to 3 ft.; rose-scented. Excellent as a standard. Hairy leaves are 5–7 lobed and further segmented. Cultivars are 'Camphor Rose', 5-lobed with a camphor scent; 'Gray Lady Plymouth', grayish leaves edged with a fine white line; 'Lady Plymouth', irregular gray leaves, splotched white; 'Variegatum', gray-green leaves, edged white and mint-scented.

P. x *nervosum* Sweet
Lime-scented geranium

Small, deep-green, sharp-toothed leaves, lime-scented. Cv. 'Toronto' with larger leaves, less sharply toothed and ginger-scented.

P. *odoratissimum* (L.) L'Her. ex Ait.
Apple-scented geranium

A crown sends off sprawling runners to 1½ ft. with foliage and umbels of white flowers with red spots; apple-scented. Excellent for a hanging basket. Roundish leaves are light-green, slightly velvety, and round-toothed.

P. *quercifolium* (L.f.) L'Her. ex Ait.
Oak-leaved geranium

A large, much hybridized pungent-scented geranium. Leaves have deep and rounded lobes as a leaf of a white oak tree. Cultivars derived by hybridization and otherwise are: 'Beauty Oak', pungent with a hint of mint and leaves with brown markings; 'Clorinda', a hybrid with P. x *domesticum*, the Lady Washington geranium; 'Fair Ellen', rough and sticky leaves with purple markings; 'Godfrey's Pride', mint-scented and large 5-lobed leaves not deeply indented; 'Pretty Polly', almond-scented; 'Staghorn', narrow veins purple and a prostrate habit.

P. *radens* H.E. Moore
Crowfoot geranium

Shrubby to 3 ft. with a lemon-rose scent. Deeply lobed leaves finely cut into very narrow segments. 'Dr. Livingston' is a larger form; makes a fine standard.

P. *tomentosum* Jacq.
Peppermint-scented geranium

Procumbent and shrubby; peppermint-scented. Velvety leaves are 3-lobed as a grape leaf.

Perilla frutescens (L.) Britt. ☉   Mint family
  Perilla
An erect, branched, aromatic annual to 3 ft.; native and cultivated in eastern Asia; naturalized around homesites throughout the Midwest and eastern United States. Broadly ovate leaves to 5 in. long, pointed, and toothed are green or purplish. Leaves of cv. 'Atropurpurea' are dark purple; cv. 'Crispa' is brightly colored purplish bronze with leaves slashed into narrow, pointed lobes. Flowers in 2-flowered whorls arranged to form a long spike.
CULTURE   Sow seed in fall to stratify; self-sows. Grows in sun or partial shade with no particular soil requirements. Prolificacy is annoying to some gardeners; banning perilla is tossing aside an easy source of purple or bronze foliage to accentuate contrast with grays and whites in a herb garden.
VIRTUES   Japanese cooking is sensitive to the color and fragrance of perilla and uses it to scent and color preserved apricots and pickled dishes; lower surfaces of leaves are dipped in an egg batter and fried in oil; fresh leaves contribute a piquant flavor in salads and rice. A leaf tea and seeds are used medicinally in Asia. Cultivated in eastern Asia for seeds as a source of a drying oil used in varnishes, printing inks, and linoleum.

Persia borbonia (L.) K. Spreng. ▲   Laurel family
  Red bay
An aromatic, evergreen shrub or tree, 30–40 ft. tall of well-drained, sandy soils in woods and open areas of the southeast c.p. Lanceolate leaves taper at the base and release a pleasant fragrance when crushed. Flowers blooming in May and June are in few-flowered clusters. Dark blue to black fruits to ½ in. in diameter ripen in September and October; they are eaten by wildlife.
CULTURE   Best propagated from softwood cuttings. Plant in a moist soil with full sun or light shade. Growth rate is medium. Fertilize in early spring with a general fertilizer. Not reliably winter-hardy from zone 7 northward.
VIRTUES   Leaves are a good seasoning substitute for bay, *Laurus nobilis*. The hard, heavy, close-grained lumber is useful for cabinet-making.

Petroselinum crispum var. *crispum* (Mill.)   Parsley family
Nyman ex A.W. Hill ☉
  Curled parsley
A biennial; native to Eurasia. Leaf stalks to 1½ ft. rise from a crown topping a taproot. Compound leaves are 3-parted, curled, crisp, and toothed. Greenish-yellow flowers in umbels top a stalk to 3 ft. and bloom in the early summer of

the second year. Var. *neapolitanum*, Italian parsley, has flat leaves and a stronger flavor; var. *tuberosum* is grown for its large, fleshy taproot which contributes fine flavor to a soup stock. Many horticultural forms exist.

CULTURE   Plant several sowings of parsley for a continual supply; sow seed in very early spring, February or March, and again in August or September to meet the need in winter when hardy parsley has the best flavor. Seed soaked in tepid water for 24 hours before sowing germinates in 7–12 days instead of the usual 24 days; self-sows. Thin seedlings to 6 in. apart. Like most members of the parsley family, transplanting is resented and is a reason for not starting seed indoors; however, by keeping a crown well above the soil surface losses are minimized. Parsley likes a bed of deep, rich, moist soil, partially shaded in midsummer; dry conditions and high temperatures invite aphid attacks. Planted close, curly and Italian parsley hybridize and a greater percentage of hybrid offspring has flat leaves. For bold contrast, border dark, rich green, curled parsley with deep-orange flowering and tumbling nasturtiums; at Thanksgiving mound orange pumpkins and bright-colored gourds all around.

VIRTUES   Parsley is one of the finest foliaged herbs to garnish a platter or embellish a herb garden. As a source of vitamin C and A as well as a food flavoring it is a very special herb. The Romans were quite right in nibbling on garlands of parsley. Parsley tea has been used medicinally. Strong-flavored stems are well-used in soups and stocks. Ubiquitous, yes—but rarely out of place.

Podophyllum peltatum L. ♃▲☠   Barberry family
Common mayapple

A rhizomatous erect perennial to 1½ ft. of mixed deciduous woodlands or moist meadows from Quebec to central and eastern United States, south to Florida and Texas. Umbrellalike deeply-lobed leaves to 1 ft. across grow in pairs at the top of stems. Beneath and between the two leaves an exquisite nodding, single white flower is concealed; blooms from March to May. Pulp of the round and yellow ripe fruit is edible. Roots, foliage, and seeds are poisonous.

CULTURE   Easily propagated by dividing the long rhizomes. In a few seasons fast spreading rhizomes provide a ground cover in a woods or damp meadow, partial shade or sun.

VIRTUES   American Indians used rhizomes medicinally; early settlers followed the example. Pharmacological investigations have resulted in a medicinal application of a semisynthetic derivative of the plant. Poisonous warnings remain valid.

Polygonatum biflorum (Walt.) Elliot ♃**△**   Lily family
   Solomon's seal
A rhizomatous perennial with arching stems to 3 ft.; native in moist woodland of central and eastern United States, south to Florida and Texas. Alternate, stalk-less leaves to 4 in. long are elliptic. Bell-shaped yellowish-white flowers hang as pendants below an arching stem in clusters of 1–4 from April to June. Globular dark-blue fruits follow.
CULTURE   Seed sown in fall to stratify through the winter germinates in spring. Divide rhizomes in spring. Plant in moist woodland soil with partial shade.
VIRTUES   American Indians used a tea made from an infusion of rhizomes for numbers of ailments which were adopted by pioneer settlers.

Polygonum bistorta L. ♃   Buckwheat family
   Bistort, snakeweed
A rhizomatous perennial to 2 ft.; native in moist soils of temperate Europe and Asia. In the twisted, creeping nature of a rhizome lies the origin of the name snakeweed and *bistorta*, "bi" twice, "tort" contorted. Basal and stem leaves are oblong-ovate to 6 in. long, bluish-green on the upper surface and gray, tinged with purple underneath. Slender wands, 12–18 in. long, terminate in striking dense spikes of flesh-colored or soft pink flowers from May to June and again in late summer. Ripe three-sided seeds are dark brown. Cv. 'Superbum' has larger flower spikes.
CULTURE   Divide twisted rhizomes in early fall or spring as a simpler and easier method than sowing seed which is slow and irregular (20–60 days) in germination. Expect plants to spread rapidly in moist soil and partial shade. Handsome as a single clump or an easy and colorful deciduous edging. An underused herb in American herb gardens.
VIRTUES   The rhizome, black on the outside, red internally, and rich in tannic and gallic acid has been used medicinally for its strong astringent properties. Early spring leaves are used in salads or as a cooked vegetable.

Poncirus trifoliata (L.) raf.   Rue family
   Trifoliate orange, hardy orange
A spiny, deciduous tree to 10 ft. with stiff and angled branches; native in central and northern China; winter-hardy from zone 8 southward in the Southeast. Aromatic leaves of 3 leaflets to 1½ in. long are elliptic. White, scented orange-blossom flowers to 2 in. across appear on thorny green twigs just before the leaves unfold in March and April. Green fruits hidden by leaves are overlooked until the leaves

fall. Then they suddenly ripen to a very fragrant yellow, bitter-tasting fruit about 2 in. in diameter. Spring branches of trifoliate orange make an impenetrable herbal thicket, fitting as a background hedge to a herb garden.

CULTURE Propagation from stratified seed is possible by planting fresh seed in a protected bed as soon as ripe, but plants are slow-growing. Propagation from soft or hardwood cuttings is practical for the establishment of a hedge. A well-drained soil and full sun produces the best hedge and abundant flowers. Shearing and pruning is necessary to obtain a planned shaped.

VIRTUES In China a decoction of unripe fruit is applied medicinally.

Poterium sanguisorba L. ♃   Rose family
Salad burnet

A short-lived evergreen perennial, 6–18 in. high; native in southern Europe and western Asia; naturalized as escapes from gardens in eastern United States. Arching leaves rising from a crown are pinnately compound with 11–12 pairs of small, round, deeply-toothed leaflets; bruised leaves smell and taste like cucumbers. Petal-less rose-colored stigmas of female flowers are in compact, globular heads while long stamens of male flowers protrude and gently sway below the head; blooms from April to July. (See plate 21.)

CULTURE Seed sown indoors germinates in 6 days; self-sows. In transplanting keep crowns well above the soil surface to prevent rot. A well-drained, neutral to slightly alkaline soil and full sun produce vigorous plants, resistant to drought; an overly moist soil causes rot and short life.

VIRTUES In times past salad burnet leaves cooled tankards of beverages that fit the phrase "cool as a cucumber." Chopped leaves introduce a refreshing cucumber flavor in a spring salad of greens; flavor turns bitter in mid and late summer. Leaves steeped in cider vinegar transfers and preserves the cool flavor to dress a salad. Herbalists attached medicinal virtues to the leaves.

Pulmonaria officinalis L. ♃   Borage family
Common lungwort

A rhizomatous, hairy perennial to 1 ft. of shaded European woodland. Ovate leaves are spotted whitish-silver. In early spring flowers to ¾ in. long in curved clusters like a scorpion's tail have pink buds that become blue when open.

CULTURE Divide creeping rhizomes in early spring or fall. Grows in a shaded position and in any soil, but spreads rapidly when the soil is fertile. A patch of leaves, spotted silvery-white, with pink to blue flowers growing at the side of a woodland path is an early spring showpiece.

VIRTUES   One of the plants supported by the Doctrine of Signatures. Exponents of the doctrine viewed the resemblance of spotted leaves to lung tissue as a sign of effectiveness in treating respiratory diseases.

Pycnanthemum incanum (L.) Michx. ♃▲   Mint family
   Mountain mint, white horse-mint
An aromatic, erect, branched perennial to 6 ft. of open woods and road banks in eastern United States, south into the mts. and pied. of Georgia, Alabama, and Mississippi. Ovate, stalked, toothed leaves to 4 in. long are a hoary frosted white toward the flower heads. Small white to pink flowers tinged with purple are in flat, dense heads; blooms from June to September. Plants have a camphoraceous scent.
CULTURE   Collected seeds sown indoors germinate in 10–15 days; self-sows. Divide clumps in spring. Grow in sun or partial shade, in open woods or a garden; drought tolerant.
VIRTUES   American Indians used a poultice of leaves for headaches and drank a leaf tea for a number of common complaints. P. *virginianum* and P. *tenuifolium*, are mint-scented, similarly used.

Rhododendron calendulaceum (Michx.) Torr. ▲   Heath family
   Flame azalea
A deciduous shrub to 9 ft. with slightly scented yellow, orange, and reddish orange flowers to 2 in. across. Blooms appear before or with emerging elliptic to obovate leaves to 3 in. long. Among native Appalachian mountain azaleas it has the most flash.
CULTURE   More detailed directions for propagation than space allows are in publications on the subject (see Bibliography). Plant new plants or transplant in late fall, early winter, or early spring; position the root ball so the top of the root base is slightly above the soil level. All rhododendrons prefer a cool, moist, acid soil (pH 4.5 to pH 5.5) and partial shade, not exposed to a hot summer sun for long periods. A well-drained soil with humus or decayed organic matter supplies nutrients and retains moisture. A mulch of pine needles or woodland litter keeps soil moist; water thoroughly in dry periods. Specialists recommend applying an azalea fertilizer (12-6-6) just before blooming and again in June or July.
VIRTUES   An infusion of peeled and boiled twigs has been used as a medicinal tea by Cherokee Indians.

Ricinus communis L. ⊙☠️   Spurge family
  Castor-bean

A fast-growing annual to 15 ft. with origins in tropical Africa; widely naturalized
in tropical and warm regions. Huge leaves with 5–11 pointed lobes and deeply
toothed are green, bronze, or dark purple according to the choice of cultivar.
Hardly noticeable flowering culminates in a spike of prickly fruits. Ripe shiny
seeds inside are colorfully marbled and shaped like an Egyptian scarab. All parts
of the plant are poisonous.

CULTURE   In zones 5–7 start seed indoors in February or March; germinates in
about 7 days. In zones 8–11 sow seed outdoors; self-sows. Keep large cultivars
at least 4 ft. apart. Enjoys full sun with warm temperatures and a sandy or garden
soil that is not too wet. The remarkable rapid growth of imposing and shade
providing castor-beans is appreciated by a gardener sitted beneath the large mass
of colorful foliage. Appropriate in a sunny corner of the herb garden or as a
spaced hedging screen in warm regions.

VIRTUES   Seeds, poisonous if eaten, yield castor oil used medicinally, in soaps,
paints, and varnishes.

Rosa spp.   Rose family
  Old roses

In Chapter 4 is a small commentary on old roses. The most ancient species and hybrids which claim a place in the herb garden are described with
cultural suggestions and virtues. From them many lovely and exquisitely perfumed old roses have been derived before 1867 which are not included. They
can be found in more complete old rose literature and in old rose nursery
catalogs.

Rosmarinus officinalis L.   Mint family
  Rosemary

The aromatic, much-branched, evergreen shrub to 5 ft. high is native in the
Mediterranean region growing among calcareous rocks on dry, warm slopes in
view of the blue Sea below. The association is evoked wherever leaves emit the
resinous scent. Closely set dark-green to gray-green, needlelike leaves to 1½ in.
long are grayish-white beneath. Light to bright blue-violet 2-lipped flowers
bloom in clusters along and toward the ends of leafy branches; blossoms are
sporadic, but most abundant from zone 7 southward in fall, winter, and early
spring. Branching varies from rigid upright to gracefully curved or prostrate
forms. The last two are well-suited for bonsai. Planting prostrate forms in a sun-

warmed stone or brick wall gives frost protection and branches have less contact with soil and moisture. Added to branching forms are cultivars based on flower color from white to deep blue and 'Majorica' which is pink. Hardiness of cultivars is variable. Cultivar names with descriptions are found in herb specialist catalogs.

CULTURE   Advantages of starting rosemarys from seed are questionable. Low seed viability of cultivars, abortive seedlings, or progeny unlike a parent are reasons for propagating from stem cuttings. Stem cuttings root in 3–4 weeks, the same time for seed to germinate, while a 3–4 in. rooted plant is potted and on its way. Because many rosemarys carry latent fungus diseases in all organs except the seed, rosemary propagators who want plant stock free of systemic fungus infected plants start from seed. Layering is very successful; peg down lower branches on outdoor plants. Give a year-round outdoor plant a sheltered position on a mound of well-drained, neutral to slightly alkaline garden soil and full sun. A teaspoon or tablespoon of bonemeal added to the soil at planting time stimulates root growth. Space plants 4–6 feet apart or allow 3 square feet for a single plant. Mix soil with pea-gravel or chopped oyster chips for a top dressing. Apply an inorganic complete fertilizer in early spring; avoid over-fertilizing and over-watering. Provide winter protection in unsheltered gardens from zone 7 northward. Hardiness varies from 20 F: to -10 F: for different cultivars and are best matched to the garden's climatic zone to avoid losses. A rapidly growing potted rosemary requires transplanting or pruning.

VIRTUES   Rosemary's penetrating aroma requires prudence in amounts added for a savory dish, from a joint of lamb to a mess of fresh, green peas. Apple jelly delicately flavored with a rosemary infusion is a fine accompaniment to poultry or ham. The spectrum in cuisine is wide; wise is the cook who uses restraint. The volatile oil is an ingredient in "eau de Cologne," and high quality oil comes from flower calyces. Dried leaves and flowers are constituents of potpourri. A wine with added rosemary was taken as a medicinal. An infusion in a hair rinse brightens black hair.

Rudbeckia hirta L. ☉, ☉, or ♃△   Composite family
   Black-eyed Susan
An annual, biennial, or short-lived perennial to 3 ft. of thin woods, pastures, and roadsides throughout eastern United States. Ovate-lanceolate leaves are rough, hairy, and coarsely toothed. Solitary, stiff, bristly stems support a daisy-like flower with yellow rays, often orange at the base, and a conical disk with minute dark purple flowers; blooms from May to July and sporadically until frost.

CULTURE Sow seed in an outdoor seedbed in late fall to stratify and expect seedlings in early spring; self-sows. Or, make several divisions of a clump-forming crown. Plant in full sun or partial shade. Sturdy, compact flowering plants grown in well-drained poor soil and under dry conditions illuminate a lightly shaded woods longer and more abundantly than those of a rich garden soil.

VIRTUES American Indians used a root tea as a medicinal. R. *fulgidum* and R. *lacinata* were similarly used.

Rumex scutatus L. ♃   Buckwheat family
French sorrel

A clump-forming perennial native to Eurasia with stalked heart-shaped, ovate basal leaves and arrow-shaped stem leaves. Flower stalks to 2 ft. high bear small reddish-green flowers on unbranched, elongated terminal spikes. Small, hard, 3-angled fruits follow.

CULTURE Sow seed outdoors in early spring; self-sows. Divide mature clumps in fall. Give sorrel a well-drained garden soil and full sun or partial shade. Fertilize established plants in spring with a complete fertilizer. Strewn wood ashes or sharp sand on the soil to a clump's periphery is a deterrent to snails and slugs that attack leaves. Unremoved flowering stalks decrease leaf development.

VIRTUES Tender, acetous leaves contribute a piquant quality in early spring salads of greens; John Evelyn wrote "it gave so grateful a quickness to a salad that it should never be omitted." Soups and sauces are equally enhanced. Oxalic acid is a contributor of sorrel's flavor; it can be harmful in large amounts. R. *acetosa*, garden sorrel, and R. *acetocella*, sheep sorrel, of the weedy wild can be substituted.

Ruta graveolens L.   Rue family
Common rue, herb-of-grace

A nearly evergreen subshrub, 1–3 ft. high; native among rocks and dry limestone hills of southern Europe and the Mediterranean region. The entire plant has a strong, bitter aroma. Glaucous blue-green leaves are deeply dissected into spatulate segments. Yellow 4-petaled flowers, ½ in. across, in flat-topped clusters bloom from May to July. Black seeds are in round 4–5 lobed capsules.

CULTURE Seed sown indoors germinates in 8–12 days; self-sows. Grow in full sun or partial shade and a well-drained soil, neutral to slightly alkaline. When lightly touched, glands dotting leaf surfaces release an acrid oil; it is known to cause a dermatitis in susceptible people. For this reason plant an inside hedging of rue plants spaced 10–12 inches apart through a portion of the herb garden which can feed the eye, but out of touch. Cut plants back to 5 in. in late fall to stimulate compact growth in spring.

VIRTUES Leaves and stalks were formerly used in medicine. Important public personages kept vermicidal rue stalks close at hand to prevent contracting pestilential vermin from the common man. In Italy rue flavored a piece of bread dipped in olive oil or a salad. Roots with alum yield a red dye.

Salvia dorisiana Standl. ♃   Mint family
An aromatic, erect, branched perennial to 4 ft. from tropical Belize. Heart-shaped, toothed leaves, 3–7 in. long, release a wonderful mingled fruit and rose volatile oil from a covering of gland-tipped hairs. Magenta flowers to 2½ in . long in an elongated cluster bloom where summer is long. Not winter-hardy from zone 8 northward.

CULTURE Propagate from stem cuttings taken in autumn to keep indoors through the winter where winter-hardiness is in question. Full sun, an ordinary garden soil, tropical temperatures and moisture keep the refreshing fragrance in a garden all through the year.

VIRTUES Dried leaves are used in potpourri.

S. elegans Vahl. ♃
Pineapple-scented sage
An erect, branched, shrubby perennial to 3½ ft. from Mexico. Ovate, pointed, toothed, and hairy leaves, 2–4 in. long, are deliciously pineapple-scented. Flowers to 1½ in. long, firecracker red, along elongated stalks, make a show from early autumn until frost. Not reliably winter-hardy from zone 7 northward.

CULTURE As for *S. dorisiana*.

VIRTUES Fresh sprigs serve as a fragrant garnish on a fruit platter or in tall glasses of iced tea. Dried leaves lose potency within a short time.

S. officinalis L. ♃
Common sage
Erect, strongly aromatic sage of the kitchen garden and symbol of longevity for its general vigor and hardiness is a shrubby perennial to 2 ft.; native along the northern Mediterranean region. Gray-green, oblong, and stalked leaves to 2½ in. long have a distinctive pebbled texture. Bluish-lavender, pink, or white flowers to 1¼ in. long and arranged in whorls bloom from April to June. Cultivars differing in leaf colors, rarely flowering, and not reliably winter-hardy from zone 7 northward are: 'Aurea' (same as 'Icterina') with leaves variegated gold and green; 'Purpurea' with purplish-green leaves; and 'Tri-color' with leaves splashed white,

pink, and green. As all have a sage aroma perfectly good to use in the kitchen, they offer colorful bonuses.

CULTURE   Seed of the species sown indoors germinates in 6–10 days. Propagation from stem cuttings, layering, or division is easy and applied to the species and to multiply cultivar stock not known to produce seed. Plant in full sun and a well-drained garden soil. Scatter a complete fertilizer around clumps after cutting back straggly branches in early spring. Guard against sage's tendency to sprawl; neat, round clumps look good and leaves remain clean.

VIRTUES   Dried or fresh leaves are a popular seasoning used in poultry dressings, sausages, with pork, or wherever a taste for sage exists. The English add sage to their cheddar cheeses. The strong smell of sage tea formerly prescribed as a medicinal folk-remedy can, by an association with an unpleasant illness, dissociate the pleasure of sage as a culinary seasoning; olfactory herbal connections evoke peculiar reactions. A bee plant.

S. sclarea ☉
Clary sage
A hairy biennial with a broad basal rosette the first year and an erect, stout flower stalk to 3 ft. the second year. Indigenous to dry, alkaline soils of southern Europe. Grayish, wrinkled, hairy leaves, 6–9 in. long, are broadly ovate. White flowers to 1 in. long with white or pale lavender bracts are in whorls along a leaved stalk; blooms from May to July. The entire plant has an intense, rich musk scent. In a moonlit garden var. *turkestaniana* is especially lovely, luminous with flowers and bracts all white and skirt of silver-gray foliage.

CULTURE   Seed sown indoors germinates in 3–5 days; self-sows. Space plants 10 in. apart in full sun and well-drained, slightly alkaline soil that is allowed to dry out; wet soil causes roots to rot.

VIRTUES   The musky scent was formerly enjoyed by eating fresh leaves dipped in cream or egg yolks and fried. Extracted oil contributes a muscatel flavor to wine. Moistened seeds are mucilaginous and were used to clear foreign particles from eyes and draw splinters and thorns from flesh. Oil distilled from flowers is important in the synthetic perfume industry as a fixative. In winter seeds in remaining dry stalks attract goldfinches.

Sanguinaria canadensis L. ♃ Δ   Poppy family
Bloodroot
Bloodroot is native in mixed deciduous woods of eastern United States; rarely in the c.p. Rhizomes and stems of the perennial bleed a poisonous red-orange sap. Elegant, pure white solitary flowers in March and April have 8–12 petals, are

1½ in. across, and precede the emergence of an expanding, single, glaucous leaf, deeply lobed into broad segments. Petals fall quickly and are followed by a long narrow capsule swollen with shiny seeds beneath the leaf canopy. A double-flowered form is available, but does not set seed.

CULTURE   Fresh seed germinates readily from self-sown seed. A shallow rhizome can be divided in summer and reset in moisture-retaining soil. Shaded woodland is best for bloodroot with benefits from light for flowering before leaves emerge on the trees.

VIRTUES   Rhizomes were used medicinally by American Indians and the red sap from rhizomes was applied as a dye and decorative skin stain. The entire plant is poisonous. Investigations and experimentation show possible worthy pharmaceutical activity.

Santolina chamaecyparissus L. ♃   Composite family
Gray santolina, lavender-cotton
An aromatic, evergray perennial subshrub to 2 ft. in the Mediterranean region that savors and fits the arid heat and glare of a dry summer. Multi-branched stems bear scented silver-gray leaves to 1½ in. long, finely segmented and hairy. Yellow button-shaped flowers borne on long stalks occur on unclipped plants. Gray cv. 'Nana' is a dwarf form of *S. pinnata* used in herb gardens; another, *S. virens*, green and less hairy, is less vulnerable to blight. It flowers more abundantly and its green leaves offer contrast to gray santolinas.

CULTURE   Easily propagated from stem cuttings in autumn to hold indoors through the winter. Give santolinas full sun and a well-drained, alkaline soil. In humid climates keep plants well-spaced on mounds; mulch with chopped oyster shells. Where humidity and associated plant diseases are not factors their compact habit is suited for interior hedgings or the convolutions of a knot garden. Single, sheared plants make a striking impression when well-spaced and mingled with clumps of shiny, green-leaved germander with pink flowers, glaucous, blue-green rue with yellow flowers, or green santolina. Cut back in early spring, shear several times through the summer, and again in fall. Clipped plants keep centers from smothering and forming hollow centers. Avoid over-fertilizing and over-watering. A well-drained, dry soil increases resistance to cold winter temperatures through zone 6.

VIRTUES   Dried stalks were placed in stored linens and woolens as insect repellents. Formerly applied medicinally as a vermifuge for children. A perfume oil is extracted from leaves and stems.

Satureja hortensis L. ⊙   Mint family
   Summer savory, "Bohnenkraut," "sarriette"
An aromatic, erect, branched annual to 18 in. of the Mediterranean region. Opposite leaves are narrow to ⅞ in. long and pointed. Tiny pale pink flowers in
whorls bloom from June to September.
CULTURE   Sow tiny seeds in spring or fall in full sun and well-drained garden
soil; self-sows. Pinch tips for compact, bushy plants.
VIRTUES   Dried or fresh leaves are a favorite sharp seasoning in central European cookery, often blended with thyme; it is said summer savory supports and
strengthens the flavor of all leguminous dishes, improves sausage flavor, and aids
digestion. Chopped fresh leaves added to chilled vegetable juices or meat dishes
act as a substitute in salt and pepper-free diets. The French call it "sarriete" and
add sprigs to new peas; the Germans call it "Bohnenkraut," the bean herb, and
grow it at the kitchen door with chive, parsley, thyme, and sweet marjoram.
Note: S. montana, winter savory, an evergreen perennial, straggling and branched
to 12 in. from the Mediterranean region is described as lacking delicacy and
sweetness by cooks partial to summer savory.

Sempervivum tectorum L. ♃   Orpine family
   Hen-and-chickens, common houseleek
Logically it is not strange for a plant that has survived the merciless glare of a sun
on barren mountain slopes of southern Europe and the Atlas range of North
Africa to find a second new habitat on rooftops or in walls with an air of per-
manency. Acceptance and actuality of houseleeks on roof-tops as a charm or
protection against fire, evil, and pestilence came down from the Greeks and Romans through the Middle Ages and onward; it is respected in Sempervivum tectorum,
"ever-living plant of the roof." The mat-forming perennial is composed of
3–4 in. wide basal rosettes. The 50–60 succulent, ovate, greenish leaves of each
rosette are often purple-tipped. A mature rosette becomes surrounded by offshoots to provide the common name hen-and-chickens. From June to September pink flowers bloom on 1½ ft. high stalks; a flowering rosette dies after setting
seed. (See plates 22 and 23.)
CULTURE   Offshoots can be detached and reset in a well-drained thin layer of
mixed loam and fine gravel. Plants spread quickly on a sunny rock garden or
from crevices of a stone wall; set offshoots in a shallow stone trough, a clay container, perhaps hen-shaped; or, in an old gardener's shoe (perhaps your own)
filled with a mixture of equal parts coarse sand and soil kept barely moist during
the growing season. Forget watering during the dormant winter season. Grows

in all but the humid Gulf coast area. Since many plants are of hybrid origin, plants from seed which readily germinate will produce a mixed progeny.

VIRTUES Houseleek rosettes have a symbolic place in herb gardens for their interconnections to ancient superstition, medicinal applications, and symbol of long life with ability to thrive despite meager resources.

Sesamum indicum L. ⊙   Pedalium family
   Sesame

An erect, unbranched annual, 3–4 ft., of Old World tropical regions. By early caravan trade and ancient Rome's movements and occupations in North Africa the entire Mediterranean region became acquainted with sesame seed as a treasure of flavor. Seed was introduced into the South during the seventeenth and eighteenth centuries by slaves from Africa as "benne," a common name in continuous use in southern states. It was coaxed into growing as a commercial corp in Texas, Louisiana, California, and Arizona and is now naturalized from Florida to Texas. A herb to grow in tropical and subtropical herb gardens of Florida and the Gulf coast. Sesame stems are crowded with ovate, coarse, fuzzy leaves. Whitish or pink flowers to ¾ in. long are borne in leaf axils. Silky smooth, pale primrose yellow seeds are in 4-grooved pods which split with a force and magic of "open sesame" to eject seeds.

CULTURE Sesame is easily grown from seed sown outdoors in loose, sandy soil of warm climates that can supply long, hot summers. Space plants 12 in. apart. A problem in commercial harvesting is the shattering of pods and scattering of seed when plants are cut; plant breeders work to develop a strain which will mature evenly and is non-shattering to avoid seed loss.

VIRTUES On buns, breads, and baked confections seeds add a delicate nutlike flavor. The real treasure is inside their smooth shells. Crushed sesame seeds yield a light, pale golden oil with delicate fragrance. It is fine for all types of cooking and salad dressings and was first used in India and warm parts of China. Sesame oil is rich in food value and low in polysaturated fats; it keeps indefinitely without becoming rancid. Oil is used to make soothing lotions. Boiled with wood-ashes it makes a soap. Chinese burned sesame oil, the soot of which made their midnight-black ink. Queen Scheherazade chose the password to secret treasure.

Smilacina racemosa (L.) Desf. ♃△   Lily family
   False Solomon's seal

A rhizomatous perennial from 1–3 ft. high; native in deciduous woodland of temperate North America south to Georgia, Alabama, and Mississippi; not in the c.p. Arching or erect stems are slightly angled at alternate, ovate leaves in a zigzag fashion. From April to June small white flowers bloom in terminal elongated branched clusters, 4–6 in. long; clusters of globose fruits, ruby red when mature, follow.

CULTURE Propagate by dividing rhizomes. Plants freely colonize in moist, woodland soil, partly shaded.

VIRTUES American Indians used infusions of rhizomes and leaves medicinally. Smoke of a burning rhizome was inhaled as therapeutic. Berries are palatable, but cathartic.

Solidago odora Ait. ⁊Δ   Composite family
Sweet goldenrod

Native goldenrods are often mistakenly considered a cause of hayfever, whereas common ragweed, *Ambrosia artemisiafolia*, is the serious culprit. And of all the goldenrods, only perennial sweet goldenrod to 5 ft. tall, widely distributed in thin woods, savannahs, pine barrens, and along roadsides, has a herbal connection. It is easily recognized by the anise odor emitted when the untoothed, lanceolate leaves to 4 in. long are crushed. Small golden yellow flowers in elongated heads are in typical goldenrod clusters.

CULTURE Propagate by dividing a root crown in late fall or winter. Expect a low percentage of self-sown seedlings in spring; it may be higher than any other method. Sun or light shade and a well-drained ordinary soil with a mulch of leaf mold or pine needles satisfies.

VIRTUES Dried anise-scented leaves have been used for a pleasant tea. Cherokee Indians applied the leaf tea as a medicinal. According to Wilbur H. Duncan and Leonard Foote, fungus infected plants of S. *odora* and other species are suspected of causing poisoning.

Spartium junceum L.   Bean family
Spanish broom, weaver's broom

A stiff, rushlike bush to 10 ft. with slender and cylindrical almost leafless grayish-green branches; native to dry slopes and calcareous soils of the Mediterranean region. Small blue-green oblong leaves, pointed at bases and tips, appear in spring and soon fall. Gloriously grape-scented and brilliant yellow peaflowers to 1 in. long borne in loose terminal clusters begin to bloom in April. Hairless, flat, many-seeded pods to 2 in. long ripen to gray-black.

CULTURE Seed, nicked and soaked overnight in water before sowing indoors germinates in 3–6 days; self-sows; viability of stored seed is very high. Plant in full sun and well-drained, slightly alkaline soil. Hardy through zone 8, and in a sheltered position in zone 7. An underused herbal plant in herb gardens of warm climates.

VIRTUES From ancient times stems have been used for basket making and for a fiber similar to hemp in weaving. An alkaloid in the paint acts as a purgative, emetic, and diuretic.

Stachys byzantina C. Koch ♃   Mint family
Lamb's ears

Plants enter herb gardens by a cachet of virtues. Aside from virtues, silver-gray foliage of lamb's ear fortuitously compliments almost any herb planted nearby. A dense covering of white-woolly hairs on gray-green, pointed, elliptic leaves to 6 in. long gives them a tactile, silky texture. A perennial in warm, arid, and rocky regions of Turkey and southwestern Asia, the hairy covering conserves moisture in the leaf and cools it. Pink to lavender flowers are borne in whorls on leaved stalks rising to 1½ ft.; blooms from April through summer.

CULTURE Seed sown indoors germinates in 4–6 days. Mature clumps can be divided in early spring or fall. Plant in a sunny position and a well-drained soil. Wet winters or a soil kept moist introduces rot; cultivated with difficulty in humid, often wet winters of southern Florida and along the Gulf. Cut back flower stalks to encourage spreading.

VIRTUES Woolly leaves were used in the Middle Ages for bandaging wounds and is referred to as woundwort in old herbals among plants similarly used.

Stevia rebaudiana Bertoni ☉   Composite family
Sweet herb of Paraguay

A low-growing shrubby annual to 18 in.; native in tropical Paraguay and adjacent regions of Brazil. Opposite leaves to 2¼ in. long are elliptic and toothed; remarkably sweet leaves retain the sweetness indefinitely after drying. Small, whitish, starry flowers in clusters are borne in leaf axils; blooms in late summer.

CULTURE Propagate from stem cuttings. Grow in sun or light shade and well-drained soil. If not pinched to encourage branching a trailing, leggy plant persists from strong roots.

VIRTUES Paraguay natives have long used dried ground leaves as a sweetening agent for bitter beverages. Water in which leaves are soaked is used for sweetening purposes. The sweet-tasting stevioside, a glycoside, is 300 times sweeter than sucrose, and reports indicate no ill effects follow use. Cultivation in Japan has begun for marketing the sweetener. The fashion for "light" and "diet" products creates a market for the sweetener long known and enjoyed by the Aztecs.

Tagetes lucida Cav. ♃   Composite family
Sweet-scented marigold
Herb gardeners in southern regions grow sweet-scented marigold from Mexico
as similar in flavor to French tarragon of western Siberian origin which is difficult
in warm climates. The Mexican plant is an easy perennial to 2½ ft. high with
unbranched stems and opposite, unstalked, oblong leaves, slightly toothed.
From late summer and into fall clusters of flowers, each with 3 yellow rays,
brighten branch tops.
CULTURE   Seed sown indoors germinates in 6–8 days. Stem cuttings are easy
to root. Divide mature clumps in early spring. Plant 1½ ft. apart in a sunny position
and a well-drained garden soil. Winter-hardiness is not a consideration where
French tarragon flourishes.
VIRTUES   Fresh leaves are used in salads. Unlike French tarragon, the aniselike
scent of sweet-scented marigold in dried leaves or in a vinegar lacks stability.

Teucrium chamaedrys L.   Mint family
Germander
An aromatic, leafy shrub to 18 in. of dry, sunny, calcareous places in the Mediterranean region. Shiny, dark green oaklike leaves to ¾ in. long are evergreen.
Pink 2-lipped flowers in 2–6 flowered whorls on loose spikes bloom from May
to August.
CULTURE   Propagate from stem cuttings; seed is slow to germinate. Plant in full
sun and a well-drained soil. For a miniature hedging space plants 4–6 in. apart,
and shear regularly during the growing season. In early spring cut back woody
stems near the soil surface to stimulate compact growth; scatter a complete fertilizer around the shrubs. Germander is easier to maintain as an edging than
santolina. Protect evergreen leaves from zone 6 northward with a straw or hay
covering in winter.
VIRTUES   Folk-medicine handed down germander as a remedy for gout, intermittent fevers, coughs, asthma, and a simple tonic. Scent made it a strewing herb.

Thuja occidentalis L. ▲   Cypress family
American arborvitae, white cedar
An aromatic, resinous, medium-sized evergreen tree to 60 ft. with gray-brown to
red bark and flattened branches. Native in moist soils from Nova Scotia south to
the mts. in Georgia. Scalelike, glandular leaves are arranged in over-lapping flat

sprays. Bell-shaped cones to ½ in. long are scaled. Horticultural forms differ in leaf color and plant form.

CULTURE   Propagate from soft or hardwood cuttings. White cedar grows in sun, partial or full shade, a soil kept reasonably moist, and a moist atmosphere. Flushes with cold water help control red spider attacks.

VIRTUES   Wood, leaves, and cones have been used medicinally by American Indians. Essential oil distilled from leaves is used in flavoring, insecticides, paints, perfume, and soaps; toxic thujane contained in the oil is removed.

Thymus spp. ♃   Mint family
Thyme

The three to four hundred species of thyme have their native habitats in the sunny Mediterranean region with greatest diversity in the Balkan and Iberian peninsulas and as far away as Greenland, Scandinavia, and the Caucasus. Some herb nursery catalogs list about 50 species and horticultural forms which make selection difficult when each one has some special appeal. For making choices it is helpful to separate thymes into two main groups, the small, upright twiggy bushes to 12 in. high from those which grow as somewhat woody perennial, prostrate creepers or in low spreading mounds. Small, evergreen, lanceolate or rounded leaves are petioled, glossy or hairy. They diffuse a fragrance from glands that carries exuberance and vigor. From April to July white to pale pink and lilac to rose purple flowers blossom in clusters at branch ends or in whorls borne in leaf axils.

CULTURE   Seed sown indoors of upright common thyme and prostrate thymes when seed is available germinates in 5–10 days; self-sows. Mix tiny seeds with sharp sand for even distribution on the medium and strew a thin covering of sand over the surface. All thyme species, hybrids, and cultivars can be propagated from stem cuttings. All can be divided by lifting plants in spring; carefully tease away clusters of woody stems with attached roots; reset in new openings with 1 teaspoon bonemeal added to the soil, tamp, and water. Peg down prostrate branches in fall and scatter a thin covering of sieved compost over the branches; keep leafy tips exposed. In spring cut away a layered, rooted branch and reset. All thymes luxuriate under a hot sun in well-drained, calcareous soil tending to be more dry than wet. Wet soil or poor drainage in winter effects greater losses than low temperatures. Except in an arid climate, upright thymes are not suited to close, mass plantings. Build or mimic a rock garden habitat, and tuck plants between calcareous rocks partially imbedded in a soil mixed with pea gravel or chopped oyster chips. Prostrate thymes drape themselves softly over rocky slopes, mounds, and banks; or persistently march along in a crevice of a flagstone path with roots reaching down for calcium. When bees are gathering nectar from flowers, tread gingerly on a carpet of creeping thyme, and reflect on the folly of an upholstered bench of flowering creeping thyme. Cut back prostrate branches after flowering in fall or early spring; cut back upright thymes to half of the previous year's growth. In autumn take stem cuttings of thymes not winter-hardy to hold indoors through the winter. Unless planted on high mounds, well-distanced among rocks, thymes are difficult to grow in the Gulf area.

T. x citriodorus (Pers.) Schreb. ex Schweigg. & Korte
Lemon-scented thyme

A shrubby hybrid of T. *vulgaris* and T. *pulegioides* with semitrailing branches, leaves narrowly ovate, and pale lilac flowers. Cultivars are: 'Aureus' with golden variegated leaves; 'Silver Queen', silver variegated. Winter protection is advised from zone 7 northward.

VIRTUES   Float fresh sprigs in a soup tureen or bowls of split pea or lentil soup for a lemon-thyme aroma.

T. herba-barona Loisel.
Caraway thyme

A flat, trailing, subshrub with tiny dark green caraway-scented leaves and deep pink flowers native to Corsica and Sardinia.

VIRTUES   Fresh leaves are an excellent roast beef or hamburger seasoning. Its epithet is derived from the medieval custom of rubbing sprigs over barons of beef. Potency dissipates when dried. A bee plant.

T. nummularis Bieb. ♃
Marjoram-leaved thyme

A mildly thyme-scented, rapidly and horizontally spreading prostrate perennial, woody at its base; native to Caucasus and very hardy. Glossy-green leaves are rounded; flowers are rose-pink. An excellent groundcover among rocks in a dry, sunny situation.

VIRTUES   A bee plant.

T. praecox Opiz. ♃
Common wild thyme

A prostrate, somewhat woody, creeping perennial; native in Europe. Leaves are rounded, flowers purple. Winter protection is advised from zone 6 northward. Subsp. *articus* (E. Durand) Jalas is native to Greenland and Scandinavia, and south to northwestern Spain. Flowers are rose-purple. Cultivars are: 'Alba' with white flowers; 'Coccineus', crimson; 'Splendens', red. Subsp. *Skorpilli* (Velen.) Jalas is native in the Balkan peninsula.

VIRTUES   All subspecies and cultivars of T. *praecox* are thyme-scented and favorites of bees. For a supply of Greek honey without the intervening bee: Cut 2 handfuls of unsoiled creeping thyme branches; examine for any extraneous matter and add them to 2 lbs. of clover honey heated in a glass container over a hot water bath until the honey is slightly warm. Remove the honey jar from the water bath and attach a lid. After 10 days reheat the opened jar over a water bath. When it is warm and runs freely strain to remove thyme and jar.

T. *vulgaris* L.
Common thyme

An erect, branched shrub to 15 in. with a rich, pungent thyme scent; native in dry, rocky limestone or clay soils of the western Mediterranean region to southeastern Italy. Gray-green, lanceolate stalked leaves, reddish underneath when young, are covered with glandular dots. Pinkish-white flowers in rounded heads and whorls bloom from April to July. Common cultivars are: 'Argenteus' with variegated silver and green leaves; 'Aureus', variegated golden yellow and green.

VIRTUES   Fresh or dried leaves, high in the essential oil known as thymol, are important as a culinary seasoning. During the Middle Ages thymol's antibacterial property was valued in the preservation and seasoning of meat in the form of sausages. Refrigeration today is reason to eliminate thyme as a preservative, but satisfying, fixed flavor combinations are not readily abandoned. Today thymol is derived from various species of thyme for antibacterial uses in medicine and as a disinfectant. Thyme oils are in perfumery for scenting soap and cosmetics, sachet powders, deodorants. Decoctions of thyme were used to wash wine vessels in Seville.

Tiarella cordifolia L. ♃ ▲   Saxifrage family
Foamflower, miterwort

A rhizomatous perennial; native in rich, acid soil of shaded woodland from Nova Scotia south through the Appalachians to Georgia; var. *collina* with stolons occurs south to Georgia, Alabama, and Mississippi. Lobed, toothed, and stalked basal leaves to 4 in. long are evergreen, red-veined in winter. Frothy clusters of white star-shaped flowers on stalks to 12 in. bloom in April and May.

CULTURE   Divide mature clumps in fall or early spring. Cut stolons (surface runners) of var. *collina* to separate clumps. Plant in partial to full shade and well-drained woodland soil high in organic matter. A mulch of composted oak leaves keeps the soil acid and moist.

VIRTUES Cherokee Indians prepared a leaf and root tea for medicinal applications.

Tillandsia usneoides L. **Δ**   Pineapple family
Spanish moss, gray moss
Alluring Spanish moss festooned in masses over live oaks is native in low woods of the southeast c.p. and southern regions of the southeast pied. An identified fungus disease is causing its decline. Long, slender, wiry stems have attached threadlike leaves. Both stems and leaves bear small silvery-gray scales which hold water and dust particles, sustaining nutrients. Small, pale green or blue flowers are solitary in axils of leaves.
CULTURE The seed plant and epiphyte, taking all its nutrition from the air, prefers to dwell in live oaks. Craggy bark gives seeds and seedlings a secure hold, and stout limbs which never loose their leaves protect the moss from wind and drying effects of the sun. To establish new parental lines tie or place collected moss on healthy live oak limbs and hope it will catch.
VIRTUES Between 1900 and 1940 Spanish moss was ginned into long dark fibers to use as horsehair for upholstery stuffing, packing material, and in fish hatcheries to collect and preserve eggs of spawning females. Used to preserve moisture in potted plants and as decorative bedding in floral arrangements. The use of unfumigated moss for campsite bedding is dangerous because chiggers are common occupants.

Tradescantia virginiana L. ♃**Δ**   Spiderwort family
Common spiderwort
A clump-forming perennial of slender, fleshy stalks, 1–2 ft. tall. Native in well-drained open woods and meadows of eastern United States, south to Georgia and Mississippi in the lower pied. Linear-lanceolate leaves are 6–12 in. long. Flowers, 1–1½ in. across in crowded terminal clusters, have 3 ephemeral blue petals, occasionally purple, rose, or white; blooms from March to July.
CULTURE Stem cuttings are easy to root at any time during the growing season; remove flower clusters from a stem cut into segments, each with at least 2 nodes, and insert in a rooting medium of moist sand; stems root in 3 weeks. Divide clumps in fall or early spring every 3–4 years. Fresh seed sown in an outdoor bed germinates in about 2 weeks. Thin seedlings, and when well-established move them to a sunny or lightly shaded position in a woodland opening or meadow. A sandy or rocky soil only slightly enriched with humus suits spiderworts. Cut away stalks with spent flower clusters for a second bloom in late summer.

VIRTUES   Cherokee Indians prepared a tea of roots and other plant material for a number of ailments. Leaf poultices were applied to insect bites. *T. ohiensis*, widely distributed in eastern United States and *T. subspera* from West Virginia to northern Florida have been similarly used.

Trilisia odoratissima (Walter ex J.F.Gwelin) Cassini ♃▲   Composite family
Vanilla plant, deer's tongue
A smooth, distinctly vanilla-scented perennial to 5 ft.; native in poorly drained pine barrens, savannahs, and thin woods of the c.p. from North Carolina to Florida, Georgia, Alabama, and Mississippi. Basal leaves are elliptic to 12 in. long. Pink-purple disc flowers (ray flowers absent) and pappus bristles in heads form more-or-less flat-topped clusters; blooms from late July to October.
CULTURE   Divide mature clumps consisting of many closely-spaced stems in spring; include one or more stems with their roots in each division; reset and water. Position plants in sun or partial shade and a moisture-retaining soil.
VIRTUES   Dried leaves, high in vanilla-scented coumarin content, are collected and sold to flavor tobacco products. A folk-medicine for a number of ailments.

Tropaeolum majus L. ☉   Nasturtium family
Nasturtium
A climbing or sprawling, slightly succulent annual reaching 6–10 ft.; native in Andean South America. Climbing is achieved by coiling leaf stalks attached at the center of roundish leaves, 2–7 in. wide. Brilliant yellow, orange, or red spurred flowers to 2½ in. long are mingled in the lush green foliage and bloom continuously from June to frost. Wrinkled 3-lobed fruits separate into 3 wrinkled seeds. Horticultural forms differ in flower color and plant habit.
CULTURE   Sow seed where plants are to grow in warm soil. Seed soaked overnight in water before sowing germinates in 7–10 days. Thin seedlings 6–10 in. apart. An enriched soil results in heavy foliage; a lean, sandy soil encourages blossoms. Full sun is preferred in cool climates; partial shade in warm climates decreases common attacks of unsightly black aphids. Sprays of cold water help by flushing them out of sight. Leaf miners may disfigure leaves, but seldom require control. Provide a trellis or pole for climbers. Spilling from a window box, from a terrace container, or a hanging basket, nasturtiums and hummingbird visitors decorate and catch attention.
VIRTUES   Chopped leaves and flowers or their buds add a sharp, peppery dimension to a salad or butter. Pickled buds and young fruits become an inexpensive caper substitute.

Tussilago farfara L. ♃   Composite family
Coltsfoot

A stoloniferous perennial of the Old World, naturalized in eastern North America, and capable of reaching pernicious weed status. Stalked, round to heart-shaped leaves, shallow-toothed and with indented margins, appear after the flowers. Dandelionlike yellow flowers on scaled stalks to 6 in. high are among the earliest spring flowers to bloom from February to April.

CULTURE   Propagate by division of clumps. Grow in woodland to benefit from a spring sun and summer shade or on a dry bank site where its limits might be controlled. The entire plant disappears by early summer. A cheering, lovely show of early yellow flowers with bright blue spikes of Scillas, sometimes through a light snow, compensates giving the invasive herb a place.

VIRTUES   *Tussilago* is rooted in "tussis," a cough. As all parts of coltsfoot are mucilaginous, a decoction of leaves boiled in water, and sweetened with honey was a sticky, common European cough remedy. Smoked dried leaves act as an antihistamine. Alkaloids present in the plant are potentially toxic in large doses. Popularity of coltsfoot in Paris is demonstrated by the painted coltsfoot flower used as a sign on doorposts of apothecary shops.

Urginea maritima (L.) Bak. ♃   Lily family
Sea onion, squill

A perennial growing from a nearly globular bulb, 4–6 in. in diameter; native in dry, rocky, sandy places along the Mediterranean seacoast and in South Africa. The bulb, only half immersed in sand or soil, sends up several slightly fleshy, strap-shaped, shining leaves to 2 ft. long in autumn after the plant has flowered. Leaves are dormant during the summer. In late summer a leafless, succulent flower stalk rises 1–3 ft. tall and terminates in a candlelike spike of starlike white flowers.

CULTURE   Seed sown indoors germinates in 7 days. Squill is slow-growing and requires transplanting to ever larger pots as the bulb develops. While you wait for a floral display, nurture a potted bulb with occasional waterings and give it place in summer sun. Move it indoors through the winter from zone 8 northward. Expect flowering three years after seed germination.

VIRTUES   A cardiac glycoside in the bulb is similar to Digitalis and was applied by ancient Egyptians in a prescription as a heart remedy. Red squill, a rat poison, is made from red-coated bulbs of a North African subspecies.

Vetiveria zizanioides (L.) Nash ♃   Grass family
  Vetiver
A rhizomatous, aromatic, perennial grass to 8 ft. high; native along river banks in
tropical India and Sri Lanka and long grown in Louisiana gardens. Odorless,
smooth, and flexible leaf sheaths enclose stiff long blades.
CULTURE Propagate by division of sweet-scented rhizomes. Give the grand
and graceful grass a sheltered position in full sun and moist soil. A plant for every
herb garden in zones 8–11; not reliably winter-hardy from zone 7 northward. A
good time to take a harvest of roots for scenting linens is every 3–4 years when
rhizomes need dividing.
VIRTUES Vetiver is cultivated for the fragrant roots woven into mats, screens, and
baskets. Distilled oil of vetiver from roots is in perfume, soaps, and cosmetics.

Viburnum prunifolium L. ▲   Honeysuckle family
  Black haw, nannyberry
A deciduous, flowering shrub or tree to 20 ft. of moist places or rich soils on
hillsides and in low woods from New York south to the pied. of Georgia, Alabama, and Mississippi. Opposite dark green, leathery, elliptic leaves to 3 in. long
are toothed and turn a lovely red-bronze in fall. White flowers in rounded clusters, 4 in. across, bloom from April to May. Oval fruits in the course of ripening
go through color changes from green to yellow to red to blue-black.
CULTURE Propagate from softwood cuttings taken in late spring. To withstand
the shock of transplanting wait until secondary roots develop before planting in
a rich, moist soil and a sunny or partially shaded position. Sucker growth of a
previous season's growth can be layered in spring to root in 1½–2 years.
VIRTUES American Indians prepared a medicinal tea of roots and stem bark.
European settlers who knew and had used European *V. opulus*, adopted black
haw as similar for medicinal usage. Fruits are toxic, but edible when cooked.

Vitex agnus-castus L.   Verbena family
  Chaste tree
An elegant, deciduous, much-branched shrub reaching to 15 ft.; native along
stream banks and moist places of the Mediterranean coast. Opposite, stalked
compound leaves of 5–7 radiating lanceolate leaflets are dark-green above and
gray-woolly below. Blue-lavender, strangely aromatic flowers in pyramidal clusters, 5–7 in. long, bloom on the current year's growth in June and sporadically
until autumn.

CULTURE Propagate by pegging down branches of the previous season's growth and originating near the soil surface. Nick slightly at the nodes, cover with soil leaving the branch tip exposed, and check for roots the following spring. Self-sown seed germinates and seedlings can be transplanted. The shrub grows in good, moisture-retaining soil and a sunny or lightly-shaded position. Winter-hardy through zone 6 and in a sheltered position through zone 5. No climate is too hot for the chaste tree, and roots can survive after frost damages the above soil plant parts.

VIRTUES Tradition has seeds used as an anaphrodisiac by men leading monastic lives. A more recent confirmed medicinal application centers on a hormone-like substance in the seed used to treat hormonal imbalances in women. The peculiarly pungent seeds are used as a pepperlike seasoning in condiments. Leaves, roots, and seeds with alum yield a yellow dye. An early printed herbal with herbs listed alphabetically and without a title is referred to officially as the "Agnus-castus Herbal," after its first entry.

Xanthorhiza simplicissima Marsh. △   Crowfoot family
   Yellowroot
A vigorously colonizing low shrub to 20 in. high with yellow stolons and bark; native in shaded moist soils from New York south to Georgia, Alabama, and Mississippi. An erect, unbranched, woody stem bears a dense mass of foliage only at the top portion. Stalked and pinnately compound leaves consist of 3–5 ovate leaflets to 3 in. long, the terminal leaflet 3-cleft, all sharply toothed. Drooping slender stalks at the base of the current year's growth bear small maroon flowers from March to May.

CULTURE Divide creeping yellow stolons in early spring or fall. Plant in partial or full shade and in ordinary woodland soil. Fast-spreading, naked stems and leafy tops that keep a regular uniform height and turn bright yellow to reddish orange in the fall make an excellent native ground cover in woodland landscaping.

VIRTUES American Indians used a root tea medicinally. Southern settlers included it in their lists of folk-medicines. Yellowroot is potentially toxic in large doses.

Yucca filamentosa L. ♃ △   Lily family
   Adam's needle, bear-grass
An evergreen perennial; native in open, dry habitats from Virginia to Florida and Mississippi. Stiffly upright, leathery leaves rising from a woody base are narrow

and pointed to 2½ ft. long with curling fibers splitting from the margins. Creamy-white pendulous flowers, 2½ in. wide, are arranged in a lose pyramidal cluster at the top of a tall upright flowering stalk, blooms from late May to June. A three-parted capsule follows with flattened black seeds.

CULTURE Propagate by separating well-rooted offshoots from the base of a mature plant. Root cuttings or a piece of root broken in transplanting and remaining in the soil gives rise to new plants. Plant yuccas in a sunny position where soil is sandy, well-drained, and ground not excessively moist in winter. Designate a pathway entrance with one or more yuccas that stand out; or, tuck them to the back of a garden and experience candelabra lighting among the herbs at night when in bloom.

VIRTUES American Indians used roots medicinally in salves and poultices. Slurries of pounded roots containing toxic saponins were put into streams to stupefy fish for easy harvest. Saponins from pounded and boiled roots were also used as soap to wash blankets. Leaves provide a fiber for twine.

When it came to feeling close to Granny, being in the garden was a sight better than sitting by her coffin. Out there amidst all the growing things, it seemed like maybe she'd just gone to the shed room to get a hoe instead of being off in Heaven.

I stood and looked for a long time. Over yonder were what she called her 'word plants'—the wild flowers she planted because they had names she liked. Creepin' Charlie, Lizzie run by the fence, love's a bustin', fetch me some ivy cause Baby's got the croup. . . . In the next bed were medicinal herbs she used in potions for sick folks: squaw weed, hepatica, goldenseal, ginseng for the brain, jewelweed for poison ivy rash, wolf milk for warts, and fleabane and pale bergamot, which Granny would rub on her face and arms to keep off mosquitos and gnats.

But on that early June morning, the heavy scent of roses was what made my heart ache. It was hard to believe the roses could be so alive and her so dead.

—Olive Ann Burns
Cold Sassy Tree

Bibliography

A Barefoot Doctor's Manual. Prepared by the Revolutionary Health Committee of Hunan. Oceanside, NY: Cloudburst Press of America, Inc., 1977.

Adroska, Rita J. *Natural Dyes and Home Dyeing*. New York: Dover Publications, 1971.

Anderson, Edgar. *The Tarragons, Cultivated and Wild*. In "Herbs for Use and for Delight, An Anthology from the Herbarist." New York: Dover Publications, 1974.

Arber, Agnes. *Herbals, Their Origin and Evolution*. Darien, CN: Hafner Publ. Co., 2nd ed., 1970.

Bailey Hortorium. *Hortus Third*. New York: Macmillan Co., 1976.

Beckett, Kenneth A., David Carr, and David Stevens. *The Contained Garden, A Complete Illustrated Guide to Growing Outdoor Plants in Pots*. London: Frances Lincoln Limited, 1982.

Bible, The. Revised Standard Version. Cleveland, OH: The World Publishing Co., 1962.

Bond, Robert E. *The Caper Bush*. Mentor, OH: The Herbarist, No. 56, 1990.

Brookes, John. *The Small Garden*. New York: Gallery Books, 1979.

Brooklyn Botanic Garden. *Dye Plants and Dyeing*, 1976.

Craker, L. E., Editor. *The Herb, Spice, & Medicinal Plant Digest*. Amherst, MA: University of Massachusetts.

Darrah, Helen H. *The Cultivated Basils*. Independence, MO: Buckeye Printing Co., 1980.

Densmore, Frances. *How Indians Use Wild Plants for Food, Medicine, and Crafts*. New York: Dover Publications, 1974.

Dickelman, J. and R. Schuster. *Natural Landscaping, A Complete Guide to Landscaping with Native Communities*. New York: McGraw-Hill Book Co., 1982.

Duncan, Wilbur H. and Marion B. Duncan. *Trees of the Southeastern United States*. Athens, GA: University of Georgia Press, 1988.

────── and Leonard E. Foote. *Wildflowers of the Southeastern United States*. Athens, GA: University of Georgia Press, 1975.

Edwards, Gordon. *Wild and Old Roses*. New York: Hafner Press, 1975.

Everett, Thomas H. *The New York Botanical Garden Illustrated Encyclopedia of Horticulture*. 10 Vols. New York: Garland, 1980.

Fernald, M. L. *Gray's New Manual of Botany*. New York: American Book Co., 8th ed., 1950.

Foster, Gertrude B. and Rosemary F. Louden. *Park's Success with Herbs*. Greenwood, SC: Geo. W. Park Seed Co., 1980.

Foster, H. Lincoln. *Rock Gardening*. New York: Bonanza Books, 1968.

Foster, Steven and James Duke. *A Field Guide to Medicinal Plants—Eastern and Central North America*. Boston, MA: Houghton Mifflin Co., 1990.

Fowler, Marie Garvey. *The Use of Herbs by the South During the War between the States*. Boston, MA: The Herbarist, No. 54, 1988.

Galle, Fred. *Native and Some Introduced Azaleas for Southern Gardens—Kinds and Culture*. Booklet No. 2 Pine Mountain, GA: Ida Cason Callaway Foundation, 1979.

Gerard, John. *The Herbal*. New York: Dover Publications, reproduced 1633 edition of T. Johnson, 1975.

Grieve, Mrs. Maud. *A Modern Herbal* 2 Vols. New York: Dover Publications 1971.

Hamel, Paul B. and Mary U. Chiltoskey. *Cherokee Plants*. Sylva, NC: Herald Publ. Co., 1975.

Hartmann, Hudson T. and Dale E. Kester. *Plant Propagation*. Englewood Cliffs, NJ: Prentice-Hall, Inc., 3rd ed., 1975.

Healey, B. J. *A Gardener's Guide to Plant Names*. New York: Charles Scribner's Sons, 1972.

Heywood, Vernon, Ed. and Stuart R. Chant, Assoc. Ed. *Popular Encyclopedia of Plants*. Cambridge: Cambridge University Press, 1982.

Hunt, William Lanier. *Southern Gardens, Southern Gardening*. Durham, NC: Duke University Press, 1982.

Inglett, G. E. *Unusual Sweetners of Plant Origin*. Concord, MA: The Herbarist, No. 48, 1982.

Kreig, Margaret B. *Green Medicine*. New York: Rand McNally & Co., 1964.

Krüssmann, Gerd. *The Complete Book of Roses*. Portland, OR: Timber Press, 1981.

Lawrence, Elizabeth. *A Southern Garden*. Chapel Hill: University of North Carolina Press, revised 2nd ed., 1967.

May, Lenore Wile. *The Economic Uses and Associated Folklore of Ferns and Fern Allies.* Bronx, NY: The Botanical Review, Vol. 144, No. 4, 1978.

Miller, Amy Bess. *Shaker herbs, A History and a Compendium.* New York: Clarkson N. Potter, Inc., 1976.

Millspaugh, Charles F. *American Medicinal Plants.* New York: Dover Publications, 1974.

Moldenke, Harold N. and Alma L. Moldenke. *Plants of the Bible.* New York: The Ronald Press Co., 1952.

Oosting, Henry J. *The Study of Plant Communities.* San Francisco, CA: W. H. Freeman & Co., 2nd ed., 1956.

Phillips, Harry R. *Growing and Propagating Wildflowers.* Chapel Hill, NC: University of North Carolina Press, 1985.

Polynin, Oleg & Anthony Huxley. *Flowers of the Mediterranean.* London: Chatto and Windus, revised, 1972.

Radford, Albert E., Harry E. Ahles, and C. Ritchie Bell. *Manual of the Vascular Flora of the Carolinas.* Chapel Hill, NC: University of North Carolina Press, 1968.

Rosetti, Gioanventura. *The Plictho, with a Translation of the First Edition of 1548* by Sidney M. Edelstein and Hector C. Borghetty. Cambridge, MA and London: The M.I.T. Press, 1969. (A book on the art of dyeing.)

Rushing, Felder. *Gardening Southern Style.* Jackson, MS: University Press of Mississippi, 1987.

Ruttle, Mabel. *Some Common Mints and Their Hybrids.* Concord, MA: The Herbarist, No. 4, 1938.

Savage, Spencer. *Calendar of the Ellis Manuscripts.* London: Catalogue of the Manuscripts in the Library of The Linnean Society of London, 1948.

Taylor, Robert L. *Plants of Colonial Days.* Williamsburg, VA: Williamsburg, Inc., 1952.

Thomas, Graham Stuart. *A Garden of Roses.* Topsfield, MA: Salem House Publishers, 1987.

Whallon, Robert E. *Oregano—Botanical and Culinary.* Falls Village, CN: The Herb Grower Magazine, Vol. XXVII, No. 4, 1974–75.

Wilder, Louise Beebe. *The Fragrant Garden.* New York: Dover Publications, 1974.

Wilson, Helen Van Pelt. *The Joy of Geraniums.* New York: William Morrow & Co., 1972.

Wrensch, Ruth D. *Boerner Botanical Gardens' Herb Information Handbook.* Milwaukee, WI: Milwaukee County Dept. of Parks, Recreation, and Culture, 1981.

Wyman, Donald. *Wyman's Gardening Encyclopedia.* New York: Macmillan Co., 1971.

Zohary, Michael. *Plants of the Bible.* Cambridge: Cambridge University Press, 1982.

Glossary

Adventive. Introduced from another region or country and not yet fully naturalized.

Alkaloid. A class of natural substances containing amine nitrogen, found mainly in plants, sometimes in animals. They are important as toxic and poisonous, but also have medicinal uses.

Alternate. Arrangement of leaves along a stem singly, on different sides, and at different heights.

Axil. The upper angle formed by a leaf or branch with the stem bearing the leaf or branch.

Basal Rosette. Leaves radiating from a central underground stem, often overlapping to form a circle.

Bract. Small, modified leaf at the base of a flower stalk or beneath a flower head; sometimes colored other than green.

Bulbil. A small bulb or bulb-like structure produced in leaf axils or in the place of flowers.

Cardiac Glycoside. A class of drug that increases the force of contraction of the heart without increasing its oxygen consumption.

Clasping. Referring to leaves partially or completely surrounding the stem.

Composite. An aggregate of flowers massed on a common receptacle (head), characteristic of the Composite family.

Compound leaf. A leaf composed of two or more leaflets. It is palmately compound when three or more leaflets arise from a common point at the end of a petiole; and pinnately compound when one or more pairs of leaflets are arranged along the sides of the axis, with or without a terminal leaflet; ternately compound when leaflets occur in threes.

Corm. A bulbous, swollen, underground stem-base bearing scale-leaves and roots; it acts as a storage organ and is a means of vegetative reproduction.

Crown. The base of a plant where stem and root tissues meet.

Deciduous. Said of plants shedding their leaves seasonally.

Decoction. An extract obtained by boiling.

Decumbent. Referring to a stem lying flat, but with the growing tip ascending.

Dioecious. Unisexual, male and female flowers on separate plants.

Disc flower. Tubular flowers in the central area of a head as distinct from the ray flowers in the Composite family.

Dormancy. The natural resting state of a mature plant or seed.

Elliptical. Oblong with ends equally rounded.

Emetic. A substance that causes vomiting.

Endemic. Native to or confined naturally to a particular and usually restricted area or region.

Entire. A smooth leaf blade margin, not toothed nor indented.

Essential oil. A vegetable oil made up of complex mixtures of volatile organic compounds that give a characteristic smell or taste to plants.

Evergreen. A plant whose leaves are functional over more than one growing season and holds them until new ones appear.

Filiform. Threadlike, long, and slender.

Glabrous. Without hairs.

Glaucous. Covered with a waxy, fine, whitish-gray or pale bluish powder.

Group. Used semitechnically in the nomenclature of cultivated plants for an assemblage of similar cultivars within a species.

Hardy. Applied to plants that survive outdoors through the entire year without protection.

Hybrid. A plant produced naturally or artificially from the crossing of two species usually within a genus that differ genetically in some marked characteristic.

Indigenous. Native.

Inflorescence. The general arrangement of flowers on a stem.

Infusion. To extract a substance by steeping in water.

Lanceolate. Narrow with tapering ends, as a lance.

Leaching. Loss of soluble fertilizers and substances as lime that are washed deep into soil out of reach of plant roots, or out of the bottom of containers by rain or continual watering.

Leaflet. One of the divisions of a compound leaf.

Linear. Long and narrow with parallel sides.

Microclimate. Climate of a very localized area, in a garden, part of a garden, or in the immediate surroundings of a plant.

Mutation. A variation within a species, not a hybrid, that appears suddenly and is heritable except in certain bud mutations (bud sports), which are then propagated by asexual methods.

Ob-. A prefix signifying a reversed position as "oblanceolate" and "obovate," with the broadest part above the middle.

Opposite. Leaves arranged on a stem opposite to each other, two at a node.

Ovate. Egg-shaped, with the narrow end above the middle.

Panicle. A loose, irregular arrangement of stalked flowers along a branched main stalk.

Petiole. A leaf stalk.

Potager. A French term for a garden that provides fruit, flowers, herbs, and vegetables for the house.

Purgative. An agent that causes evacuation of the bowels.

Raceme. An alternate or spiral arrangement of stalked flowers along an unbranched, elongated stalk having an actively growing tip.

Ray flowers. Flowers on the margins of Composite flower heads with a straplike petal above a very short tube; they surround the disc flowers.

Rhizomatous. Producing or possessing rhizomes, modified underground stems bearing roots and leafy shoots; also referred to as rootstocks.

Sessile. Without a stalk.

Simple. A medicinal herb, or medicine made from a herb; (archaic).

Solitary. Flowers borne singly, one to a stalk.

Spike. The arrangement of unstalked flowers along an unbranched, elongated stalk having an actively growing tip.

Stoma (pl. Stomata). Openings in the epidermis of a leaf or stem through which gases are exchanged and moisture is given off.

Subshrub. A low shrub with stems woody only at the base; treated as a perennial because tender new growth dies back seasonally.

Succulent. Fleshy and usually thick with water reserves.

Taproot. A main root, growing vertically deep into the soil.

Tender. A plant that can be injured by cold weather or frost.

Trace elements. Essential elements for plant growth in minute quntities and present in minute quantities in a soil.

Transpiration. The giving off of water vapor through openings (stomata) on the epidermis of leaves and stems.

Umbel. An umbrella-shaped arrangement of stalked flowers radiating from the top of a main stem; in a compound umbel secondary umbels arise from one

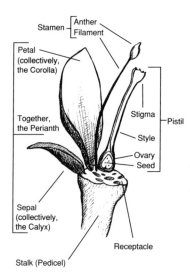

Stamen { Anther
         Filament

Petal
(collectively,
the Corolla)

Stigma

Pistil

Together,
the Perianth

Style

Ovary
Seed

Sepal
(collectively,
the Calyx)

Receptacle

Fig. 16. Diagram of flower from which all but one member of flower parts have been removed.

Stalk (Pedicel)

point and give rise to several terminal flower stalks. Umbels are a defining characteristic of the parsley family.

Uniform species. A species not inclined to variation.

Variegated. Leaves or flowers patterned with different spots, blotches, or lines in one or more colors.

Whorl. Flowers or leaves arranged in a circle of three or more around a single node.

Useful Addresses

Mail-order catalogs as sources of herbal seeds and plants.

Boyce Thompson Southwest Arboretum, Superior, AZ 85273. Seeds of plants adapted to aridity.

Edgewood Farm & Nursery, Rt. 2, Box 303, Stanardsville, VA 22973. Herbal plants and perennials.

Flowerplace Plant Farm, P.O. Box 4865, Meridan, MS 39304. Native woody and perennial plants as well as non-native herbal plants.

Gardens of The Blue Ridge, P.O. Box 10, Pineola, NC 28662. Native plants.

Hastings, 1036 White St., S.W. P.O. Box 115535, Atlanta, GA 30310-8535. Seeds & plants.

J.L. Hudson, Seedsman (A large collection of seeds from around the world), P.O. Box 1058, Redwood City, CA 94064. Seeds.

Native Gardens, Rt. 1, Box 494, Greenback, TN 37742. Native plants, some seeds.

Native Nurseries, 317 Theard, Covington, LA 70433. Native plants of the Gulf Coastal Plain.

Niche Gardens, 1111 Dawson Rd., Chapel Hill, NC 27516. Specializes in native plants.

Pickering Nurseries, Inc., 670 Kingston Rd. (HWY. 2), Pickering, Ontario, L1V 1A6, Canada. Old rose specialists. (New legislation may forbid shipment of roses from Canada into the United States.)

Roses of Yesterday and Today, 802 Brown's Valley Rd., Watsonville, CA 95076-0398. Old rose specialists.

Salter Tree Farm, Rt. 2, Box 1332, Madison, FL 32340. Trees, shrubs, & vines; mostly native.

Sandy Mush Herb Nursery, Rt. 2, Surrett Cove Rd., Leicester, NC 28748. Herbal plants and some seeds.

Shepherd's Garden Seeds, 30 Irene St., Torrington, CT 06790. Herbal seeds; some herbal plants.

Sunnybrook Farms Nursery, 9448 Mayfield Rd., P.O. Box 6, Chesterland, OH 44026. Herbal plants and some seeds; perennials.

The Flowery Branch, P.O. Box 1330, Flowery Branch, GA 30542. Herb seeds.

Thompson and Morgan, P.O. Box 1308, Jackson, NJ 08527. Includes herbal seeds and is an excellent source; since shipments are often too late for spring sowing in the Southeast, plan for fall sowing.

W. Atlee Burpee & Co., Warminster, PA 18974. Herbal seeds & plants.

Wayside Gardens, 1 Garden Lane, Hodges, SC 29695-0001. The complete catalog includes old roses and herbal plants.

We-Du Nurseries, Rt. 5, Box 724, Marion, NC 28752. Specializes in herbaceous southeastern natives and world-wide rock garden plants.

Well-Sweep Herb Farm, 317 Mt. Bethel Rd., Port Murray, NJ 07865. Herbal plants & seeds.

Woodlanders, 1128 Colleton Ave., Aiken, SC 29801. Offers a large number of trees, shrubs, vines, and perennials native to the Southeast or other warm-temperate parts of the world; herbal plants are in the collection.

For ready reference, enter the name of your state and/or county agricultural agent below:

NAME   ADDRESS   TELEPHONE

Arboreta, botanical gardens, and other gardens of herbal interest.

Agecroft Hall, 4305 Sulgrave Rd., Richmond, VA 23221. A herb garden of the Tudor period.

Atlanta Botanical Garden, Piedmont Park at the Prado, Atlanta, GA 30357. Herb garden, Mediterranean house, outdoor garden for plants from arid climates, rock garden, native aquatic plant pond, native woodland.

Birmingham Botanical Gardens, 2612 Lane Park Rd., Birmingham, AL 35223. Potager with herbs, old rose garden, garden of southeast natives.

Alfred L. Boerner Botanical Gardens in Whitnall Park, 5879 S. 92nd St., Hales

Corners (Milwaukee), WI 53130. Notable herb garden, old rose garden, restored prairie.

Brooklyn Botanic Garden, 1000 Washington Ave., Brooklyn, NY. Comprehensive herb garden.

Callaway Gardens, Rt. 27, Pine Mountain, GA 31822. Herb garden.

Chicago Botanic Garden, P.O. Box 400, Lake Cook Rd., east of Edens Hwy., Glencoe, IL 60022. Extensive, well-designed herb garden.

Medieval Herb Garden at Bonnfont Cloisters of the Metropolitan Museum of Art, Ft. Tryon Park, NY 10040.

Colonial Williamsburg, Williamsburg, VA. Special herb gardens associated with the Governor's Palace, houses, tavern, and apothecary shop.

Crosby Arboretum, Picayune, MS 39401. Ecological landscape in the Gulf Coastal Plain.

Heritage Herb Garden, Ozark Folk Center, P.O. Box 500, Mountain View, AR 72560.

Indian Herb Garden, James H. Barrow Field Station at Hiram College, Hiram, OH 44234.

Kanapaha Botanical Gardens, 4625 S.W. 63rd Blvd., Gainesville, FL 32068. Herb garden.

Missouri Botanical Garden, 2345 Tower Grove Ave., St. Louis, MO 63110. Herb garden, Mediterranean house, scented garden of raised beds; an adjunct, the Shaw Arboretum, is an ecological reserve and environmental education facility.

New York Botanical Garden, 200th St. and Southern Blvd., Bronx, NY 10458. Herb garden features plants for industrial use.

North Carolina Botanical Garden, University of North Carolina, Totten Center 457-A, Chapel Hill 27514 (U.S. 15-501 bypass at Laurel Hill Rd.). Herb garden of raised beds; replicated habitats for native plants.

Old Salem Herb Garden, a Moravian restoration in Winston-Salem, NC 27108. Design follows a 1761 medicinal garden plan patterned after medieval physic gardens.

State Botanical Garden of Georgia, 2450 S. Milledge Ave., Athens, GA 30605. Herb garden.

Tennessee Botanical Gardens and Fine Arts Center, Nashville, TN 37205. Herb study garden.

Tullie Smith House restoration, 3101 Andrews Dr. N.W., Atlanta, GA 30305. Choice, historical (1836–1860) herb garden.

United States National Arboretum, 3501 New York Ave., N.E., Washington, DC 20002. The important herb garden features ten specialty gardens and an old rose garden.

Wing Haven, 248 Ridgewood Avenue, Charlotte, NC 28209. Herb garden and old
   rose garden within a bird sanctuary.

   Additional current addresses that specialize in herbs and herb gardens or contribute information sought by a herbist can be supplied by local horticultural
societies, nurseries, botanical gardens, and state universities.

General Index

Plant Index

Geranium maculatum (Wild geranium, wild cranesbill), 203–04

German chamomile. See Matricaria recutita

Germander (Teucrium chamaedrys), 74, 257

Giant garlic. See Allium scorodoprasum

Giant hyssop. See Agastache foeniculum

Gillenia stipulata (American ipecuc), 204

Gillenia trifoliata (Indian physic, bowman's root), 204

Ginseng (Panax quinquefolius), 237–38

Golden Marguerite (Anthemis tinctoria), 75, 165

Golden oregano (Origanum vulgare 'Aureum'), 66

Goldenseal (Hydrastis canadensis), 209

Gravel root. See Eupatorium purpureum

Gray moss. See Tillandsia usneoides

Gray santolina (Santolina chamaecyparissus), 43, 74, 252

Grecian foxglove (Digitalis lanata), 194

Greek oregano (Origanum onites), 237

Hamamelis virginiana (Common witch hazel), 47, 86, 204

Hardy orange. See Poncirus trifoliata

Hedeoma pulegioides (American pennyroyal), 205

Helianthus tuberosum (Jerusalem artichoke), 118

Helichrysum angustifolium (Curry plant), 43, 205

Heliotrope (Heliotropium arborescens), 54, 144, 206

Heliotropium arborescens (Heliotrope), 54, 144, 206

Helleborus foetidus, 206

Helleborus niger (Christmas rose), 206

Helleborus orientalis, 206

Helleborus viridis, 206

Hen-and-chickens (Sempervivum tectorum), 253–54

Hepatica acutiloba, 207

Hepatica americana (Round-lobed hepatica, liverleaf), 207

Herb-of-grace. See Ruta graveolens

Hercules club (Aralia spinosa), 167

Hesperis matronalis (Rocket, dame's rocket), 207

Heucheria americana (Alumroot, rock geranium), 207–08

Himalayan musk rose (Rosa brunonii), 71

Holly (Ilex), 210–11

Honesty (Lunaria annua), 104, 150

Horehound. See Marrubium vulgare

Horn-of-plenty (Datura metel), 192

Horsefly. See Baptisia tinctoria

Horseheal. See Inula helenium

Horseradish (Armoricia rusticana), 167–68

Horsetail (Equisetum hyemale), 53, 87, 197–98

Humulus lupulus (Common hop, European hop), 208

Hydrangea arborescens (Wild hydrangea, sevenbark), 208–09

Hydrastis canadensis (Goldenseal), 209

Hyssop (Hyssopus officinalis), 3, 47, 75, 104, 209–10

Hyssopus officinalis (Hyssop, European hyssop), 3, 47, 75, 104, 209–10

Ilex cassine (Dahoon), 210

Ilex (Holly), 210–11

Ilex opaca (American holly), 86, 210, 211

Ilex paraguariensis (Yerbe-mate, Paraguay tea), 211

Ilex vomitoria (Yaupon, cassine), 210

Illicium floridanum (Purple star-anise, purple anise, Florida anisetree), 47, 67, 211–12

Illicium verum (Star anise), 212

Indian apple (Datura inoxia), 191

Indian physic (Gillenia trifoliata), 204

Indigo, 215

Indigofera tinctoria (Indigo), 16

Indigo (Indigofera tinctoria), 16

Inula helenium (Elecampane, horseheal), 212

Ipomoea tricolor (Morning-glory), 212–13

Iris cristata (Crested dwarf iris), 85, 213

Iris pallida, 71, 214

Iris prismatica (Blue iris), 84